WINDOWS ON THE PAST

Windows on the Past

HISTORIC LODGINGS OF NEW MEXICO

Sandra D. Lynn

UNIVERSITY OF NEW MEXICO PRESS ALBUQUERQUE

For the men and women who put time, hard work, money, heart and soul
into saving New Mexico's historic lodging and their stories

FIRST EDITION

Library of Congress Cataloging-in-Publication Data

Lynn, Sandra, 1944–
Windows on the past : historic lodgings
of New Mexico / Sandra D. Lynn. — 1st ed.
p. cm.
Includes bibliographical references and index.
ISBN 0–8263–2000–7 (pbk.)
1. Hospitality industry—New Mexico—History.
2. Hotels—New Mexico—History.
3. Resorts—New Mexico—History.
4. Dude ranches—New Mexico—History. I. Title.
TX909.L96 1999
647.94789'009—dc21
98–48956
CIP

CONTENTS

ACKNOWLEDGMENTS

Many people have generously helped me in many ways while I was researching and writing this book.

From the very beginning, Mike Pitel, Program Officer with the New Mexico Department of Tourism, encouraged me and made his files available to me. Mary Ann Anders, architectural historian with the Historic Preservation Division, Office of Cultural Affairs, patiently answered questions and helped me locate information in the division's files. Sandra Dallas Atchison read and commented on portions of the manuscript in its earliest stages and spurred me on.

I extend thanks to everyone listed in the interviews section of the bibliography. Over a period of years I interviewed dozens of people at length, and without their willingness to share their time, memories, and knowledge, this book would not have been possible. George C. Pearl was particularly gracious in submitting to hours of interviews and sharing his experiences, his love of historic hotels, and his files with me. Many of the people interviewed also checked drafts of chapters for accuracy, though any errors that escaped notice are my responsibility and not theirs. I would especially like to note that Audrey Alpers read the chapter on the St. James Hotel in manuscript and shared with me her family's collection of historic photographs—all while struggling bravely with serious illness. Janaloo Hill was not only kind enough to grant interviews but continued long afterward to respond fully to questions and requests for additional materials. Katherine (Kak) and Wid Slick provided interviews, tours of buildings, and supportive interest over a long period.

The Pennzoil Company helped a great deal with my research on Vermejo Park Ranch. Jim Charlesworth made it possible for me to use and photocopy historic documents at the ranch, and Tom Powell and H. M. (Mickey) Gentry provided information and valuable materials.

Betty Lloyd, formerly with the Arthur Johnson Memorial Library in Raton, and Marie Wuersching, Curator of the Sacramento Mountains Historical Museum in Cloudcroft, assisted with searches through files and efforts to locate photographs. Claude Morelli and Sally Kabat shared bibliographical information. In the often frustrating search for photographs, I turned for special help to several people, to whom I am grateful: Steven M. Hilton, Vice President for Programs of the Conrad N. Hilton Foundation; Roger Myers with the University of Arizona Library's Special Collections; Arthur L. Olivas, photographic archivist with the Museum of New Mexico; Mo Palmer, photographic archivist with the Albuquerque Museum; and Virginia (Goldie) Kayser of Mountainair. Mr. and Mrs. Kenneth Laird of Raton presented me with a wonderful batch of memorabilia from the 1930s and 40s from several of the hotels in this book. Others who provided special help with my research for this book were Ken and Louise Blair of Taos, Alton Bryant of Clayton, Thomas Burch and Emily Hughes of Raton, Jackie Shaffer Hudgeons of Queen Valley, Arizona, Diana Stein of Las Vegas, Betty Thompson of Socorro, and Margaret Wall of Cloudcroft. Special thanks go also to Robert Torrez, State Historian, and to Jan Dodson Barnhart, Mary Davis, John Grassham, David Kammer, Dan Scurlock, Paul Whiteman, Chris Wilson, and the staff of La Posada, all of Albuquerque.

The Research Allocations Committee and the Department of English at the University of New Mexico assisted with travel and research expenses.

My editor, Larry Durwood Ball, has proven to be unfailingly patient and reassuring while offering skilled guidance. DeL, Rick, and many friends encouraged and supported me in a variety of ways during this long labor of love. Thanks to you all.

Sandra D. Lynn
MAY, 1998

[N]o church or capitol or university or fort or hospital has so known the heart and blood circulation of history as a great hotel, where all the people, famous and petty—but especially the famous, since they must travel most—have rested and made plots, forgotten their masks in the exhilaration of wine, whispered in darkened chambers, and roared at banquets in the admiring presence of all the press and dignitaries.

SINCLAIR LEWIS FROM *Work of Art*

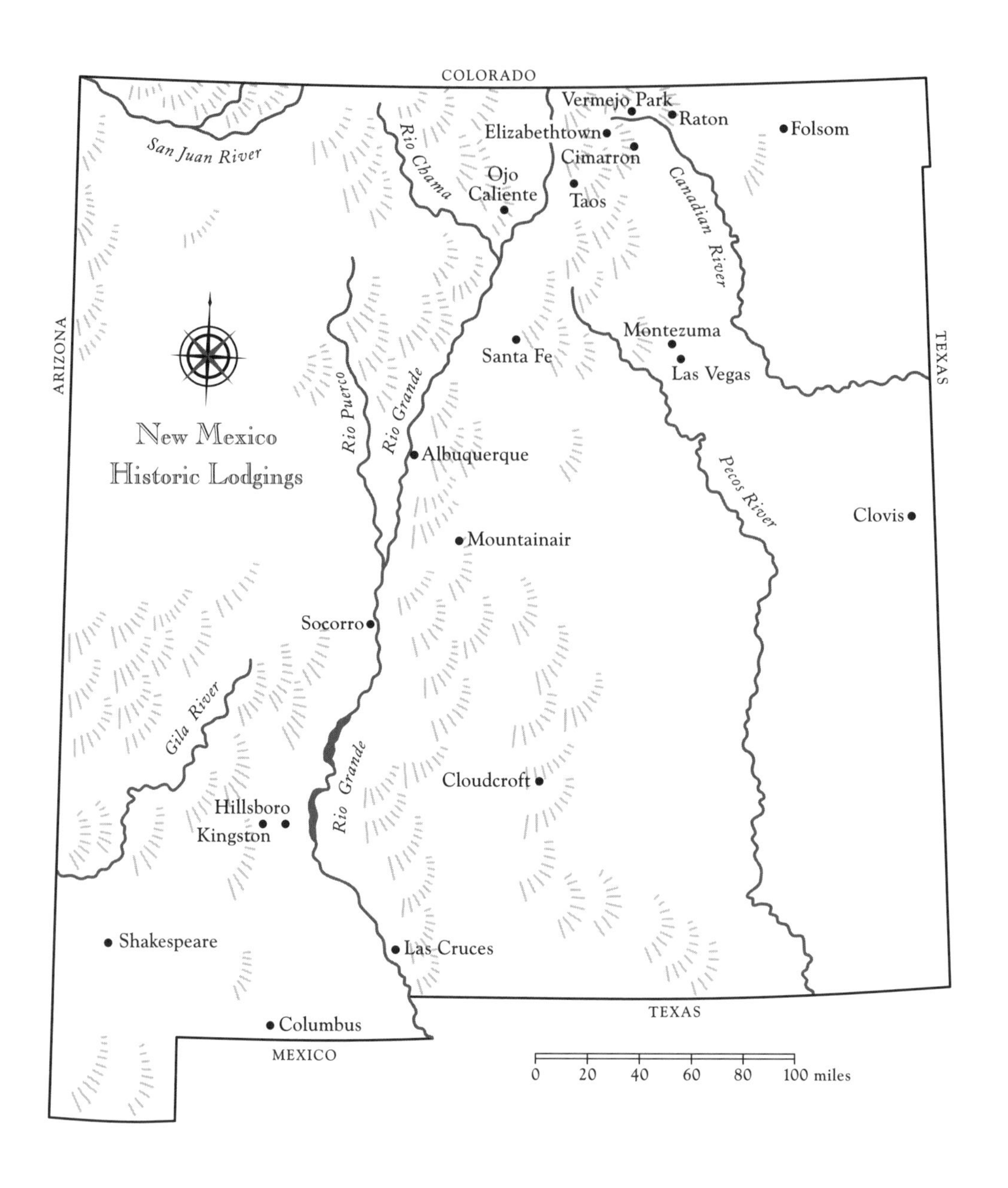

New Mexico
Historic Lodgings
COLORADO
ARIZONA
TEXAS
TEXAS
MEXICO
San Juan River
Rio Chama
Rio Puerco
Rio Grande
Rio Grande
Canadian River
Pecos River
Gila River
Vermejo Park
Raton
Folsom
Elizabethtown
Cimarron
Ojo
Caliente
Taos
Montezuma
Las Vegas
Santa Fe
Albuquerque
Mountainair
Clovis
Socorro
Cloudcroft
Hillsboro
Kingston
Shakespeare
Las Cruces
Columbus
0
20
40
60
80
100 miles

Preface

My son once received as a birthday gift a jigsaw–puzzle map of New Mexico. We dropped its pieces into a gold, pink, green, and orange heap and began working it at the margin. The outline of the state emerged, and outside its borders appeared pictures of the state gem, the turquoise, and the state flower, the yucca. Inside, the assembled puzzle pieces bore familiar place names: Santa Fe, Albuquerque, the Navajo Indian Reservation, Carlsbad Caverns National Park. But scattered among those names stood out some we had not expected: La Fonda in Santa Fe, the Shaffer Hotel in Mountainair, the Stratford Hotel in Shakespeare, the St. James Hotel in Cimarron. According to this jigsaw version of New Mexico geography, old hotels merit prominence in the landscape. In time I came to agree.

Writing this book was like working the puzzle map. When I began, it seemed no one knew how many historic lodgings still existed in the state or where they all were, much less how their stories might fit together. Why did I want to look for them? Because I remembered what such places had meant to me.

As a girl growing up in a small town in Texas, I took a trip with my father to the Adolphus Hotel in Dallas. My hardworking father had little time for hobbies, but one of his favorite pastimes was listening to music on a sound system he built, famous among our friends as the very latest in hi-fi. So he took me with him to the Adolphus for a high-fidelity equipment show. I didn't know that when the Adolphus was built in 1912, it was considered "the most beautiful building west of Venice, Italy." I only thought how fine it seemed that my friend Lucy and I were allowed to go with Daddy to a city hotel with such a grand name and so many acres of carpet and antiques. I also remembered staying with my mother in the Hotel Galvez in Galveston, where large rooms overlooked sunlit sheets of open water, the Gulf of Mexico. I remembered hanging out with other writers in the shadowy machismo of the Menger Hotel Bar in San Antonio, a short walk from the Alamo. I remembered anniversary interludes when my husband Rick and I escaped to historic hotels: a lodge perched in the mountains, a two-story brick hotel set down in golden cattle kingdoms of grass, and an inn posted like a lighthouse beside a funky, workaday port. Each one had seemed to distill some essence of its place for me.

Such memories led me to years of travel and research looking for New Mexico's historic lodgings. A batch of apparently unconnected names and dates gradually fit into a multicolored portrait of the state, past and present.

Just as with the puzzle map, I encountered the expected: stops on the Santa Fe Trail, railway hotels, boomtown relics in long-abandoned mining districts. But almost as often, I met with the unexpected. At the southwestern border of the state, in Columbus, I found a small adobe hotel, the Hoover. It had escaped the fires of Pancho Villa's raid across the border into the town in 1916, just as Villa himself escaped General John J. Pershing's expedition into Mexico to search for him. Then diagonally across the state at its northeastern edge, I happened upon another small hotel, constructed of native sandstone, the Folsom Hotel. A local citizen, George McJunkin, a black cowboy and ranch foreman, featured in its history. McJunkin, whose parents had likely been slaves in Texas, headed farther west after the Civil War, hoping to find freedom in the grazing lands of New Mexico. In an arroyo a few miles from Folsom, after a flood, McJunkin spotted some unusual, large bones. He tried to interest others in his find, but it was not until after he had lived out his last days and died in the Folsom Hotel in 1922 that scientists would name the place where he discovered the bones Folsom Site. They would recover there important evidence of the antiquity of human habitation in North America.

The historic lodgings I sought are hotels, inns, lodges, stage stations, resorts, or guest ranches built and functioning before 1940. Thanks to good luck, hard work, and sometimes the fortunate side of poverty—not having enough money to destroy old buildings in order to erect new ones—New Mexico can boast more than sixty of these survivors. Not included here are the many bed-and-breakfast inns recently established in historic homes. Theirs are stories of residences more than hostelries.

The lodgings whose histories comprise this book are

—reminders of the long continuum of travel and tourism in the Southwest
—markers of community change and sense of identity
—gathering places established before the automobile dominated American culture and separated travelers from one another
—symbols of the lure of the Southwest's natural resources and multicultural traditions
—testaments to the everyday and the extraordinary efforts of individuals who founded, managed, saved, and restored them.

Readers will find in these pages places to stay that offer a genuinely regional experience. Unlike contemporary chain hotels and their ilk, which promote predictability and homogeneity, these long-lived lodgings incorporate all the diversity and idiosyncrasy that arise from belonging to a place and its past. The special qualities of regional culture they offer reinforce a sense of community for the local citizens who enjoy them for meals, meetings, and celebrations. They also provide for tourists one of the benefits of travel—a chance to find out just a little about how people have lived differently in New Mexico than they have in New Jersey or Michigan or Washington.

This book has space for histories of only a

few of the state's enduring hostelries. But it covers a wide range of them. It includes a little mud and rock hotel keeping company with the creosote bushes and pastel distances of the Chihuahuan Desert. It also embraces the conifer-forested and coal-veined acreage of Vermejo Park Ranch, one of the largest privately owned properties in the United States. Some of the buildings still enjoy the constant traffic and central position in their communities they have known for more than half a century, while others attest in silence and decay, or even by their absence, to failed ambitions and neglect.

The chapters are arranged roughly chronologically according to founding dates, except for chapter 1 on the life and death of the Alvarado Hotel. It is the only chapter in the book dealing with a building that no longer exists and is placed out of sequence at the beginning because I believe its history can provide a valuable perspective from which to view the later chapters.

I located the historic lodgings in this book and many others by searching through old and new guidebooks, exploring, following leads, and being nosy. I dogged the footsteps of whoever would take me through a building, even if it meant climbing a ladder to crawl through a second-story window. I pestered owners, historians, museum curators, state officials, librarians, anyone with sharp eyes for remnants of the past or a long memory.

In the process of locating and researching these buildings, of working through the puzzle, I became aware of the fourth dimension in my surroundings, time. Some aspects of a place may be directly sensed: qualities of light and space, colors and textures, terrain, plants and animals. Other aspects are more elusive. They are experienced through knowledge and tradition rather than the senses alone. Knowing the story behind the place makes a big difference in what you see. For instance, if you know where to look with binoculars, you can spot a scrap of wall from Interstate 25 near Raton. With those few adobe bricks in view—all that remain of the stage station, Clifton House—you can summon to your imagination the era when hospitality there welcomed travelers who had struggled for days just to cross Raton Pass.

I also became aware of how often the history of hotels has been merely a hearsay history. Stories adhere to houses and to their larger cousins—hotels, inns, resorts—and accumulate over the years because in homes our most intimate dramas occur, and in homes-away-from-home intimate dramas intersect with public life. Seldom does anyone investigate the truth of the stories; they are simply repeated, with errors and embellishments compounded year after year. These accretions of tales provide entertainment and spice up sales brochures and guidebook entries, but sometimes they mask more revealing stories that lie buried beneath them, the ones that are not distortions of remembered events or invented for amusement or advertisement. These truer stories are almost always more interesting than hearsay because they are more surprising and complex—if one can learn enough to flesh them out fully. But hearsay is useful to the writer; it points in the direction of pay dirt.

I have sought stories for this book and

found many. I have dug beneath the overburden of hearsay and located veins of true material. Not being very skillful at juggling abstractions, I won't ponder here how we discern what is Truth. I just went looking for questions to fit to the shapes of the answers and enjoyed the resulting adventures.

I hope this book will inspire visitors and residents to pursue their own adventures, beyond the most frequented parts of New Mexico into smaller towns and byways and the less advertised life of our region. I hope, too, that its stories of the people who have struggled to protect and revive these buildings will encourage awareness of the value of historic places in our public and private lives.

Introduction

A Brief History of Hospitality and Lodgings in New Mexico

Historic buildings offer windows in the walls of the relentless here and now. Like eyes gazing back at us from old photographs, they allow us to slip for a moment into the otherness of the past. We sense possibilities and values much different from ours and yet simultaneously recognize connectedness, the family resemblance. Historic buildings hint at places beyond the horizon of our immediate perceptions and limited life-spans. Because of the American propensity for demolishing the physical remnants of the past and sealing off their fragments in museums, surviving structures are all the more crucial to their communities. They can be keys to unlocking forgotten rooms that remind us where we have been.

Where We Have Been

Welcome to New Mexico, where cultures met, clashed, and learned to live together even before the region's participation in that complex national experience we simplify with the terms *frontier* and *Wild West*. Though remote from population centers, New Mexico possesses exploitable natural resources and the rich, and equally exploitable, cultural resource of ancient traditions. Its landscape offers the dramatic beauty of contrasts, such as white-mantled mountains hanging like luminous mirages above a tortuous black lava *malpais* or the Rio Grande traversing the brown desert with its retinue of green.

Although it fit into larger patterns of travel and commercial hospitality occurring across the West, New Mexico made some special contributions all its own. Just as the jigsaw puzzle came together more easily by starting with the outline of the state, the lodgings in this book are best viewed within an outline of the region's travel history.

Natural Oases and Private Hospitality

When the ancestors of the Tewa-speaking pueblos migrated southeastward from the Four Corners (where today New Mexico meets Arizona, Colorado, and Utah) toward the Rio Grande, they lingered at a place they would call *Poseuinge* or "village at the place of hot springs." They liked the spot—blessed by steaming springs with mossy banks, near a river, surrounded by low, rose-colored hills layered against blue peaks. In the fourteenth century they

Ojo Caliente, New Mexico, ca. 1885–1895. *Photo by Dana B. Chase. Courtesy of the Museum of New Mexico, Santa Fe, New Mexico. Negative No. 9646.*

erected blocks of rooms on a bluff overlooking the springs. The springs have been the location of a popular spa ever since, now known as Ojo Caliente Mineral Springs.

Later, in the last years of the sixteenth century, Don Juan de Oñate left his home in Zacatecas in the Spanish colony of Mexico to lead a caravan of livestock and settlers in groaning wagons up the *Camino Real* (Royal Road) into what would become New Mexico. The colonists paused at natural oases that became established campsites, or *parajes*, along the *camino*, eventually a thoroughfare for missionaries, more colonists, soldiers, and traders. No wayside inns punctuated the long journeys to Santa Fe, and hospitable haciendas or ranchos could be days of travel apart.[1]

In 1846–47 Susan Shelby Magoffin accompanied her trader husband along the Santa Fe Trail into New Mexico and then down into Mexico. At that time wayfarers found courteous, sometimes lavish, hospitality in private homes along the way. Susan wrote in her journal of being a guest in a home in El Paso del Norte:

> [I]ndeed we are so free and easy, 'tis almost a hotel, meals are served in our own room, one of the ladies always being in attendance to see and know if we are propperly attended to; the dishes are often changed and well prepared.

The Beginnings of Commercial Hospitality

Yet even as Susan Magoffin arrived in Santa Fe in 1846, the era of travelers' reliance on private hospitality was ending. The United States's occupation of New Mexico had begun, and more and more newcomers would arrive, needing places to stay. In order to house them, hotels and inns were built from Raton Pass in the north to Las Cruces in the south. Haulers of freight, stage coach passengers, prospectors hustling to gold and silver mining regions looking for luck, well-heeled tourists in search of the "American Alps"—

they all wanted rooms. Several forms of commercial lodgings became common—stations along stage routes; inns, hotels, and wagonyards in towns; and solitary guest ranches sprawling over mountain valleys and rangelands.

STAGE STATIONS

Not all stage stops offered overnight accommodations. Swing stations located every ten miles or so provided the driver with places to change horses and the passengers a chance to put their feet on firm ground again and wash the grime off their faces. Home stations, situated farther apart, thirty to fifty miles, could supply exhausted travelers with lodging, food, and offices where they could buy tickets or post letters.

Manville Chapman, an artist who painted murals on historical subjects in the Shuler Auditorium in Raton under the auspices of the WPA, envisioned the Clifton House stage station near Raton as having been an exciting place where "globe trotters" were continually arriving in their "expensive clothes," providing diversion for the local ranchers. However, historian Richard Orman, relying on the reports of such globe trotters as Mark Twain traveling in the West, described the accommodations stagecoach passengers might expect as distinctly unexciting—"foul" sleeping arrangements, "wretched" and "high-priced" food, and "slimy" liquor, just when a traveler could use a good drink.[3]

Little has been published about stage stations in New Mexico, but it is known that both swing and home stations were often added on to structures such as ranch buildings, hotels, and forts, though some separate stations were constructed. In the 1940s, Roscoe and Margaret Conkling, authors of a study of the Butterfield Overland Mail route, were able to locate across southern New Mexico ruins of adobe and stone stations with attached corrals.[4] The Corn Exchange Hotel/Bean Butterfield Building in Mesilla, once the most important stop on the Butterfield Overland Mail route between El Paso del Norte and Los Angeles, still serves the public today as La Posta Restaurant. In northern New Mexico I have visited several sites believed to be stage stops, with ruins of both adobe and frame buildings.[5]

By the middle of the nineteenth century conditions were improving for travelers in the West. After 1848, in New Mexico Territory, stage stations became more frequent because of military protection along travel routes.

HOTELS

Another change throughout the West was the dissemination of an American invention—the hotel as we know it today, complete with desk clerks and bellhops, indoor bathrooms supplied with soap, and room keys. The earliest modern, first-class American hotel—distinguished from the European-style inn by its size, staff, and conveniences—was Boston's Tremont House.[6] It opened its doors in 1829, just a few years after the Santa Fe Trail opened trade between Mexican Santa Fe and the United States. Then a few years after that, from 1833 to 1837, Mary Donoho, the first Anglo woman known to travel along the Santa Fe Trail from Missouri to Santa Fe, ran a hotel at the end of the trail with her husband William. But their hostelry, the forerunner of present-day La Fonda, bore little resemblance to Boston's luxurious Tremont House. It probably offered to the Santa Fe trader a bed, a fireplace, food spiced with plenty of chiles, opportunities for gambling and dancing, and the lice freely available in all Santa Fe lodgings.[7]

In the 1830s and 1840s hotels spread rapidly across the United States and began to extend even into the rawest and most isolated settlements in the West. They were at first puny and primitive by Tremont House standards but eventually included establishments on a regal scale. In Europe comforts and finery lavished upon travelers had been considered the exclusive prerogative of the upper classes, but Americans hit on how to run "palaces of the people" as large business enterprises. Americans used them for everything from weddings to political rallies. They became "as public as the parks."[8]

Hotels were among the first structures to sprout in western boomtowns, and they followed the rails all the way to the Pacific. Several New Mexico hotels date from this era of rapid expansion from the 1830s through the 1880s: hotels that evolved from frontier fortlike structures, the Stratford Hotel in Shakespeare and the Amador Hotel in Las Cruces; hotels that developed to serve Santa Fe Trail and rail traffic, such as the St. James in Cimarron and the Plaza in Las Vegas; and a palatial health resort, the Montezuma Hotel in Gallinas Canyon near Las Vegas.

WAGONYARDS

Another sort of stopover, the wagonyard, was apparently a precursor to the autocamps that later developed into motels. Bonnie Barnes Houston, whose family moved from Texas to New Mexico in 1918 in a big, canvas-topped wagon, recalled in an oral history interview that her father would try to find wagonyards along the way. She described these as being "a motel sort of . . . where you could wash clothes, take a bath, and let the horses rest. We would usually lay over on Sunday."[9] Travelers could sleep in bunkhouses or in bedrolls in or near their wagons. Information about wagonyards is scarce, but they may have originated from livery stables or home stations, probably not until late in the nineteenth century.[10]

By the turn of the century, stage stations, hotels, and perhaps some wagonyards provided lodgings for the flood of tourists and emigrants, the curious and the committed. They arrived by stagecoach, train, or in their own wagons, laden with dusty bags of clothing, clutching parcels of fruit and tins of biscuits, often shepherding children. Of course, many were headed for land or business opportunities, but by the 1880s tourism had become an American pastime. Americans crowded Paris streets and Florida beaches, and they hungered to see the Wild West and relics of the struggle to tame it.

GUEST RANCHES

Some of these Easterners came West to taste the pleasures of the wilderness, to hunt abundant game in magnificent surroundings with all the comforts wealth could command. Such notables as Jim Bridger, Buffalo Bill Cody, and General Philip Sheridan led hunting parties outfitted with French cooks, chilled wine, and table linen. By the 1870s and 1880s cattle ranches in the northern Rockies began taking in paying guests, hunters and outdoor enthusiasts like Theodore Roosevelt, who first became acquainted with the Dakotas as a dude-ranch lodger.[11]

By the mid-1920s several guest ranches (the term more often used in the Southwest) were operating in New Mexico, offering visitors the opportunity to experience life on a working ranch while enjoying elaborate facilities for hunting, trout fishing, riding, and indulging in ample food and alcohol, despite Prohibition. One of the earliest and most remarkable guest ranches in New Mexico, Vermejo Park Ranch, still hosts guests today in original stone buildings in the Sangre de Cristo Mountains near the border between New Mexico and Colorado.

New Mexico's Contributions to the Development of Commercial Hospitality

By the 1870s and early 1880s small hotels could be found along the travel arteries of New Mexico Territory. In Las Cruces on the ancient route downriver to Mexico, touring theatrical troupes amused freight haulers staying in Don Martin Amador's lodgings. In Cimarron on the Santa Fe Trail businessmen preoccupied with gold mining and troubles on the Maxwell Land Grant paused at the National Hotel.[12] At that time commercial hospitality in New Mexico differed little from stage stops and hotels elsewhere across the West, except perhaps for the predominance of adobe as a building material. But when the Atchison, Topeka, and Santa Fe Railroad crossed Raton Pass in 1879, a new era began in which the New Mexico Territory would make two of its own contributions to the history of the American hotel.

First, some of the finest and most distinctive of Fred Harvey's railway hotels would be built in New Mexico, and the Harvey approach to attracting visitors to them would change the nature of tourism in the Southwest. Second, America's greatest hotel magnate, Conrad Hilton, was born in 1887 in San Antonio beside the railroad tracks. His family's adobe home would turn into the first Hilton hotel.

HARVEY HOUSES

To understand the changes wrought by Fred Harvey in the comforts available to rail passengers, it helps to have some idea of what early rail travel in the West was like. Passengers disembarked from the train for meals at eating stations along the route, and some of them have left accounts of the quality of the food and the haste with which they had to consume it.

One passenger wrote of alighting from the train for breakfast covered with "white, salinous dust" from crossing the Nevada desert and then of being allowed only twenty minutes to wash up and eat. Lady Duffus Hardy, after praising a roast of black-tailed deer served at the Cheyenne, Wyoming, eating station, wondered why all were not so well managed and supplied: "We have thrown away many a noble appetite on tough, tasteless steak and watery soup that had scarcely strength to run down our throats."[13]

Fred Harvey, an immigrant Englishman employed by the Chicago, Burlington, and Quincy Railroad in the 1870s as a freight agent, would have agreed with Lady Hardy about better management at meal stops. He traveled most of his workweek on the railroad and was all too well acquainted with dirt, discomfort, and distasteful food. Because he had management experience in restaurants, including railroad eating houses, he decided he could improve food and service for passengers.

In 1876 and 1878 he arranged with the Atchison, Topeka, and Santa Fe Railroad to operate a lunchroom in Topeka, Kansas, and a railroad division point restaurant/hotel at Florence, Kansas. They proved to be the beginning of a very influential and successful line of railroad dining rooms that eventually expanded into fine hotels and other tourist services. Harvey innovations produced high quality food and excellent service all along the route of the Santa Fe, which advertised, profited by, and subsidized "Meals by Fred Harvey" served by smiling Harvey Girls in prim white aprons. Harvey became known as "The Great Civilizer" of the American West because he introduced extraordinary improvements in the way travelers' meals were prepared and presented, in the reading material available to them through Harvey newsstands, and in the supply of intelligent, attractive, and upstanding young women in the masculine outposts of the frontier.[14]

Later, Fred Harvey's luxury hotels in New Mexico at Las Vegas, Albuquerque, Lamy, Gallup, and Santa Fe became famous for their regionally inspired architecture and interior design. The company also developed effective new techniques for marketing Southwestern travel and introducing Native American arts and crafts to tourists.

During the six decades from the railroad's advent into New Mexico Territory until World War II, the Santa Fe Railway, Fred Harvey, and other civic and commercial promoters devised for New Mexico and the Southwest a new identity. It became known for its healthful climate, especially for tuberculosis sufferers; its dramatic scenery; and time-hallowed sites—from cliff dwellings to ghost towns. And conveniently for tourists, its native peoples still lived in their centuries-old villages and created arts and crafts that didn't have to be admired in glass cases in museums but could be bought and carried home. New Mexico became, by the second decade of the century, not just a new state but an exotic destination.[15]

When Mary and William Donoho had offered hospitality in the 1830s, it was to Santa Fe Trail traders who arrived in the city of Holy Faith muttering prayers of thanks. They had managed to pass, though unwelcome, through the country of the plains tribes and survive the hazards of sickness, lack of water, and Raton Pass. Nearly a century later, in the 1920s in Santa Fe's new La Fonda, adventurous train travelers signed up for the first "Indian Detours," automobile side trips. They risked a few bumps and flat tires, but a 1929 Harveycar Motor Cruise brochure pointed out to them that the Southwest had now been made safe and accessible. There was nothing to stop them from experiencing in comfort "the lure . . . that lies beyond the pinched horizons of [the] train window."[16]

The image of New Mexico sold to travelers since 1880 has capitalized on and embellished the state's multicultural traditions, especially those of the arts and crafts, its frontier history, and its compelling landscape. That image still draws American and international tourists in the last years of the twentieth century, but today's crowds of shoppers are encouraged to feel the lure of highly publicized "Santa Fe Style" beyond the pinched horizons of their credit cards.

Though Fred Harvey's marketing strategies not only emphasized but, to a degree, invented the now-familiar attractions of New Mexico and the Southwest, the most influential of the New Mexico Harvey Houses, the Alvarado Hotel in Albuquerque, was demolished in 1970. Other bastions of civilized Harvey territory are gone now, too, such as El Ortiz at Lamy and El Navajo at Gallup. But some still stand: the Montezuma Hotel near Las Vegas, the Castañeda in Las Vegas, Santa Fe's La Fonda, and the Gran Quivira in Clovis.

The family of Conrad Hilton: (l to r) Felice, mother Mary, Conrad, Carl, father Gus, and Eva. (no date) *Courtesy of the Conrad N. Hilton College Archives and Library, University of Houston.*

HILTON HOTELS

While Fred Harvey's hotels and restaurants were catering to the needs and wants of railroad passengers, Conrad Hilton was a young man doing just the same, only he was toting heavy trunks and drummers' showcases for passengers stepping down into the sunbaked streets of San Antonio.

Born on the Rio Grande, Hilton was nearly 20 when the currency panic of 1907 wiped out his father's success as proprietor of a general store. Gus Hilton had pioneered in what his son later described as "a huddle of mud houses hugging the river's edge" [17] because of a bridge across the Rio Grande. Across this bridge, Gus Hilton figured, would flow traffic—trappers, coal miners, and ranchers—needing access to the trains. He figured right. But in 1907 even canny Gus Hilton was left with stock on the shelves he couldn't sell. Luckily, he had other assets: a big adobe house directly across from the railroad station, two sons old enough to work hard, and his wife Mary's good cooking. So the family went into the innkeeping business, and Conrad Hilton and his brother met trains whenever they arrived and hauled luggage.

Having experienced only the bellhop's

Sagebrush Inn, Taos, New Mexico, 1931.
From the author's collection, a gift from Helen Kentnor.

view of it, young Hilton didn't think much of the hotel business. He yearned to be a banker—until he bought his first hotel. He found it while shopping for a bank, in Texas, in the days when the post–World War I oil boom was tearing like a tornado through towns like Wichita Falls and Cisco. All that mattered to Hilton or to his guests was locating just enough floor space to accommodate a bed. Hilton described his Mobley Hotel in Cisco as "a cross between a flophouse and a gold mine" and was glad "the people around town have so much oil in their eyes they can't see it."[18] Only after the gain and loss of a fortune or two and the unfolding of an obsessive desire to acquire hotels with a past and a pedigree did Hilton come to appreciate the characteristics that give a hotel what he called its soul: "[T]here is an indefinable quality that must be found and supplied else you have the most elegant ice-house in town."[19]

Among the many hotels Conrad Hilton built was the one originally known as the Albuquerque Hilton, now La Posada de Albuquerque. He decided to add it to his collection in 1939 and said this about it:

> I once built a hotel in Albuquerque and the first thing I said to the architect [Anton F. Korn] was that I wanted it to stand for the Southwest: in line, color and material. I visioned mellow sand-colored walls, red tile floors, polished smooth, native woods and tile roofs. That is the tradition of the area.[20]

Thanks to a 1984 restoration the red clay tile floors of the La Posada still sound to the click of heels across the lobby and some of the original woodwork and murals still grace it. The hotel persists, a tribute to one of New Mexico's most successful sons.

Not Just for Tourists

Hotels, inns, lodges, resorts and guest ranches were built to serve the needs of travelers and to advertise the Southwest as the place to come for wealth, health, and, despite the apparent contradiction, comfortable adventure. But these outposts in the foreign and wild country of mesas and pueblos did as much for their neighbors as for those signing the guest register. They often stood, architecturally and culturally, for local ambition and tradition. They served as symbols of the regional landscape, of hopes for personal and community success, of the enduring appeal of the West and, as the decades passed, each survivor became a repository of some part of its community's sense of identity. These institutions supplied beds, meals, liquor, podiums, cotillions, courtrooms, infirmaries, and funeral parlors.

For instance, the Sagebrush Inn in Taos was built in 1929 by Frank and Helen Kentnor, who hired local craftsmen and women to use traditional techniques and native materials. They shaped adobe bricks for walls and peeled bark from logs from the mountains for the roof beams, known as *vigas*.[21] The twelve-room inn echoed in its structure the visual cadences of the mesas seen from its windows across miles of sagebrush.

One recent weekend at the end of September a wedding reception filled the patio of a now much-expanded Sagebrush Inn. Celebrants gathered under the tower room, where Georgia O'Keeffe lived and painted one summer, and just outside the lobby bar, where some have long believed Julius and Ethel Rosenberg were arrested for selling secrets of the Manhattan Project at Los Alamos to the Soviets. This tale told about the Rosenbergs is not true (though in fact, Conrad Hilton's hotel in Albuquerque played a pivotal role in the Rosenberg case; but that's another story, related in chapter 10). However the rumor was born, its longevity indicates the way such an inn becomes a locus, real or imagined, for historic moments. A singer strummed his guitar and serenaded the guests. The sun warmed their backs even while a storm hovered over the already snow-dusted mountains to the west. The newlyweds raised their glasses in a toast.

Like all the historic lodgings in this book, the Sagebrush Inn is not just for tourists. These lodgings provide links between their natural surroundings, indigenous crafts and architecture, community memory, people and events of world importance that briefly touch them, and milestones in the lives of local people. All are windows on a shared past.

ALVARA

CHAPTER ONE

The Alvarado Hotel in Albuquerque

Prologue—The Montezuma Ball

1908

Were there no other public displays for the Sixteenth National Irrigation Congress, this building alone is worth traveling to see. The entire front of the Alvarado Hotel, every window, every arch, stands out against the night, outlined with small electric bulbs. Above them all the Santa Fe Railway's emblem is emblazoned, white against deep blue. Electricity has been available in Albuquerque for more than twenty years, but only now are many residents making the change from gas to electric lighting in their homes. They are dazzled by the novelty of the Alvarado's incandescent splendor.

It is early October; the lights sparkle in crisp air. For weeks the city has been caught up in its own surge of electricity, the momentum of events of national and even international importance and sheer hoopla. The headlines have heralded, "Distinguished Visitors Pouring Into City, Will Be Largest Gathering of Men of World-Wide Note Ever Held in the West"; "French Engineer and Party Are in City, Much Interested in Irrigation Construction in the U. S."; "Sugar Pyramid at Exposition Ground—130,000 Pounds of the Crystallized Beet."[1]

But the excitement is almost over—the trains constantly disgorging illustrious visitors at the Alvarado's doorstep and its porticoes jammed with people listening to the Mexican Army Band. Even the territorial fair is over, except for the traditional Montezuma Ball.

For the ball the Alvarado's dining room on this October night is graced with Navajo rugs, evergreen branches, a pyramid of whole lobsters crowned with a quivering globe of jelled lobster salad—and fair women and brave men, or so the paper will proclaim tomorrow. To the strains of the Twenty-first Infantry Band and Orchestra, Governor George Curry leads the grand march.[2]

1916 AND 1917

October and time again for the annual Montezuma Ball, "The Climax of Social Gaieties" at the close of the fair (since 1912, a state fair). In 1916 a courtyard on the east side of the Alvarado is enclosed in canvas and transformed with twinkling, multicolored lights and Japanese lanterns suspended in a cross, the insignia of the Santa Fe. Governor William C. McDonald leads the grand march.[3]

But by October of the following year, the *Albuquerque Morning Journal* has been filled with black-bordered notices that read "Enlist Now. Your President Calls You. The Country Needs You." The state fair has been cancelled, replaced by Patriotic Week: "Come and see the boys before they go away. Come and see what will be going on in the trenches." In wartime there will be no Montezuma Ball at the Alvarado nor will there be one again for more than half a century.

1969

By now the Alvarado has become rather dreary. Long extension cords for lamps meander across the floors because there are too few wall sockets. The beloved gardens, once compared to those of the Alhambra, are reduced to the basics: shrubs, trees, grass. But for this evening, all have been cut and pruned. Everywhere among them are lights, yes, once again the lighted fairyland gardens everyone remembers from Montezuma Balls of the past. Even the long-dry Moorish fountain flows again, repaired just for this evening.

The tradition of the Montezuma Ball has been revived. In 1968 the Albuquerque Museum Association celebrated the opening of the museum with the first Montezuma Ball held since World War I. Now, September 6 of the following year, it is being held once again at the Alvarado.

Eighty-two-year-old native son Conrad Hilton decides to fly from his home in California to attend the party with Mrs. Olive Wakeman, his administrative assistant. But a few difficulties arise. Hilton wants to stay, not in the aged Alvarado, but rather in the aging Albuquerque Hilton, which he opened thirty years before. The Hilton, like the Alvarado a few blocks away, has become embarrassingly shabby, so someone from its staff calls up Richard Worthen, a cochairman of the Montezuma Ball, and complains, "We've got to do something because Hilton is coming to that damn ball you're giving."[4]

Worthen, a professional interior designer, decides to "totally rehab a suite on one of the middle floors [of the Hilton]. But to get Mr. Hilton from the elevator to the suite is a problem, so I fly in floor covering and we give the corridors on that floor an overnight facelift."

So it is that Conrad Hilton is able to get on the hotel elevator during his stay, get off at his floor, and walk down the only refurbished hall to the only refurbished suite. The fears of the hotel manager—that someone on the elevator with Hilton will get off at another floor and thus reveal to his discerning eye the discrepancy between floors—do not materialize.

But TWA has managed to lose Mrs. Wakeman's luggage en route from Beverly Hills. She does what she must: goes on a shopping spree.

And so it is that an unperturbed Conrad Hilton and a reoutfitted Olive Wakeman open the dancing at the Montezuma Ball with the "Varsoviana," Hilton's favorite dance.

Despite slow ticket sales at first, many people decide in the last week or so that they, like Conrad Hilton, *must* attend the party.

Conrad Hilton dancing the "Varsoviana" with Olive Wakeman, his administrative assistant, on the Merv Griffin television show in 1964. *Courtesy of the Conrad N. Hilton College Archives and Library, University of Houston.*

The crowd swells to the point that Max Apodaca and his orchestra have to move out of the way, up on the train track platform above the hundreds of partygoers seated at tables, walking, talking, and laughing in the gardens.

With all the preparations for the ball completed, Worthen relaxes and enjoys the party immensely. Albuquerque still retains something of a small-town atmosphere (though in retrospect it may only seem that way because the city will swell by a third in the next decade), and it seems to Worthen the guests have come together at the Alvarado like family for this one evening. A train passes. Worthen wonders what the passengers must think gazing out the windows and seeing dancers in their finery right up there on the platform, under the lapis lazuli sky, the grand old hotel spanning their view bedecked with lights.

The Shining Jewel in the Santa Fe's Crown[5]

By the mid-1890s the Santa Fe Railway, reorganized under a new president, E. P. Ripley, had become well aware of the golden goose it sheltered—Fred Harvey's superbly run dining facilities. The railroad recognized what a draw Harvey's excellent food and service were to its passengers and embarked on a program designed to lure even more visitors to the West. The Santa Fe would persuade them to spend time and money in a new line of luxury station hotels to be built from Las Vegas, New Mexico, to the Grand Canyon.[6] These fine hotels would supersede Harvey lunchrooms established earlier and offer not only the customary high-quality food but also a carefully created *experience* of the Southwest: regionally inspired architecture and design along with opportunities to catch a glimpse of the native cultures. The first Harvey House in Albuquerque, a red frame building built near the depot in the 1880s, would be replaced on a grand scale. "How great an improvement the splendid new depot is upon the dingy little red building which did duty for so many years," the *Journal Democrat* proclaimed.[7]

The new train station/Indian Building/Alvarado Hotel complex was designed and built between 1901 and 1904 in a popular style. During the previous decade California architects had cultivated an interest in the Spanish Colonial and Native American mix of architectural forms and building techniques found in the Franciscan missions of California. This interest spread to other parts of the country and developed into the California Mission and Spanish Colonial Revival styles, which included elements of Moorish and Italian design as well.

The Santa Fe, Southern Pacific, and Union Pacific Railroads began building Mission-style buildings in southern California as early as 1894.[8] Charles Whittlesey, chief architect in charge of stations and hotels for the Santa Fe Railway, continued this trend when he designed the Alvarado complex.[9] Its spreading group of frame and rough-surfaced stucco buildings were joined and unified by graceful arched arcades. The impression was one of horizontality, earth-bound structures punctuated with parapets and towers derived from California missions. Though the style was said to be "indigenous," the Alvarado's architecture was not native, as it did not spring from the Spanish and Pueblo blend of adobe architecture actually found in New Mexico (and used in later Harvey Houses) but rather from California models. Yet the traveler arriving at the Alvarado for the first time met with an architecture, while not really drawn from New Mexican sources, that suited its larger region and offered an experience quite different from eastern hotels. David Gebhart, in his studies of the architecture of Harvey Houses, put it this way:

> On alighting on the platform the visitor encountered not the usual neo-Roman or neo-Renaissance station so characteristic then of the eastern sections of the country, but instead he was faced with a low two or three story structure, almost domestic in character. He . . . found before him a simple unpretentious stucco covered building, often enclosing small intimate gardens and court yards, with shaded loggias, textured brick and tile floors, broad fireplaces and wood beamed ceilings.[10]

While the Alvarado was being constructed, its architect lived in Albuquerque and designed the El Tovar Hotel, a Harvey hotel spectacularly located on the rim of the Grand Canyon. He also planned a rustic log and stone residence for his family. The Whittlesey home (now the Albuquerque Press Club) bears a striking resemblance to El Tovar. Whittlesey said both were in the style of a "Norwegian villa."[11]

In 1902 Fred Harvey wired Mary Jane Colter in St. Paul, Minnesota, to come to Albuquerque. The company wanted a decorator "who knew Indian things and had imagination"[12] for the new hotel's museum and salesroom for Indian handicrafts, the Indian Building. Colter had attended the California School of Design in San Francisco. While there she apprenticed in a local architect's office just at the time when California architects were calling for a new approach to building design—not copying the latest from Europe but developing a regional style that would grow out of California traditions and be suited to its landscape. Mary Colter absorbed these views as a student and would, in years to come, transform them into her own distinctive approach to design. When the Harvey company offered her the Alvarado job, her acquaintance with the company was casual—she had a friend who worked in a company gift shop—but she was eager to go all the way to Albuquerque to work for them. A summer job arranging Indian pottery, baskets, and blankets for the Indian Building turned out to be the beginning of a forty-year career with Fred Harvey and the Santa Fe Railway.

The New Alvarado Hotel

Captain Hernando de Alvarado had arrived in the Tiguex Province in the late summer of 1540, having accompanied Francisco Vasquez de Coronado on his explorations of this remote northern outpost of colonial New Spain. Dispatched to the Rio Grande by Coronado, who was headquartered at Zuni Pueblo, Alvarado followed orders to lead a reconnaissance party into the land of the Tiwa Indians. Captain Alvarado wrote the first description we have of the region where Albuquerque would later be established in a letter to Coronado: "This river flows through a broad valley planted with fields of maize. There are some cottonwood groves. The houses are of mud, two stories high. The people seem good, more given to farming than war."[13]

In May of 1902, 362 years later, there were still cottonwoods along the Rio Grande, low adobe houses, and good people who grew corn. There was also an impressive new hotel in what had once been Tiguex Province, a hotel said to be "the finest structure of the famous Spanish mission style of architecture now in existence."[14] It was named for Captain Alvarado. The *Albuquerque Journal-Democrat* printed the first full description we have of it.

The Alvarado Hotel stretched a block and a half from south to north and more than a block from east to west. It was situated in the midst of New Town, a district engendered by the arrival of the railroad and fast growing into a downtown that looked like it could have been planted in Iowa or Pennsylvania (if one did not pay too much attention to the five knobby volcanoes across the river or sand and gravel outwash from the ten-thousand-foot Sandia Mountains.) The newcomers who had ridden the rails into town to seek their fortunes wanted Albuquerque to resemble the places they came from. It is an odd footnote that the Alvarado, which would become an icon of regional identity, was built just at a time when Albuquerque New Town in the heart of New Mexico Territory was trying very hard to cast itself in the mold of a respectable older town in the East or Midwest.[15]

An arcade extended from the hotel to the Indian Building (still unfinished when the hotel opened) and on to the train station. Massive gates on the north and west driveways allowed for automobile and carriage access. Gardens had not yet materialized, so the gray, red-tile-roofed building at first looked stark. It contained eighty-eight guest rooms, a large dining room, two parlors, offices, a lunchroom, kitchens, laundry, reading and writing rooms (for this was an era when travelers still read for entertainment and wrote lengthy letters home), a barber shop, and living quarters for Harvey employees.

The furnishings were specially manufactured for the building out of heavy, dark oak, and the woodwork was black. It might be imagined the rooms were thus gloomy, but the *Journal-Democrat* reported that "myriad brilliant electric lights" (here the theme of lights first appears) with green opal globes enhanced what it termed "the subdued effect" of the interior. And low-ceilinged guest rooms proved to be "airy and well lighted."

Fred Harvey As Benefactor

When the Alvarado opened in 1902, Fred Harvey himself had died the previous year, but the business he founded (always called simply by his name) was becoming legendary for its service, food, and fine new hotels. Fred Harvey received and kept in its company files numerous log entries, notes scrawled on menus, and letters from satisfied customers over the decades, many of them from guests of the Alvarado. A reader of the correspondence is struck by how often the writers thanked Harvey managers for attention to their special needs—women traveling with babies, elderly guests, and those who became ill en route or had to travel while still convalescing. Apparently, Harvey employees readily ministered to them.

The acclaimed Harvey Girls enjoyed working at the Alvarado. The money was good, and the women, many from Kansas, found living in exotic New Mexico and working in proximity to famous visitors a heady experience. Since the Alvarado was on a main route between Hollywood and the East Coast, many celebrities stopped briefly or stayed at the hotel. Over the years local photographers managed to snap, among others, Wallace Beery, Norma Shearer, Zazu Pitts, Jack Dempsey, Rudolph Valentino, Gary Cooper, Betty Grable, and Rin Tin Tin.

But there were also the ordinary railroaders and cowboys to contend with every day. C. M. Graham, a fireman for the Santa Fe who began eating at the Alvarado in 1916, told a story about the Harvey lunchroom. The checks consisted of a strip of coupons marked with amounts from five cents to a dollar. The waitress would tear them off up to the total of the bill. About 1917 Fred Harvey began charging for bread and butter and coffee, which until then had been gratis. One day a cowboy came in and ordered ham and eggs, thirty-five cents. The Harvey Girl, Nell, asked him if he wanted bread, butter, and coffee. He did. When she handed him the check showing he owed forty-five cents, he yelped that she was overcharging him. She tried to explain that the coffee, butter, and bread had added ten cents to his bill:

"Oh," said the cowboy, sarcastic like, "I had salt and pepper too."

"That's right," says Nellie and tore off another nickel from the check.[16]

The Indian Building

An entire complex of buildings dedicated to the traveler, resembling a mission transported from the misty coastal mountains of California to dry New Mexico. All the superlatives of Harvey service. What more could anyone ask? Fred Harvey came up with an answer: goods and experiences to buy.

Santa Fe Railway passengers shopping for Indian crafts at the entrance to the Indian Building, Alvarado Hotel. *From the Fred Harvey Company Papers, University of Arizona, N-5015. Folder 4. Special Collections, Tucson, Arizona.*

The traveling public, at the turn of the century, had left their Victorian rooms crammed with feathers, photographs in ornate frames, figurines, and crocheted table scarves to go in search of the West and its "primitive cultures." In 1899 Herman Schweizer, a former news agent and buyer for Fred Harvey, carefully considered that fact and acted upon it. He commissioned some silver Navajo jewelry to be sold through the Harvey gift shops. Collecting and using authentic pawn silver as a guide, he had silver pieces created in a lighter style than the traditional and thus more likely to please Easterners. The year Fred Harvey died, the company opened an Indian Department, founded by his son-in-law, John Frederick Huckel, and went into the business of merchandising Indian arts and crafts. Schweizer and Huckel envisioned that tourists would want to take home to their already stuffed parlors some mementos of their travels—not only jewelry but also basketry, pottery, blankets.

So when the Alvarado was designed it included an Indian Building—part museum, to display the company's growing collection of artifacts, and part salesroom. The collection itself became quite significant and attracted researchers, museum staff seeking acquisitions, well-heeled collectors like William Randolph Hearst, and even President Theodore Roosevelt. Huckel and Schweizer (who became known as "the Harvey anthropologist") spent five years accumulating North American Indian arts and crafts, both ancient and modern. They also acquired items from the South Pacific, such as Cook Island ceremonial adzes, and specimens of every mineral and gem found in New Mexico, Arizona, and Colorado.[17]

The salesroom designed by Mary Colter presented quantities of goods artfully arranged—blankets hung like tapestries, rugs with geometric designs spread on the floor, cone-shaped baskets dangling, heavy pots on benches and shelves, and a settee hung from the ceiling in front of a fireplace like a porch swing. But most compelling of all was the presence of the Native American artisans themselves at work: Navajo weavers and silversmiths, Acoma and Laguna potters. The

Indian Building was positioned between the hotel and the train station, so when the train stopped and passengers headed for the lobby or alighted for a stroll and a breath of air, they would be drawn to the Indians seated in front of the building selling handicrafts. The curious would then wander inside the building, lured by the prospect of watching a Navajo woman at her loom or a silversmith hammering a bracelet.

At first travelers, unaccustomed to Indian arts and crafts, showed little interest. So Herman Schweizer took to standing on the platform like a carnival barker exhorting them to see the Indian Building. Soon the venture succeeded in creating a market. Native American craftspeople acquired a new source of income and tourists a new taste for their well-wrought goods. The Alvarado's Indian Building with its Curio Rooms would have a lasting effect on the livelihoods of many Native Americans and the growing commerce of tourism in New Mexico.

One of the strongest attractions of the Alvarado lay in its evocation of a sacred site. It seemed one of the ancient missions summoned up from the past, where native artisans "undisturbed by the eager gaze of the tourist," worked or performed their chants and dances.[18] The Indian Building even contained a replica of a Hopi altar, though some Hopis objected to its construction and believed the man who built it was punished for his sacrilege with a swollen tongue that hung out of his mouth.[19]

The California Mission style was first associated in people's minds with an idyllic indigenous past that in turn became connected with tourism and recreation.[20] In addition, the Santa Fe Railway and Fred Harvey's "commodification"[21] of the Indian Southwest appealed to the longings of the public to touch something of a lost primeval America. It was "image-making freighted with the scent of earth and evocative aspects of Native American life."[22] Passengers wanted to step off the train and leave behind the rigid timetables, the soot and steam, the screaming brakes. They wanted to stroll into the quiet, ordered gardens and corridors of the past, into an imagined time when native peoples must have lived comfortably in the shadow of the Spanish mission. No reminders in this idyll of coercion, disease, or cultural loss.

Royal Reception

Even Theodore Roosevelt wanted to see the Alvarado Curio Rooms. He was driven right up to the doors, with troopers to hold the crowds back, and enjoyed a private tour for half an hour. Elle of Ganado, the most famous Navajo weaver at that time and a prime attraction herself at the Indian Building, presented the president with a wool saddle blanket woven in red, white, and blue. In big white letters it announced:

THE PRESIDENT
HONORARY
MEMBERSHIP CARD
COMMERCIAL CLUB
ALBUQUERQUE, N.M.
MAY 5, 1903.[23]

Roosevelt's two-and-a-half-hour stopover provided statehood boosters an opportunity to publicize their cause. When the president mounted the speaker's stand erected at the north entrance to the Alvarado, he saw before him a Statehood Tableau. It consisted of forty-six little girls, forty-five of them standing together surrounded by a fence, with one child outside the fence, arms outstretched beseechingly toward her companions. The message was clear: New Mexico Territory yearns to join the Union.

If President Roosevelt experienced at the Alvarado what the *Journal-Democrat* called a "Royal Reception," the same cannot be said of William Howard Taft.

There were certain similarities in the visits. Taft, in October of 1909, was, as Roosevelt had been six years earlier, traveling across the country and New Mexico Territory was fortunate enough to be en route. Once again, the territorial politicians seized the opportunity to make their perennial case for statehood. Taft, like his predecessor, was presented with Navajo blankets by the Commercial Club of Albuquerque and made an appearance at the Alvarado Hotel.

A banquet was arranged for the president there. On the agenda for the evening: blue point oysters shipped from the Atlantic seaboard, the presence of the most prominent political men (no women invited) in the territory, and a numbing number of speeches.[24] Albert Bacon Fall, an influential figure in New Mexico's public life, was scheduled for the best slot of the affair, the last speech. A tall, forceful man with heavy brows and mustache and long curling hair, Fall wasted no words on gallantry. To the dismay of those who had hoped to impress the visiting president, he called Taft's honesty into question. Doubting Taft's word that he supported New Mexico's bid for statehood, Fall reviewed the frustrating history of the territory's efforts to be admitted to the Union.

Taft jumped to his feet in angry self-defense and assured Fall and the shocked audience of his friendship to New Mexico. The main dining hall in the Alvarado where this event took place became known as "Taft Hall." In spite of his reception there, the offended president later signed the bill that admitted New Mexico into the United States, and the new state constitution was approved in Taft Hall.[25]

The Largest Hotel in the Harvey System

Mary Colter, who had one summer made the Curio Rooms so appealing when the Alvarado was brand new, became a permanent employee of Fred Harvey as a designer and architect. By the time she was asked to return to the twenty-year-old Alvarado and do some remodeling, Colter had designed the interiors for the company's station hotel at Lamy, New Mexico (El Ortiz), and three buildings at Grand Canyon—the Lookout, Hermit's Rest, and Phantom Ranch. She created buildings and interiors that seemed to grow out of the natural and cultural heritage of their settings. This became the hallmark of her work.

In 1922 the Alvarado was expanded to double its original room capacity, making it the largest Fred Harvey hotel. The lunchroom was completely renovated and made three times larger. Colter had the countertops covered with a black Belgian glass that resembled onyx. But the dark oak furniture in the lounge and lobby was discarded, and she tried to brighten those interiors. Despite what the newspaper had said at the hotel's opening about how the rooms were amply lighted, she felt they were too dark.[26] The changes extended into the gardens, with a lily pond and a wall fountain added and, by the following year, the "most extensive landscape gardening project ever attempted in Albuquerque for a hotel."[27] The landscape work was supervised by Paul Thiene of Pasadena, California, an authority on Spanish gardens and the designer of the San Diego Exposition grounds. Sixty-five varieties of shrubs, numerous flowers, and Lombardy poplars, spruce, juniper, and probably honey locusts were planted. The gardens many would later remember as one of the most pleasing parts of the Alvarado complex were taking shape—a cool, green oasis amid the dust and glare of an arid city.

Meals in the larger, modernized lunchroom changed too. Santa Fe employees had been accustomed to special rates at Harvey House lunchrooms, and they had enjoyed their camaraderie with the Harvey Girls, even ordering by code names. Scrambled eggs on toast had been "Adam and Eve on a raft and wreck 'em." A railroader might have called out "one Rio Grande on ice" for a glass of ice water or "one graveyard stew" for milk toast, so called because it was a favorite dish of the "lungers" or tuberculosis patients who hoped to evade the graveyard by coming to New Mexico. But after 1926 the Alvarado began to phase out the railroaders' discount, reducing it from 25 percent to 15 and then to 10, at the same time prices were hiked.[28] Fewer of them came into the Alvarado for a slice of pie or to kid their favorite Harvey Girls.

Soldiers at the Alvarado

The Depression years closed smaller Harvey Houses in stops like Emporia, Kansas, and Waynoka, Oklahoma, but the Alvarado remained open and busy. In fact some of the laid-off Harvey employees from elsewhere on the Santa Fe line were sent to the Albuquerque or Las Vegas or Grand Canyon hotels during those hard times. The Harvey system was in decline, but it was not so apparent in the heartland of the Southwest.

After the United States entered World War II, the necessary movement of troops across the nation provided a shot of adrenaline to Fred Harvey. In 1943 the *Santa Fe Magazine* wrote, "Every month more than a million meals are prepared in diners, in hotels and restaurants operated by Fred Harvey, and most of these meals are for Uncle Sam's fighting citizens."[29] The company shouldered the emergency job of feeding and housing military personnel. Some of the closed Harvey Houses were reopened and did a land-office business. Military officials approved menus in advance for troops. Their arrival at a Harvey lunchroom or dining room superseded all other activities while

Soldiers and civilians at the Alvarado Hotel and Albuquerque Depot, ca. 1943. *Courtesy of The Albuquerque Museum. Ward Hicks Advertising Collection, Gift of John Airy. Neg. No. 82-180-226.*

regular employees aided by volunteers fed them. Ads in *Life*, *Newsweek*, and *Fortune* featured a fictional Private Pringle to represent the thousands in uniform traveling by train and eating at Harvey establishments. The ads were intended to allay criticisms of the company, whose legendary high standards were being undermined by severe rationing and man- and woman-power shortages.

The Alvarado Hotel dealt with the scarcity of potential employees by hiring Harvey Girls from groups little represented in its work force before—Hispanic and Native American women. Houses that were major troop-train stops—the Alvarado was one of them—added staff known as troop-train girls. They served only the traveling soldiers and started right to work under emergency conditions on twenty-four-hour call; they did not undergo the traditional training of a Harvey Girl.[30]

Because Albuquerque was an aviation and military research center, housing of any kind was hard to come by. So the Air Transport Command as well as commercial airlines kept rooms on reserve to house pilots and their families as necessary.[31]

Opal Hill, a Harvey Girl who came to Albuquerque in 1941, recalled in an interview in 1969 that Clark Gable and Jimmy Stewart were both stationed at Kirtland Field and visited the Alvarado during the war. She also spoke of the work:

> In those days soldiers were dining and dancing every night at the Alvarado. Sometimes we were feeding trains at midnight or at 5 o'clock in the morning. There were no hours for us—we worked when we had to. On some days we have fed as many as 1,900 soldiers a day. Tables were set everywhere, on the outside, under the porch, and even in the kitchen. . . . Then there were days when the mortuary trains [would] pass by and we knew that some of these very boys

we had in the Alvarado were on these trains.[32]

Barbara Peterson, later the manager of the Coffee Shop, told an anecdote about the mix of troops and tourists in the Alvarado. One evening enlisted men were eating outside on the porches, officers were dining inside, and a fancy party was in progress near the dining-room fireplace. The party guests made no secret of their indulgences: lobster, baked Alaska, champagne. On her rounds Peterson overheard one of the soldiers remark, "So that's the hardship on the homefront."[33]

The Fifties

In 1940 Mary Colter once again returned to the Alvarado where her long career with Fred Harvey had begun. She designed and decorated a new cocktail lounge called La Cocina Cantina. She intended it to resemble an early southwestern kitchen, so she included a recessed brick fireplace in the style of the old ranchos and tables capped with copper. She decorated it with Mexican tiles that spelled out sayings in Spanish, rare old bottles, and lights set in parrot cages. Colter had a gift for the touches that transformed an ordinary public space into a memorable place.[34] The ambience of the Cantina attracted many regulars in the war years, including Albuquerque's nationally known journalist and war correspondent Ernie Pyle.

But the fifties were not kind to the Cantina. In May of 1952, newspaper headlines reminded readers, "Alvarado Hotel 50 Years Old; Changes Few Since Its Opening." But in its fiftieth year the Alvarado had to endure a major makeover. Guest rooms were redecorated and air-conditioned. The beloved Cantina was remodeled and rechristened "The Spotlight Room." With new paneling, glass and chrome, it acquired all the charm of an operating room. "Many people didn't like the new place," Harvey Girl Opal Hill recalled. It had lost what Mary Colter had been able to give it—character.[35]

By 1959 television sets had been added to all suites with living rooms (cost: $20 to $30 per night). Albuquerque was not just a town anymore; its population had burgeoned to 175,000. And the Municipal Airport served not only TWA but also Continental and Frontier Airlines.[36] Added amenities, population growth, increased opportunities to attract tourists—none could help the Alvarado. Travelers drove in from Santa Fe or from Tucumcari or, as I did with my parents in August of 1952, from Kingman, Arizona. But we all buzzed like crazed June bugs around the snazzy, neon-lit motels, even though the venerable Alvarado was located right on Route 66. Its part of downtown was deteriorating and some potential guests felt uneasy.

Wallace Stegner once said that a place is not a place until things that happened in it are remembered in history, ballads, yarns, legends, or monuments. The Alvarado had truly become a place. It was remembered in history and yarns, was in fact a monument itself to the city's past, but the crowds driving through Albuquerque in their Fords or Nash Ramblers didn't know or care.

The Alvarado Buildings Have Had Their Day

JUNE 8, 1969
The Alvarado Coffee Shop closed. It had once been the Harvey lunchroom, serving a thousand passengers a day. Since the previous year the Alvarado had been the sole surviving active Harvey House in the state.[37]

JUNE 26, 1969
The cochair of the second revival of the Montezuma Ball, Richard Worthen, announced to the press, "The days of the Alvarado are numbered, we all know, and we feel the atmosphere will help make the event a social highlight of the year."

LATE AUGUST, 1969
Santa Fe Railway spokesman Pat Hill said no decision had been made yet about the fate of the Alvarado. The hotel's manager Ted Arrelanes said, "As far as I know we'll be in operation for some time."[38]

SEPTEMBER 19, 1969
Despite the manager's optimism and while memories of the revived Montezuma Ball remained fresh, the Santa Fe Railway announced the Alvarado would be closed at the end of the year: "The decision to close the hotel was a difficult one but the demonstrated preference of travelers for more modern motel facilities situated away from the downtown area has made continued operation of the facility unduly burdensome." The *Albuquerque Journal* pointed out that the announcement had been expected for more than a year.

SEPTEMBER 22, 1969
Richard Worthen was apparently the only one consulting a crystal ball. On this date he wrote to Pete Domenici, Chairman of the City Commission:

> We cannot stand by idly and see the bulldozers do their worst. . . . If everyone else who should be jumping up and down in despair is sitting this one out, then I'll totter down First Street and lie down in front of the bulldozer. . . . We hold our heads and mourn the loss of so many traditions in our valley. This is one time we might have to say "we tried and failed" but how much better to have tried.

He urged Domenici to call together some concerned citizens.[39]

SEPTEMBER 26, 1969
An inspection report on the Alvarado Hotel from the city's Division of Building and Inspection concluded the building was "in good shape structurally," the basic wiring "in fair shape," and the plumbing and gas systems "acceptable."[40]

OCTOBER 1, 1969
The State Planning Office wrote to Santa Fe Railway President John Reed expressing concern about the Alvarado and pointing out its importance to the historical heritage of New

Mexico. George Cox, Santa Fe Railway vice president, replied, " . . . our engineers are firmly of the opinion that the building is too old to warrant remodeling or rehabilitation and while we plan to raze it, no time has been set for its demolition; neither have we decided what, if anything, to do with the property after it has been cleared."[41]

OCTOBER 27, 1969
Van Dorn Hooker, President of the Albuquerque Chapter of the American Institute of Architects, wrote to Pete Domenici:

> The Alvarado has national historical importance because it is the best extant example of the unique type of railroad center developed in the west by the Fred Harvey System. Locally the Alvarado was for many decades the social, as well as the transportation, center of the city.[42]

DECEMBER 8, 1969
The City Commission adopted a resolution to appoint an Alvarado–Santa Fe Station Complex Advisory Committee "to study the feasibility of planning" the preservation of the buildings. Pete Domenici appointed seven members, and Richard Worthen served as its chairman.[43]

JANUARY 2, 1970
John Reed, president of the Santa Fe Railway, was selected by *Modern Railroads Magazine* as the Railroad Man of the Year for 1970.[44]

The Alvarado closed.

JANUARY 5, 1970
At last the Alvarado–Santa Fe Station Complex Advisory Committee held its first meeting.

JANUARY 12, 1970
Mary Olin Harrell, manager of an Albuquerque typing service, wrote to Maria Blachut, city planner:

> I have read with much interest and nostalgia (since I am a native) the stories about the possibility of the Alvarado being torn down. This to me would be one of the greatest mistakes the downtown could make. What a tourist attraction it would be, and within walking distance of the new Convention Center. . . . I also feel it is so important to hold onto that bit of greenery in the patios and garden. The fountain area was a favorite spot of families in the early days. I can remember what a treat it was to walk down there on a summer evening, perhaps have dinner, and then enjoy this sheltered garden. . . . [45]

JANUARY 13, 1970
In answer to a letter from City Manager Richard H. Wilson, John Reed, Railroad Man of the Year, wrote, " . . . a professional appraisal has convinced us that the Alvarado buildings have had their day and that a small fortune would have to be spent in order to make them safe and satisfactory for any future use by the public."[46]

JANUARY 16, 1970

The State Cultural Properties Review Committee nominated the Alvarado for inclusion on the National Register of Historic Places and asked for fast action.

JANUARY 17, 1970

Several hundred people waited to get into the proposed National Historic Place for the auction of its furnishings. Bidders shopped for souvenirs and conversation pieces. A brass table lamp went for $12. Blank menus with the hotel's name on them sold for $6.[47]

JANUARY 19, 1970

The Alvarado–Santa Fe Station Complex Advisory Committee, whose unwieldy name had been shortened by the newspapers to "the preservation committee," met with George Cox, vice president of the railroad, to talk terms. According to the *Albuquerque News*'s post-mortem, oilman Robert Anderson, who was looking into the possibility of buying the Alvarado property, had been "privately quoted" a price of one million dollars. Richard Worthen, who attended that meeting, recalled a figure of just under a million. At the meeting, however, George Cox claimed he didn't know where that figure came from, that the railroad wouldn't accept less than 1.5 million. "At that point Anderson picked up his hat and coat and walked out," Worthen remembered.[48]

JANUARY 20, 1970

Architect and "preservation committee" member George Pearl examined the Alvarado at the request of the local chapter of the American Institute of Architects. Pearl found the building to be "well designed and well constructed." On the other hand, architects in the employ of the railroad pronounced the Alvarado unsound and not worth rehabilitating.[49]

JANUARY 26 AND 28, 1970

The city declined the offer to buy the Alvarado at the asking price of 1.5 million and asked the Santa Fe Railway to donate it. John Reed wired back his refusal.

JANUARY 31, 1970

Demolition began. The Coronado Wrecking and Salvage Company began to remove roof tile from the building named after the earlier Coronado's Captain Hernando de Alvarado.

FEBRUARY 1, 1970

Craig Andrews, American Institute of Architects, Society of Architectural Historians, wrote to Pete Domenici:

> I believe it was worth preserving and could have been preserved if leadership for such an effort had formed in time. The dilemma which the Santa Fe Railway faced was certainly predictable five years ago. Preservation efforts might well have started then.

Senator Clinton P. Anderson wired from Washington that the Alvarado had been put on the National Register of Historic Places.

Demolition of the Alvarado Hotel, February 1970. *Photo by Gordon Ferguson. Courtesy Museum of New Mexico, Santa Fe, New Mexico. Neg. No. 58706.*

Citizens were removing tile wainscoting and counter stools from the Coffee Shop.[50]

FEBRUARY 4, 1970

At a public meeting in Civic Auditorium a number of citizens testified about the Alvarado crisis. A city planner explained that Albuquerque possessed two landmark areas surviving from the past—Old Town, the Spanish Colonial settlement dating from the early eighteenth century, and New Town, the late nineteenth-century railroad town. While Old Town was already protected by a zoning ordinance, New Town was "crumbling" without any protection. Clearly a new ordinance was needed.

George Pearl recalled the room was packed with people who spoke out in favor of the salvation of the hotel but, after all was said and done, of the $50,000 thought necessary to get the Santa Fe's attention, only about $500 was raised. Actually, a few picket signs and petitions later, the total rose to $2,800.[51]

FEBRUARY 9, 1970

Citizens for Saving the Alvarado presented to the City Commission its recommendations: that the city file a temporary restraining order or injunction against the railroad and the wrecking company to halt the demolition and that the City Commission establish an historic zone to include the hotel and thus ultimately save it. The citizens' proposal cited a number of reasons for intervening on the Alvarado's behalf, listing not just its architectural and historical value but its potential economic contributions and the value of its human scale in a downtown dominated by institutions and towering office rectangles. It would offer fountains, foliage, a gently curving roof line, a refuge for a lunchtime stroll.[52]

FEBRUARY 16, 1970

John Reed wired the city that demolition had gone too far to be stopped. The historic zone proposal was rejected when the urban renewal director and the chairman of the Planning Commission argued that passage of such an ordinance could delay federal approval of the city's proposed urban renewal project. The Alvarado had not been included within the project area because, ironically, it was still considered "one of the best facilities of its kind in the city."[53]

SOMETIME IN FEBRUARY, 1970

Richard Worthen, chair of the "preservation committee," collapsed and went into the hospital suffering from exhaustion.

Afterlife—More Than a Hotel

The Santa Fe Railway had indicated the property would be used for a parking lot, but only temporarily. Five and a half years later, in September of 1975, the *Albuquerque Tribune* noted, "The site is an unpaved parking lot with no plans in view," and went on to point out what *was* in view—broken beer bottles, litter, weeds, sand.[54]

The physical remains of the Alvarado not trucked away as rubble were transported into people's homes. A decade after the demise of the hotel, writer Ruth Luhrs set out to find them. She located at homes and ranches the tile lions from lobby colonnades, candelabras, brass stools from the Coffee Shop, an oak guest-room door, and a Spanish settee purchased by Mary Colter for the hotel, among an array of other items. The owner of the settee explained her affection for several remnants in her ranch house: "The Alvarado was a home away from home for us. . . . It was more than a hotel, you know. The Alvarado was a tradition."[55]

Twenty-five years later notices appear fairly regularly in the classified ads listing Alvarado artifacts for sale. It sometimes seems everyone in town owns a piece of the vanished hotel. A frequent occurrence, when visiting someone's home for the first time, is to be shown the resident relic. The Alvarado not only was but still is, even in its absence, a tradition, a genuine cultural phenomenon.

The emotional legacy can also be traced. Richard Worthen recalls, "I was terribly angry for many years, but I've overcome my anger." He muses, "I don't know that there's a lesson, unless . . . the public has learned that they can't sit on their hands and let things like this happen without making an effort. I feel better because the effort was made. We certainly tried. God knows we tried."

The effort was made but not soon enough. So many have pondered the "if only" possibilities. V. B. Price, a journalist and regular commentator on Albuquerque's environment, summed up those regrets:

> If Albuquerque's fragmented leadership could have formed a consensus at the

> end of World War II to accommodate growth while preserving the downtown's unique identity, New Mexico would have two major "historic cities," one a diorama of Southwestern imagery and cultural mythology, the other a Western American downtown complete with adobe hotels, 1920s neoclassical style banks, and a 1950s curtain wall skyscraper. . . . and three luxury Southwestern hotels . . . all of them powerful draws for visitors, one-of-a-kind places you remember and write home about.[56]

Price later wrote that the destruction of the Alvarado initiated the destruction of Albuquerque's downtown and thus the city's identity.[57] Of the "three luxury Southwestern hotels"—the Alvarado, the Franciscan (annihilated soon after the Alvarado), and the Albuquerque Hilton—only the Hilton, now La Posada de Albuquerque, remains.

Epilogue

It is January 16, 1995. A quarter of a century ago today the State Cultural Properties Review Committee nominated the Alvarado Hotel for inclusion on the National Register of Historic Places and requested fast action. They got it. But today you have to know what you're looking for to find any clues that the designated Historic Place ever existed.

Though it is a sunny day, the wind bites. I stand shivering in the gravel parking lot and look east toward the train tracks where I can see niches in the gray wall below the platform where Max Apodaca's orchestra played for the last Montezuma Ball. One of them must have been for a fountain—I can make out the remains of a sculpted fish. When I scuff about in the gravel and blowing trash I find some of the brick that once outlined the lawn.

Exactly two weeks from today will be the twenty-fifth anniversary of the day the wrecking company moved in to prepare for demolition. Standing here in the empty space I recall the words of Lawrence Clark Powell:

> Where do I take my stand when I survey the Southwest? . . . It is at the heart of hearts, the *cor cordium*, in Albuquerque, New Mexico, that ancient crossing on the Rio Grande. I will be even more precise and say just where it would be in Albuquerque: on the station platform of the Alvarado, one of the last of the Harvey Houses and the most beautiful of them all, old gray stucco with the turquoise trim, its cool courts and shady patios inviting siesta, its Indian museum packed with old Pueblo artifacts, its slow heartbeat the coming and going of the Santa Fe trains.[58]

CHAPTER TWO

La Fonda in Santa Fe

"The world walks through our lobby!"
—*La Fonda advertisement*

Countless pairs of sneakers and cowboy boots cross the smooth pattern of chile-red and sand floor tiles. A pony-tailed man strides through wearing a belt with conchos the size of hubcaps. A bridesmaid hurries by with a white bouquet. The flow of denim is punctuated occasionally by a chic black dress. People gather in knots, reading brochures for Jeep tours, Taos Ski Valley, the Cumbres and Toltec Scenic Railroad. Sunlight from La Plazuela pours into the lobby, illuminating the canvas of a painter working in oils. On a wall hangs a portrait in wood marquetry of Jose Ronquillo, a driver for Indian Detours for many years, its plaque explains, who took a daily stroll through the hotel. Oliver La Farge once reported that, "during the Fiestas of 1958, three young ladies rode their ponies into the lobby of La Fonda, passing over the spot where, ninety-one years earlier, Chief Justice Slough fell with his derringer in his hand."[1]

Simone de Beauvoir, who despised American hotels, wrote

> The La Fonda is the most beautiful hotel in America, perhaps the most beautiful I have ever seen in my life. The patio is surrounded by cool walkways paved with a mosaic of tiles and Spanish-style furnishings; here, an Indian stands in the lobby who has been selling fake turquoise and pieces of petrified wood to tourists for years.[2]

Spanish Colonial Period

The lobby of La Fonda is the heart of a building at the heart of a city with a long life. The date generally accepted for the founding of Santa Fe is 1610, making it one of the oldest European settlements in the United States. So La Fonda's piece of earth, above which now lie the lobby's "mosaic of tiles" from the 1920s, has seen nearly four centuries of foot traffic.

The Spaniards who carved a foothold into a remote frontier of their empire in the New World named this city Villa de Santa Fe or City of Holy Faith. To the east rise the Sangre de Cristo, or Blood of Christ, Mountains. The city lies just below their dark green slopes, where the rose-tinted foothills are dotted with junipers and piñon pines.

As in other Spanish colonial towns, the earliest buildings were constructed around a plaza. Of the structures located where La Fonda stands today at the southeast corner of the plaza, little remains. In the mid-1980s a three-story parking garage was planned for La Fonda on the site of the hotel's open-air parking lot. John A. Ware of the Laboratory of Anthropology arranged with Sam Ballen, chief executive officer and chairman of the board of the Corporación de La Fonda, to do some exploratory archeological excavations on the proposed building site. Despite hopes that remnants from homes of the territorial period (1846–1912) would be unearthed, none were found. Over the years they had been thoroughly razed. The early Spanish Colonial period (before 1680) yielded some findings but only from a trash pit that contained animal bones, blacksmithing slag, Indian pottery sherds, and European-made artifacts such as lead shot.[3]

Jose Urrutia's map of Santa Fe for a later Spanish period, the oldest extant map of the city, dated about 1766–68, shows a row of connected buildings along the south side of what is now San Francisco Street between the church and the plaza.[4] They were probably residences. A descendent of an owner of one of those residences, which stood on the present site of La Fonda, has carefully researched the home of the Juan Bautista Alarid family and constructed a model of it in adobe. It now stands in the lobby of La Fonda.[5]

Americans Arrive in a Mexican Town on the Santa Fe Trail

Susan Magoffin was, in 1846 and for 141 years afterward, thought to have been the first Anglo-American woman to cross the plains and enter the city at the end of the Santa Fe Trail. But in 1987 historian Marian Meyer found evidence that a woman from Missouri, Mrs. William Donoho, Mary Dodson Donoho, had traveled the trail and arrived in Santa Fe in 1833, thirteen years before Susan Magoffin. Mary Donoho left no journal, as did Susan Magoffin, of her time there, but according to their son, she and her husband ran a hotel on the plaza, the forerunner of the Exchange Hotel and La Fonda.[6]

Mexico had declared its independence from Spain in the spring of 1821, and word of this enormous event finally trickled north as far as Santa Fe by September of that year. Life changed, even in the hinterlands so distant from the turmoil of a nation in the making. No longer restricted by Spanish xenophobia, trade with the United States burgeoned, and the main route for goods was through Santa Fe. Americans rented stores in the summertime on the south side of the plaza to sell calico and gingham, American-style mirrors, boots, and muslin shirts to people who had managed before without them. The women of Santa Fe began to wear fashionable, fitted gowns instead of their customary loose blouses and skirts, and bonnets instead of *rebozos* or shawls. Santa Feans in turn offered to the Americans the pleasures of dancing at *fandangos* and gambling at *monte* tables.[7]

All these Americans coming and going in Santa Fe required lodging, and Marian Meyer concluded that the hotel run by the Donohos must have provided it. An 1836 list of Santa

Fe property owners includes mention of a house called *Los Estados Unidos* (the United States) on what is now the south half of La Fonda property. It would have been convenient to the American traders' rented shops on the south side of the plaza, so perhaps this was where the Donohos offered commercial hospitality to them.[8]

For a view of the neighborhood of "the American *fonda*" nearly a decade after the Donohos left the city, we can look to Susan Magoffin's journal of her travels along the Santa Fe Trail and into Mexico as an eighteen-year-old newlywed with her husband Samuel, a veteran trader on the route. When she arrived in Santa Fe at the end of August 1846, Susan Magoffin was well aware she was arriving at a crucial time in its history, just two weeks after General Stephen Watts Kearny had entered the city and claimed it for the United States.

Santa Fe tradition holds that the house the Magoffins stayed in for more than a month was the one nearest the *parroquia* (parish church, located where St. Francis Cathedral stands now) on the block presently occupied entirely by La Fonda and its Carriage House. They occupied a house Susan described as being "under the shadow of '*la iglesia*'" and definitely within earshot of its bells, which seemed to her to be chiming all day and all night.[9] They had four rooms, one of which served as "reception room, parlour, dining-room, and in short room of all work."[10] All the rooms had dirt floors, plank ceilings, and whitewashed walls. Her "room of all work" had calico tacked to the wall up to a height of six feet. Susan thought it looked "quite fixy."[11] Because the seats were mostly benches against the wall, the calico saved coats and dresses from the whitewash. She liked the coolness of the bedchamber for an afternoon siesta and the pleasant demeanor of her household servants. In short, she was satisfied with her temporary home in Santa Fe.

The house she described, if it was in fact the one across the street from the church, would subsequently become the property of several families, the best known being the Fiske family, who lived there for thirty years. Eugene A. Fiske was a prominent attorney and political figure who acquired the house in 1881. It was demolished to make space for the La Fonda parking lot in 1949, a few years more than a hundred after Susan and Samuel Magoffin entertained General Kearny and his soldiers in their parlor. On the evening before the house that had come to be known as the Fiske-Magoffin House was razed, Santa Feans gathered there to mourn its passing and celebrate its past, not with speeches or commemorative plaques but, characteristically, with a costume party.[12]

1840s and 1850s—The Pulse Quickens

When General Kearny entered Santa Fe, "there was but one Public House in the place," said the *Santa Fe Republican* in September of 1847, "and it was so badly supplied that but few paid it a second visit now we have several, the Missouri House, the Santa Fe House, Beck & Redmans Hotel, and the German Hotel, also several private

Boarding Houses."[13] If there was a *fonda* on the southeast corner of the plaza before 1847, it may have been the hotel run by the Donohos discussed earlier, or it may have been the badly supplied Public House mentioned above. But by the end of the 1840s, the pulse of Santa Fe had quickened with the constant flow past its adobe walls of Americans traders, gold seekers en route to California, and soldiers. Providing food, lodgings, and diversion for them became a necessity and a business opportunity. In a process repeated again and again across the West, a small, agricultural town was being irrevocably altered by an influx of newcomers impelled by forces generated far beyond its borders.

The public house that would always later be known as "the American *fonda*" was, early in the American occupation, named the Santa Fe House. We can get some sense of the newly heightened activity in slow-blooded Santa Fe by the fact that its innkeeper advertised meals available at any hour of the day or night, oysters and sardines always on hand, cooked if desired.[14]

By June of 1848 Santa Fe House had already changed hands, been repaired and renovated, and become the U.S. Hotel. Its proprietors, listed in an advertisement as "Humphrey & Coulter," laid claim to having ample beds, large and ventilated rooms, the best of liquors, and the only ice house and large corral in town.[15]

The reality may have been somewhat less restful. William R. Goulding, a member of the Knickerbocker Exploring Company of the city of New York, bound for the gold fields of California, arrived in Santa Fe one night in 1849 and spent it at the U.S. Hotel sleeping, not in a well-ventilated room, but in the billiard parlor, where mattresses were tossed on the tables and below them. Billiard play presumably ceased as sojourners bedded down for the night, but gaming continued in an adjoining room, where twenty or thirty Americans and locals played cards on tables heaped with dollar bills. Goulding learned that the gaming license cost the proprietors a thousand dollars a year, but they raked in a hundred dollars a night.[16]

By far the most colorful descriptions of the U.S. Hotel, soon to become the Exchange Hotel, were provided by New Mexico attorney and historian Ralph Emerson Twitchell. In a lengthy and fascinating footnote in his history of Santa Fe, he tells us much about the hotel established in a building leased from a member of the Pino family. The one-story building surrounded a patio and included a dining room, a large corral, and stables on the south side. The stagecoaches from points east always stopped first at the "American *fonda*."

A postcard from the 1930s (see color section) depicts the stage pulled by a team of six horses arriving at full gallop in a swirl of dust at the entrance. This postcard was supposedly based on an "old original photo."[17] I believe it likely that the photo was one dated 1855, now in the Museum of New Mexico archives, that shows the Exchange Hotel and the Seligman and Clever store across the street. The postcard scene's angle of view is a bit different, and for sales appeal, the stagecoach's arrival has been added. Also, the men loitering around the hotel entrance have been ren-

The Exchange Hotel (center of photo), southeast corner of Santa Fe's plaza, 1855. *Courtesy of the Museum of New Mexico, Santa Fe, New Mexico. Neg. No. 10685.*

dered more exotic, wearing sombreros in the postcard rather than the ordinary felt hats with broad brims of the 1850s seen in the photograph.

The main entrance where stage passengers alighted was at the northwest corner of the building, catercornered from the plaza. After they entered the hotel, they would find, on three sides of the interior patio, a *portal* (long, roofed porch) offering them a place amid flowers and vines to escape the dirt and smells of the street and collect their wits. In cages swinging from the *portal vigas*, or beams, mockingbirds ran through their repertoires. "Loungers sat there in their black American broadcloth, rakish hats, and full whiskers, tilting their chairs back with their feet up on the portal posts in native American manner, picking their teeth after a family-style meal."[18]

But it was the hotel's gaming rooms that summoned historian Twitchell's eloquence. He described the "gaming devotees" as coming from every walk of life from justices of the supreme court to sheep herders, all gathered under the kerosene lamps before the dealer and his associates, who sported "immaculate linen" and "resplendent solitaire" diamonds.[19]

James A. Bennett, a New Yorker enlisted in the First Dragoons and sent to New Mexico, arrived in June of 1851 at the "American *fonda*," which had changed its name again, burned in March of that year, and then been quickly rebuilt.[20] It was now the Exchange Hotel, a name it would retain through all subsequent vicissitudes for nearly 70 years, until World War I.

Bennett's experience of the Exchange Hotel proved to be less inspiring than Twitchell's. He wrote of his evening there:

> Several persons were seated in the hotel. A person came in, took a glass of brandy, turned from the bar and commenced firing his pistol at random, and

> could not be stopped until he had fired four shots which wounded one lawyer in the abdomen and another man in the arm. He was asked the reason for so doing and replied, "A friend of his from Texas was killed at Santa Fe and that all the inhabitants of the place were cut-throats, robbers, and murderers." He was a Texan. He was placed in jail. Later in the night, the Texan was taken from the jail and hung by the neck in the back yard of the Exchange. I suppose it was done by friends of the lawyer.[21]

1860s and 1870s—More Violence in the Exchange Hotel

In December of 1867 John P. Slough, New Mexico's chief justice, felt that he was being insulted by members of the territorial legislature, recently convened in the capital. They had failed to request that he administer their oaths of office and then added insult to injury by passing resolutions claiming the chief justice to be unjust, unfair, and bad-tempered. Slough did not welcome these legislative pronouncements on his alleged character flaws. He particularly objected to a speech by W. L. Rynerson from Doña Ana County and unburdened himself of these feelings to a friend at the Exchange Hotel. The *Santa Fe Weekly Gazette* reported that he had called Rynerson a liar. Other reports indicated that he made unflattering remarks about Rynerson's military record.

Within hours Rynerson, concealing a Colt revolver, showed up at the Exchange Hotel. He paced up and down in front of the door leading to the billiard saloon until Slough appeared from one of the inner rooms. Rynerson demanded a retraction. The chief justice refused and tried to draw his derringer, but Rynerson shot too fast. The bullet ripped into Slough's abdomen. The chief justice died a lingering death. Rynerson was granted a change of venue to be tried in Las Vegas, New Mexico, and was finally acquitted of the charge of murder on a plea of self-defense.[22]

Another murder at the Exchange Hotel that jolted tranquil Santa Fe into what a contemporary called "an agitated sea"[23] was committed by the nephew and namesake of the renowned Archbishop Jean Baptiste Lamy, the protagonist of Willa Cather's novel *Death Comes for the Archbishop*.

The archbishop brought to the humble, earth-embracing architecture of Santa Fe certain aspirations. He desired a stone cathedral built on the site of the old adobe *parroquia* that would speak of the soaring religious art and architecture of his memory—of his native France and perhaps of other places from his own history.[24] But the dream was very slow in realization. Lamy could lay his hands on too little money to carry the project forward with any speed. Antoine Mouly, the chief architect, began to lose his eyesight and had to return to France. In the midst of all this difficulty, another French architect, Francois Mallet, came to Santa Fe in 1878 to "correct and perfect the design of the cathedral."[25] He drew up a new set of plans.

He came alone, so young Jean Baptiste Lamy, the archbishop's nephew, befriended him, inviting him to the home he shared with his wife, Mercedes Chavez de Lamy. They lived near the cathedral-in-progress on San Francisco Street on the portion of the block now occupied by La Fonda's Carriage House. The house was part of the estate inherited by Mercedes Chavez de Lamy from her wealthy mother only a year before Mallet's arrival.

Mallet often visited them. Too often. The frequent presence of the architect, described as a man "of prepossessing appearance with a flow of brilliant language,"[26] seemed too welcome to his wife for Jean B. Lamy's comfort. So he informed his wife that Mallet could no longer be their guest. Mercedes Chavez de Lamy did not quietly accept this dictum from her husband. She, after all, was a woman who had perhaps married beneath her. From a prominent and well-to-do Santa Fe family, she had married an industrious but poor fellow from France (though undoubtedly rendered a more desirable match because of his relationship to the archbishop). She pointed out to her husband that their home was actually her home, and she could entertain whomever she pleased, when she pleased. She went further. She told her friends that in marrying Jean B. Lamy she had made a misalliance. She moved out of the house (probably into the Exchange Hotel on the same block), filed for divorce, and continued to see Mallet. Some gossiped that they planned to go to Denver and marry after the divorce. Lamy's friends reported later that he became distraught and did not seem himself.

On the evening of September 1, 1879, Mallet ate dinner at the Exchange Hotel, as was his custom, and then stationed himself at the entrance, looking out on the plaza to watch Santa Fe stroll by. Lamy entered the hotel office behind Mallet, circled it as if trying to work up his nerve, and then stepped directly behind Mallet and shot him in the back of the head.

Mrs. Lamy, after she had learned of this, tried to kill herself by taking aconite but was saved by Dr. Robert Longwill. Her husband Jean B. Lamy stood trial. After three attempts to render a properly worded verdict, a jury acquitted him by reason of insanity. All of this trouble within his family—and this latest blow to progress on the cathedral—caused Archbishop Lamy to be "cast down with sadness."[27]

1880s—Renovation

The Exchange Hotel was sold in 1881 to Dr. Robert Longwill and Abraham Staab, a leading merchant and one of the largest landowners in town. Staab had immigrated to the U.S. from Germany in the 1850s with his older brother, Zadoc. By 1859 the two had begun a retail business in Santa Fe and joined the small but very influential fraternity of Jewish merchants in New Mexico who became leaders in their communities. By the 1880s Z. Staab & Brother, Dealers in General Merchandise, had grown into a major business enterprise.

The hotel was dilapidated when Abraham Staab became co-owner of the building. So the Staabs began to exert some of their considerable clout in the Jewish community to raise money for a major renovation. Zadoc Staab contributed $5,000, and others with locally well-known names such as Ilfeld and Seligman and Spiegelberg put up more than $9,000 altogether out of $28,700 in total subscriptions.[28]

The money was used to make substantial changes in the building, primarily enlarging it. Shops were added on San Francisco Street, and general improvements made. The Exchange now had to compete with the elegant, new, three-story, mansard-roofed Palace Hotel on Washington Avenue, and no one had ever described the Exchange Hotel as elegant. In fact, one writer said its outward appearance "impresses the visitor as being the last place to find good hotel accommodations."[29] But the Exchange offered a venerable reputation and, in addition, sought to please its guests with food such as this on an 1885 menu: "Colorado Head Cheese, Baron of Beef, Stuffed Turkey, Calf's Brains Scrambled with Ranch Eggs, Brown Potatoes, Pumpkin and Grape Pie, Cocoanut Jumbles, and Pine Apple Snow."[30]

The Rise of Santa Fe Style

Decades later, the long-lived Exchange Hotel—which by now had done time as a meat market, a rooming house, and Nancy Thornton's "eating house"—was again deteriorating.

At the same time a new spirit was arising in Santa Fe, an enthusiasm for the city's and the region's past and the distinctiveness of New Mexico's architectural traditions. This zeal for uncovering and reclaiming Santa Fe's heritage would ultimately determine the city's architectural destiny, and along with it, that of any successor to the old "American *fonda*."

Faced with a declining population, the city needed to find economic salvation. Tourism seemed to offer it. One way to attract tourists would be to fashion a new image from old materials.

In 1912 an exhibit known as "New Old Santa Fe" at the Palace of Governors presented the results of recent research into the characteristics of the region's architecture, despised in earlier decades by visitors and even by its own archbishop. The intent of the exhibit was to encourage support for the Santa Fe City Planning Board's proposal that same year to stimulate tourism and improve civic life through emphasizing historic preservation and a Santa Fe building style. To tell the truth, Santa Feans had not been particularly aware of how they built their buildings or why they might be considered special. They simply built in traditional ways or borrowed styles from the eastern U.S. that rode into town with Anglo-Americans.

But the researchers behind the exhibit were not local folks born and bred to the look of the ancient townscape. Rather they were newcomers to New Mexico, archeologists and photographers. With unaccustomed eyes they appreciated its unique mix of Pueblo and Spanish Colonial "primitive" architecture: single- and multi-story, flat-roofed, adobe buildings with *portales* and with projecting *vigas* originally hand-hewn out of ponderosa pine. They wanted to preserve and restore what they found and photographed; they also wanted to carry traditional patterns into the future by incorporating them into new construction. A "Santa Fe style" was being devised.

Buildings in the California Mission style, such as the Alvarado Hotel in Albuquerque, had been popular for years and familiar to travelers. But a New Mexico Mission style? That, in effect, is what the proponents of the "New Old Santa Fe" exhibit had in mind. New Mexico's own native and colonial architecture would be restored, preserved, reproduced, and creatively used in a selective version of Santa Fe's past.[31]

Gentlemen, the child is born!

In the midst of all this enthusiasm for the old, the old Exchange Hotel—certainly an example, if not an inspiring one, of indigenous architecture—met an ignominious end. It could be said to be a casualty of World War I, for it died as a result of injuries from a two-man tank nicknamed the Mud Puppy.

It happened in a burst of patriotic fervor at a Victory Bond rally in the spring of 1919. Stores were closed for the occasion, and Santa Feans gathered in a holiday spirit to hear speeches and exhortations to support the war effort by buying Victory Bonds. The Mud Puppy provided incentive. Every time a hundred-dollar bond was sold, the tank would bash against the hotel, sending up dust and bringing door and window frames and sections of the worn adobe wall on Shelby Street crashing down. The crowd must have loved it.[32]

They apparently loved equally well the idea of building a fine new hotel on the site after the demolition of the old. Before the end of 1919, the president of the First National Bank announced the successful completion of a subscription drive to raise $200,000 for the building of a new hotel: "Gentlemen, the child is born!"[33]

The *Santa Fe New Mexican* was impressed that a small town could raise so much money in such a short time. T. B. Catron, who had been elected to the U.S. Senate when New Mexico became a state in 1912, expressed his opinion: the new hotel ought to be plain, substantial, four stories high, and have good elevators.[34] Catron was not aware that elevators would pale in significance beside Santa Fe style.

The architectural firm given the commission for the new hotel—Rapp, Rapp, and Henrickson—had not originally been at the forefront of the movement to develop a new building style that clearly proclaimed New Mexico. Indeed, Isaac Hamilton Rapp, the designer and head of the firm, had made a name for himself in southern Colorado and in Santa Fe by designing public buildings, including the New Mexico territorial capitol of 1900, in conformance with the styles typical of the period. But the firm had attracted attention from the planners of the "New Old Santa Fe" exhibit with, of all things, a warehouse. It was designed for the Colorado Supply Company and stood near the train tracks in Morley, Colorado, in clear view from the train as it ascended Raton Pass. I. H. Rapp had based his plan for the warehouse on the San Esteban Rey mission church at Acoma, in ruins at the time he drew his inspiration from it. Admiration for this building of Rapp's, plus the Rapp firm's solid reputation in Santa Fe, resulted in commissions that would prove important to the development of Santa Fe style. I. H. Rapp's design of the 1916 Museum of Fine Arts on the plaza was particularly significant in popularizing it.

Rapp's last major commission was the design of the new hotel, to be called officially as its predecessor had long been unofficially, La Fonda. He planned the building around an interior courtyard, like the old Exchange. It was not made of adobe, though, but of reinforced concrete and hollow tile covered by cement stucco, earthen colored to resemble adobe. It included a walled patio on San Francisco Street, terraced roofs, balconies, and projecting *vigas*. Contrary to T. B. Catron's opinion, it was not plain, and at first there was no elevator.

Worse yet, forty-six rooms were not enough to ensure its success. The new hotel, the pride of Santa Fe but plagued with financial difficulties, closed after only two years.

Indian Detours

> Harvey hotel service, Harvey hotel food, Harvey hotel standards—these are fixed and unchangeable and their fame is as wide as travel itself.[35]

The *Santa Fe New Mexican* exulted over the purchase of La Fonda by a subsidiary of the Santa Fe Railway, the Santa Fe Land Improvement Company, which would in turn lease it to Fred Harvey to operate. But survival for La Fonda would not depend only upon the Harvey reputation but also upon an innovation in travel known as the Indian Detours. They would attract hundreds of thousands of visitors to northern New Mexico, to automobile tourism, and to La Fonda, some of them sophisticates already acquainted with world-famous cities, travelers such as Eleanor Roosevelt, Albert Einstein, and John D. Rockefeller Jr.[36]

The Santa Fe Railway had already established in the public mind a corporate image that suggested a strong connection with Native American culture. This association was fostered by the sale of Native American crafts at the Indian Building at the Alvarado Hotel in Albuquerque and the evocative use in company advertising of paintings of Indians in their southwestern landscape.

Train travel was still the dominant mode of transportation for tourists coming to New Mexico in the 1920s, but they longed for an escape from the train, a chance to venture into the distant mountains and mesas only glimpsed through its windows. What they wanted, the Santa Fe Railway reasoned, was the Indian Detour, which allowed rail passengers to make two- or three-day excursions by car into the "real" New Mexico, where the Indians on the railroad's posters actually lived and worked.

The Detours began in May 1926. La Fonda played a key role from the outset, as they were initially conducted between the Castañeda Hotel in Las Vegas and the Alvarado

Hotel in Albuquerque, with an overnight stay at La Fonda and touring of pueblos between the three towns.

Travelers, called "dudes," climbed into luxurious big Packards and Cadillacs bearing Thunderbird logos. These "Harveycars" were driven by men wearing riding breeches that seemed more appropriate attire for a fox hunt than an exploration of cowboy country. But never mind, the drivers were courteous, according to reports from travelers, and able to deal with the rigors of auto travel in northern New Mexico at the time, an adventure that included sandy washes, muddy arroyos, high altitude engine trouble, flat tires, and mighty tight turns on the road down La Bajada between Santa Fe and Albuquerque.

Young women guides called couriers also eased travelers' introduction to exotic New Mexico. Writer Charles F. Lummis described them in a booklet published by the Santa Fe Railway in 1928:

> Fine, clean, thoroughbred, lovely young women of old families, inheriting love and comprehension of their native State, and put through a schooling in its history and nature—they give the tourist such insight and understanding as not one traveler in 500 ever got before.[37]

This schooling was initially provided quite successfully by Erna Fergusson, daughter of a prominent Albuquerque family and veteran operator of her own automobile touring outfit known as Koshare Tours. Her trained couriers accompanied the "dudes" on their excursions, which first began with pueblos and ruins near Santa Fe (such as Puyé) and eventually branched out to other sites and went further afield, to the archeologically rich Four Corners area of northwestern New Mexico or southeast to Carlsbad Caverns. Couriers had to handle deftly all sorts of questions, such as "Why did the Indians build their pueblos so far from the railroad?"[38]

When Detourists returned to La Fonda for the night they could visit the room known as the lecture lounge. A large map of the Southwest, books, lantern slide shows, and lectures provided information to help them understand what they were seeing. Being a "dude" resembled taking a short field course in Southwestern studies, and apparently many were delighted to be students.

Fred Harvey's files accumulated letters and more letters from travelers who enjoyed the Detour experience. One such writer wrote with breathless enthusiasm:

> The romance and picturesqueness of the old Santa Fe Road itself, the excellent service of both Pullman car and cuisine, and the charm of the Southwest Indian country 300-mile motor ride over 'roads to yesterday' and delightful visit to our quaint artistic Pueblos and fascinating prehistoric Indian ruins, as well as the unsurpassed hotel service at the Alvarado and La Fonda, and the gracious hospitality of couriers, made my trip one never to be forgotten.[39]

The Indian Detours corralled some of the untamed aspects of New Mexico and turned them into the likes of trail horses for dudes. One result—whether for better or for worse is still being argued—was the further encouragement of an internationally significant tourist industry centered in Santa Fe.

Another was that La Fonda was losing $500 a night having to refer guests to other hotels for lack of rooms.[40]

John Gaw Meem and Mary Colter

The bold corporate imagery of the Santa Fe Railway—Indians standing before their stacked adobe dwellings gazing into a sunbathed distance—appealed to many. One was a young man in New York City. He had contracted tuberculosis while working in Brazil and had just been informed that he would have to go to a sanatorium in North Carolina, the Adirondacks, or New Mexico. He must choose. Walking along the street mulling it over, he passed a Santa Fe Railway ticket office. Struck by one of their advertisements, he went in and bought a ticket.[41]

The young man was John Gaw Meem, and soon he was living in Sunmount Sanatorium in Santa Fe under the care of Dr. Frank Mera, one of a group who were fomenting interest in traditional Santa Fe arts and architecture. Dr. Mera not only treated his patients' bodies but also provided them with a creative environment that ministered to their minds and sensibilities. In that setting John Meem, who had been educated as an engineer, began to develop an interest in architecture, especially in the historic architecture of New Mexico. He became well enough to venture to Denver to work with an architectural firm there and to attend courses in design. But when that schedule strained his health, he had to return to Sunmount.

Meem decided to start his own architectural firm in a spare building at the sanatorium and entered into partnership with an accountant and fellow patient, Cassius McCormick. He also became active in historic preservation with an organization known as the Committee for the Preservation and Restoration of New Mexico Churches, which was involved in extensive repairs on the mission church at Acoma from 1927 to 1930.[42]

At that time La Fonda needed more space in order to accommodate the numbers of tourists arriving for Indian Detours. Plans called for a new kitchen to be constructed and the former kitchen converted into a bigger dining room. A new wing was to be added onto the south side and a fifth floor, more than tripling the number of rooms. John Gaw Meem obtained the commission for the project.

Meem was undertaking his first major commission as an architect, but he would be working with a veteran. Designer Mary Colter had begun her career with Fred Harvey one summer a quarter of a century before when she had planned the arrangement of goods in the Indian Building at the Alvarado Hotel in Albuquerque. Her familiarity with the needs of hotel guests, such as size and layout requirements for their rooms, was helpful to Meem.

Colter definitely wanted to change some aspects of the Rapp-designed La Fonda. She considered the Rapp version of Spanish Pueblo Revival style to be "too nervous and indented" and told Meem she thought simpler lines would be more effective. He agreed. His emphasis would be more on mass than ornament. He observed that the design of the tower at the southwest corner of the building recalled the towers at the Acoma church, which were then being reconstructed under his direction. His simultaneous work on the church at Acoma and the tower at La Fonda provided an opportunity for each design to influence the other.[43]

In fact, he faced the difficult problem of successfully linking the tall, solid mass of his new wing to the lower, very broken lines of the older portion of the hotel. Another of his concerns was that the much larger, remodeled La Fonda not compete with St. Francis Cathedral or interfere with the scale of other nearby structures. He tried to keep the new construction from being too massive-looking by stepping back the walls of the suites on the top floor and by interjecting balconies.[44]

Mary Colter was dealing with problems of her own. Just before her assignment to decorate La Fonda, she had been riding to her office in Kansas City in a taxi that crashed into a streetcar. So her work at La Fonda had to be done from the confines of a wheelchair. She also worried about how her work would hold up under the scrutiny of Santa Fe's artist colony, confessing to a friend that she was "scared to death."[45] One of those artists, Olive Rush, was brought in to paint murals and panes of glass—sunlight would shine through the colors as if through stained glass.

Colter thought the stained wood of the lobby too dark and urged Meem to open the room to more light. She removed the old furnishings and replaced them with Mexican-style furniture, custom-made to her specifications and hand-painted by Kansas City artist Earl Altaire. He painted a remarkable 798 pieces.[46]

In 1928 workers digging the basement for the expanded La Fonda unearthed an 1886 loaded revolver, many very old bottles of whiskey, a four-inch cannon ball, and a human skull—all reminders of the rough old days of the Exchange.[47] But Mary Colter was creating a far more opulent hotel than the *fonda* at the end of the Santa Fe Trail had ever been before. She worked out a unique design and color scheme for each one of the 156 guest rooms. For the expensive suites on the fifth floor she acquired Spanish antiques, such as an eighteenth-century Catalan bed; she said that even though she knew it was "not customary to use such furniture in hotels, the temptation was too great."[48]

Work had begun on the enlargement plan in May of 1928, and the hotel reopened in June of the following year. Both Meem and Colter had risen to the challenges facing them in the project. Meem, at the beginning of what would become an outstanding career in New Mexico, quickly rose to prominence with the successful blending of existing and new structures in La Fonda's Spanish Pueblo Revival style. As architectural historian Bainbridge Bunting put it, "La Fonda aspired to be more than merely eye-catching; its architecture and interior appointments were intended as serious interpretations of the region. One might see it as John Meem's 'master work.'"[49] Colter, already well established in her career and respected for buildings and interiors from the Grand Canyon to Union Station in Chicago, had demonstrated once again in La Fonda her creativity and sensitivity to the cultural context of her designs.

Only Twenty People in Santa Fe Were Downright Interesting

In spite of Mary Colter's concern about how the artists of Santa Fe would accept her work, they soon made it clear that the grander La Fonda suited them just fine. Thus the hotel was able to provide for its Detour guests not only a lecture lounge but also a bonus, close-up view of the cultural elite drawn to the capital from about 1915 to 1940.

Well-known journalist Ernie Pyle explained it this way:

> Life among the upper crust centered by daytime in the La Fonda Hotel. (La Fonda is Spanish for "The Hotel," but people don't pay much attention to that. They just go on saying The-the Hotel-Hotel.) You could go there any time of day and see a few artists in the bar, or an Indian that some white woman loved, or a goateed nobleman from Austria, or a maharaja from India, or a New York broker, or an archaeologist, or some local light in overalls and cowboy boots. You never met anybody anywhere except at the La Fonda.[50]

Pyle also commented that his friends told him that only twenty people in Santa Fe were downright interesting, but he generously allowed as how that was "probably more than you'd find with a strict yardstick in any other American town of fifteen thousand."[51]

One of those twenty interesting people in Santa Fe in the early 1930s must have been Konrad Allgaier, the chef at La Fonda, because people kept pestering Ernie Pyle to write about him. Pyle didn't want to because he didn't care much about food. However, he did care about being overcharged for food he didn't care about, so he wrote a column griping about the cost of breakfast at La Fonda. He had paid ninety cents for orange juice, one egg, bacon, toast, and milk and thought that called for public complaint. Allgaier and his colleagues read the column, decided Pyle was right, and changed the menu. Ah, the power of the press.

Pyle was so surprised and pleased by their response he agreed to go to La Fonda for a special luncheon. Afterward he got acquainted with Allgaier and learned that he had emigrated in 1922 from Germany, where he had served in the Kaiser's kitchen. He could cook food from many of the world's cuisines and said he never had a request from the dining room that stumped him. Long-time habitués of La Fonda still recall his best dishes, one of them being, oddly enough so far inland, Lobster Newburg.[52]

Several years before Ernie Pyle observed the upper crust and sampled Konrad's "turkey so tender you could cut it with a glance"[53] at La Fonda, another writer ensconced herself there. She would claim New Mexico as her territory to such a degree that visitors to the city would read her *Death Comes for the Archbishop* as if it were a guidebook and history and not a fiction.

Willa Cather, born in Virginia and transplanted to the Nebraska prairie as a young girl, first discovered in 1912, during a visit to her brother in Arizona, the landscape of New Mexico. It would haunt her. She would in time describe it so simply and powerfully that generations of readers would view the novel as an essential portrait of the Hispanic and Indian villages, grasslands, mountains, and wide skies of the region.

It was more than a dozen years after that first visit that Cather and her companion Edith Lewis spent a summer in New Mexico, and she began to think about a particular figure in the landscape, Archbishop Jean Baptiste Lamy. She and Lewis stayed in La Fonda, a stone's throw from the stone cathedral that Lamy had willed into being and that said so much about his origins and aspirations. Going in and out of the hotel, she passed the bronze statue of Lamy in front of his unfinished cathedral. His fine, well-bred face interested her. His life seemed to her a story waiting to be told.[54]

The two women returned again the next summer, again living at La Fonda but traveling around as they had the first summer. They went to the green villages nestled along the Rio Grande in the Española Valley; followed the tumbling river on up to Taos, situated between the mountains and the expanse of sagebrush plain gashed by the river's dark gorge; ventured into the Sangres north and east of Santa Fe to pueblo ruins and ancient towns. These places and others Cather visited were shaping themselves into the setting of a novel. By the second summer *Death Comes for the Archbishop* was underway.

Writer Paul Horgan told on several occasions the story of how he came upon Willa Cather and Edith Lewis in lounging chairs on a La Fonda balcony surrounded by books and papers. Embarrassed that the two women seemed annoyed by his inadvertent intrusion on their work, he left quickly.

Of the writers who frequented La Fonda in the 1920s and 1930s, I mention here only four who left more than a memory. Ernie Pyle put his comments into newspaper columns that outlived their newsprint and became books. Willa Cather bequeathed us *Death Comes for the Archbishop* (though some New Mexicans are more troubled than pleased with the legacy of Cather's revision of history according to her own lights). Nobel Prize winner Sinclair Lewis embedded some of the details of life in La Fonda in a novel about hotelkeeping entitled *Work of Art.*[55] B. B. Dunne—writer, collector, and eccentric extraordinaire—was a fixture in the hotel's lobby for years and is memorialized in that space by his alpaca coat and a portrait painted by E. Horace Akin.

Decline for Fred Harvey but not for La Fonda

After World War II, passenger rail traffic declined rapidly, and Fred Harvey had to close several Harvey Houses, but the hotels at Grand Canyon and in Albuquerque and Santa Fe remained open and popular. In fact, La Fonda needed to be enlarged again. Some seventy rooms were added to the newer wing, rooms that would later be considered too small.[56]

In 1948 Mary Colter retired at the age of seventy-nine. She had been with Fred Harvey for forty-six years. She had just settled into a house in Santa Fe when Fred Harvey called on her one more time—to decorate a new cocktail lounge for La Fonda to be called La Cantinita.

If you go into the French Pastry Shop and Creperie on La Fonda's San Francisco Street side, you can see more of Colter's work in that room, once La Cantinita, than anywhere else in the hotel. The bricks of the fireplace came from the old state capitol building, and you can easily see how unevenly they are mortared. According to Colter's biographer, the contractor and chief engineer for the Santa Fe Railway who were in charge of the project returned from lunch one day to find the brick wall looking as if the masons had been drinking on the job. They apologized to Colter and offered to have it done over. She replied, "No, no, that's just the way I want it."[57]

Huge copper pots Colter placed on the mantel are still there in what Colter called her "pots and pans" room (some have been moved to the alcove just outside). So are the chandeliers, designed to resemble those in Mexican inns that would be lowered at night by pulley so that guests could take the candles and light their way to bed.

During changes in La Fonda almost all of Colter's work disappeared. A few important art works from Santa Fe Railway and Indian Detour days remain in the Santa Fe Room: the terra-cotta reliefs over the mantel and around the doors by sculptor Arnold Ronnebeck and Gerald Cassidy's illustrated map of New Mexico.

Maintaining a Balance

By the mid-1960s the Santa Fe Railway was ready to sell La Fonda. In 1968 the Corporación de La Fonda purchased it. Fred Harvey, which had always leased from the railroad, remained in the building until the following year.

I asked Sam Ballen, chairman of the board of the Corporación, what changes had been made in the hotel in the nearly thirty years since 1968. Ballen, a genial man in his early seventies, was wearing with his lavender sweater a silver bolo tie in the shape of a flower like the ones carved on the registration desk, with the words La Fonda written across it. He answered quickly, as if he had been waiting for the question. "Well, even I can hardly believe it." He reached into his desk, pulled out some papers, and read, "Since 1968 we have made $15,485,000 worth of improvements in this building.

"We're proud of doing something new but making it appear old. People say to me, 'I'm so glad you kept the lobby the same,' but we've changed everything in the lobby. It's just that we tried to make it look like it always did.

"What did that $15 million go for? I could start listing: air-conditioning; the parking structure; the ballroom; computerizing the hotel; remodeling in order to make larger rooms, reducing 212 rooms to 167, and refurnishing them; replacement of the boiler; installing a sprinkler system and smoke alarms; providing shops. When we came there were only two shops in the building.

"In the 1960s nobody wanted this hotel.

Hotel management companies were approached and turned it down. It was an old property in a time when old wasn't attractive. They wanted chrome and glass. And it was downtown, another disadvantage. Once we bought it, we couldn't just preserve it. In order to survive we had to make substantial changes in order to maintain a balance between convenience and preservation."[58]

One of the most visible changes in La Fonda on behalf of convenience was the addition in 1985–86 of the parking structure, the Carriage House. Because the hotel is located in such a prominent position in the historic district, on the plaza and across the street from the cathedral, there was considerable concern about whether a 205-space, three-level parking garage could fit in gracefully. After a number of plans and revisions of plans, the present structure, which includes a roof-top garden and a corridor from the parking area into the lobby, was built. The *Santa Fe New Mexican* expressed its editorial approval: "La Fonda has been a good corporate citizen in this community, recognizing its civic responsibility for maintaining the standards of the city's historical zone."[59]

A Public Space

> [T]he city had converted its history into an asset of commerce. As such, it was seen by the traveler as a mixture of the true and the contrived. . . . [60]

In the twentieth century Santa Fe became, as John Jakle put it in a history of tourism, "a place that would be what it never was." It strictly adhered to one architectural style as if nothing else ever had been or ever could be built in the historic district. That effort to devise a static image has been both praised and decried. No matter which position you defend, you can agree that the city succeeded in achieving what Jakle terms *legibility*. By this he means a place whose landscape and culture are so closely allied that visitors easily read and remember them. Jakle claims, "The more legible a city, the more positive the tourists' reactions."[61]

As early as the 1930s some visitors thought such self-consciousness likely to be destructive of the essence of Santa Fe's appeal. Lewis Gannett, who traveled West in his Ford V-8 and wrote a book about it, arrived in Santa Fe in the heyday of the artist colony. He wrote:

> But the artists, who rediscovered the primitive beauty of old Santa Fe . . . seem doomed, despite themselves, to ruin whatever they discover. They bring hordes of tourists in their wake; they make the Mexican and Indian conscious of their charm, which destroys it; they invite the Eastern mob to see what they have found, and it ceases to be.[62]

Today, walking and window-glancing anywhere near the plaza, these "hordes of tourists" see astonishing price tags on Kachina Christmas tree ornaments, Hopi golf ball markers, neon cacti, West Coast cocktail party concepts of Western chic, and turquoise-studded everything. They correctly conclude that Santa Fe has turned itself into an adobe boutique. La Fonda actively participates in this fantasy merchandising, but it retains two characteristics that keep it rooted in New Mexico reality.

One is its allegiance to its human, and not just its stylistic, past. Many examples may be found in the public rooms: B. B. Dunne's coat; Jose Ronquillo's portrait; the murals in the restaurant, La Plazuela, painted in 1978 by Yugoslav Vladan Stiha, who was connected with the hotel through an art gallery in the building; a photo of Amarante Chavez in retirement, accompanied by a plaque that reads:

> Serving La Fonda's guests as busboy, waiter, and maitre d' from 1929 to 1989, greeted by thousands, including John F. Kennedy, Greer Garson, Paul Newman, Maria Martinez, Lady Bird Johnson, and scores of wonderful local eccentrics who sweetened the days of old Santa Fe.

The hotel management has succeeded in keeping employees for decades. Besides Chavez, another is Ernesto Martinez, La Fonda's full-time artist, who says of his work that the "whole hotel is my gallery."[63]

Martinez has painted in the hotel for more than forty years, from the large Mimbres-inspired panels in the Lumpkins Ballroom to companionable little figures on closet doors and in hallways. He has painted bedsteads, bar tables, and the window panes that surround La Plazuela with splashes of color. Descriptions of La Fonda often play up the murals by Santa Fe artist Olive Rush, commissioned by Mary Colter, or the works by Gerald Cassidy, a pioneer of the artist colony in Santa Fe whose paintings done for the Santa Fe Railway hang in the hotel. But Ernesto Martinez, with little fanfare, has had more effect on the appearance of the hotel than any other painter, creating a folk art environment that extends into every cranny of the building.

A second special quality of La Fonda that grows out of its history is its centrality as a public space in Santa Fe. In a culture that tends to neglect the public realm in deference to private ones—radio music through earphones, the automobile, the family room with the television on—La Fonda's public rooms offer a momentary sanctuary for the sense of urban, and urbane, community.

From the days of the American occupation, the Santa Fe Trail, and Fred Harvey's Indian Detours, gamblers, soldiers, legislators, artists, writers, and all sorts of travelers have mingled in the several versions of *la fonda*. Today people who were born about the time the present La Fonda opened can remember Chef Konrad, the annual crowds of Fiesta de Santa Fe celebrants, snow softly falling on a nativity scene in the once-open-air courtyard, wedding parties, and on holidays or any day, the plain pleasure of eavesdropping and people-watching.

La Fonda's rooms are full of past visitors. As writer Anais Nin once said about the Hotel Crillon in Paris, "They remained like a perfume in the air, in rooms that had been lived in." [64]

CHAPTER THREE

The St. James Hotel in Cimarron

If you were traveling from Elizabethtown to Taos in 1870, you might glimpse a cabin through the shivering leaves of the aspens at Palo Flechado Pass. If you knew that one Charles Kennedy lived there, the proprietor of a frontier version of a bed-and-breakfast, you might be tempted to stop for the night.

Allow me to tell you the story of some travelers who did.

In September of 1870, the woman who lived with Kennedy suddenly appeared in a saloon in E-town. She had escaped from him and made her way through the mountains on foot for help. To the men in the saloon she gasped out a story of horror. Kennedy had been killing and robbing strangers who stopped for the night, and in a rage he had just murdered her small son. Grief and terror had at last goaded the woman to flee the charnel house Kennedy's cabin had become.

Her listeners saddled up and rode to the cabin. They seized Kennedy and searched his place, uncovering the remains of a body and some bones. Jose Cortez, who had stayed there months earlier and had seen a fellow guest shot, revealed what he knew of Kennedy's hospitality, and a Taos Indian reported that he had found a skeleton in the cabin. Outraged local citizens forced a "trial" on the spot and hauled Kennedy from the jail to a slaughterhouse, where they lynched him.[1]

If this story sounds familiar, it should—its essential elements have become durable goods in the lore of New Mexico. Perhaps the story's best known retelling appears in Willa Cather's *Death Comes for the Archbishop*, where Charles Kennedy has been turned into a loathsome fictional creature, Buck Scales, whose name suggests a reptilian redneck. He was "tall, gaunt, and ill-formed, with a snake-like neck, terminating in a small, bony head. . . . [T]his head had a positively malignant look."[2]

But this macabre story doesn't end with Kennedy's head at the end of a rope. Clay Allison, a rancher and gunfighter notorious in Cimarron, cut off Kennedy's head and stuffed it in a sack. Allison then strode into Henry Lambert's saloon in Cimarron and emptied the bloody contents of the sack before the appalled saloonkeeper. Allison, so the story goes, ordered Lambert to post the head outside his community gathering place as a warning to evildoers.

So Lambert's saloon, soon to become the St. James Hotel, proclaimed with a shriveled head stuck on a fence what could befall travelers and those who preyed on them. Many years later, a white marker greeted guests climbing out of their cars in front of the hotel with this announcement:

Charles Kennedy
Beheaded
January 16, 1871
by
C. Allison[3]

Lucien Maxwell

To search out the story of the St. James Hotel from its beginning we must go back to the mining boomtown of Elizabethtown, for just as Charles Kennedy's grisly story is linked to the flood of travelers and gold prospectors through E-town, so is Henry Lambert's. But even that isn't far enough—we must go all the way back to Lucien Maxwell's mansion.

By the 1860s Lucien Bonaparte Maxwell not only owned more land than anyone else in New Mexico Territory, but also more than any other individual landowner in the United States—1,714,764.93 acres of northeastern New Mexico and southern Colorado.[4] Maxwell obtained the land grant through inheritance from his father-in-law Charles Beaubien and the purchase of shares belonging to other heirs and Beaubien's original partner in the grant, Guadalupe Miranda.

Maxwell built a mansion in Cimarron, on the Santa Fe Trail, from which he managed a thriving business of supplying beef and other necessities to the United States Army at Fort Union and other frontier forts and to Indian tribes. He also traded with caravans passing through on the trail. In the 1860s Maxwell's home was referred to as "the first civilized stop on the [Santa Fe] trail in New Mexico."[5]

Zane Grey described a visitor's view of Maxwell's headquarters in his novel *Fighting Caravans* that agrees pretty well with descriptions found in other, nonfiction accounts and with historic photographs.

> The main ranch house appeared more like a white-walled fort than the home of one man. . . . Maxwell and his guests, who were always numerous, lounged on the shady porch and gazed out across and down that gray, endless, purple-horizoned prairie, as if they could never tire of it. . . . His dining room would seat a hundred and it often did.[6]

So the most renowned hostelry in Cimarron in the 1860s was the sprawling home of landowner Maxwell, but he sold his fabulous grant and home to the Maxwell Land Grant and Railway Company in 1870. About the same time a French chef named Henri Lambert would establish a business next door to the Maxwell mansion that would eventually replace it as the social center of town.

In Which Henri Lambert Discovers the Best Use of Pans

Lambert's biography was a bit unusual. Born in Nantes in 1838, the Frenchman had run away from home as a boy. He began his career as a chef through apprenticeship to a ship's cook, eventually enlisting in the French navy and serving as a chef on a gunboat that landed him in Uruguay. Although this sounds more like Everyboy's Runaway Tale than a biographical sketch, Lambert joined a circus in Montevideo, still as a cook, bound for the United States. He eventually rose to the position of chef for General Ulysses S. Grant in 1862. On Grant's recommendation Lambert moved up to the American pinnacle of his profession—to the White House to prepare food for President Abraham Lincoln's table, whether or not the careworn president had the appetite to relish Lambert's efforts.

For some reason Lambert abandoned his prestigious post at the White House and joined the mad rush westward for gold, ending up staking his mining claim on the Maxwell Land Grant. But apparently he decided early on that "a talented man could accumulate more gold out of a panful of food than a panful of gravel."[7] He opened a roughboard, two-story hotel in E-town, where it became known for its dining room, and then moved on to Cimarron to found the St. James.[8]

Lambert's St. James began as a saloon and eating establishment in a small building across the street from Lucien Maxwell's mansion. Though the exact date is hard to pin down, it probably commenced in 1870.[9]

Two Henrys. Henri Lambert, founder of the St. James, in front with arms crossed and behind him another man coincidentally named Henry Lambert, a friend. *Courtesy of the Alpers Collection, Cimarron, New Mexico.*

Cimarron in the 1870s

Henry (no longer Henri) Lambert may have realized that E-town's golden days were numbered when he shifted his hospitality business to Cimarron. He may also have recognized that Cimarron would gain importance. In 1872 the county seat of Colfax County was relocated from E-town to Cimarron, a business center for local ranchers, the Maxwell Land Grant, and travelers on the Santa Fe Trail. Perhaps Lambert foresaw that with Lucien Maxwell gone from his role as purveyor of hospitality, presiding over the daily dining and gaming at the commodious tables in his home, Cimarron would need a new place for locals and visitors to gather. But he could not have foreseen how much bloodshed would accompany the prospering of his enterprise.

In American Spanish *cimarron* means "wild, unmanageable," an apt name for the town.[10] Guns and alcohol kept disorder simmering most days and nights, and political conflict on the Maxwell Land Grant often brought it to a boil.

An enormously valuable chunk of real estate with uncertain boundaries and ownership, the Maxwell Grant invited opposing claims. Because it had been granted by the Mexican government to Charles Beaubien and Guadalupe Miranda, it had to be validated by Congress after New Mexico became a United States territory. In 1857 Surveyor General William Pelham confirmed the validity of the Maxwell Grant and its original, extraordinarily vague description—a description that would eventually allow certification of the inclusion of far more land than the original grant recipients had imagined.[11]

Maxwell had tolerated settlement on his vast grant, exacting payments, usually in produce from farmers and ranchers and in rentals and royalties from miners, but making little effort to oust claimants who refused to recognize his title. But after the discovery of gold on the grant, Maxwell's empire attracted the attention of capitalists in the United States and Europe. When he sold the property, its new owners, an English syndicate, made it clear that settlers who did not arrange for payment to the financially struggling company would be ejected.

The region became polarized: settlers and their sympathizers against the Maxwell Land Grant and Railway Company. Powerful men in Santa Fe who sought to profit by controlling land grant claims added the ingredient of politics to an already volatile brew. Years of turmoil resulted, with land claims, counterclaims, and violence. These conflicts often poisoned daily life in Cimarron, including what went on inside the St. James Saloon.

More Grisly Stories

While some of the stories that follow clearly reveal the influence of the explosive tensions that became known as the Colfax County War, all of them demonstrate something else just as telling. Though this observation will not be welcomed by nostalgia buffs or those enamored of what they see as the romance of frontier violence, all of these stories of the St. James Saloon and Hotel show how little has changed in the last century or so. The same stories will crop up in tomorrow's newspaper. The plots are disturbingly familiar: the discharged employee whose resentment leads to a sorry end, the desire for vengeance locking men into a murderous cycle, the lethal mix of guns with strong drink and racism, and the tragedies of admirable men who make bad choices.

Coal Oil Jimmy

Historian Marc Simmons has pointed out that an outlaw with the moniker of Coal Oil Jimmy has not received his fair share of notoriety for his brief career as a highwayman in the neighborhood of Cimarron in 1871.[12] James Buckner or Buckley, a.k.a. "Coal Oil Jimmy," played a role in the history of criminality in northeastern New Mexico and unwittingly perpetuated a certain unfortunate trend at the St. James.

The short, slick-haired James B. sought work in Cimarron and found it with the local stage station. But he was fired, for drinking or stealing or both. He threatened revenge, and

(top) Gran Quivira Harvey Hotel, Clovis, New Mexico.
Courtesy of Lake County (Ill.) Museum/Curt Teich Postcard Archives.

(bottom) Central Patio, Alvarado Hotel, Albuquerque, New Mexico.
Courtesy of Lake County (Ill.) Museum/Curt Teich Postcard Archives.

"Pioneer Days" Arrival of Stagecoach at La Fonda, Santa Fe, New Mexico. *Postcard from author's collection.*

(opposite, top) La Fonda, Santa Fe, New Mexico, ca. 1923. *Courtesy of Lake County (Ill.) Museum/Curt Teich Postcard Archives.*

(opposite, bottom) Patio, La Fonda, Santa Fe, New Mexico. *Courtesy of Lake County (Ill.) Museum/Curt Teich Postcard Archives.*

The Castañeda Hotel, Las Vegas, New Mexico. *Courtesy of Lake County (Ill.) Museum/Curt Teich Postcard Archives.*

(opposite, top) The first Lodge at Cloudcroft, 1908. *Postcard from author's collection.*

(opposite, bottom) The present Lodge at Cloudcroft, probably 1914. *Postcard from author's collection.*

6987
CLOUDCROFT,
NEW MEX.
The Lodge

The Lodge." CLOUDCROFT, N. M. Altitude 9,000 feet
PHARMACY
Hand-Colored

HILTON

The Val Verde Hotel, Socorro, "on Highway Between Carlsbad Cavern and the Grand Canyon."
Courtesy of the Rio Grande Historical Collections, New Mexico State University Library, Las Cruces, New Mexico.

(opposite) The brand new Hilton Hotel, Albuquerque, New Mexico.
Courtesy of Lake County (Ill.) Museum/Curt Teich Postcard Archives.

The Swastika Hotel, Raton, New Mexico.
Courtesy of Lake County (Ill.) Museum/Curt Teich Postcard Archives.

sure enough, within a few days stage line horses had been stolen. Soon it became clear that James B. had either turned, or returned, to a life of crime and was holding up stagecoaches between E-town and Cimarron. He and a partner named Tom Taylor were not only taking the stages' cash boxes but passengers' lives as well. (With Charles Kennedy and Coal Oil Jimmy around, these were not good years to be touring the territory around Cimarron.)

Coal Oil Jimmy and his partner did not pursue their vocation for long, though, thanks to a couple of Texas cowboys. Hoping to add to their meager pay with the reward on the outlaws' heads, the cowboys pretended to want to join up with them but then shot them instead. The Texans hauled the bodies to Cimarron and the St. James Hotel to exchange them for $3,000. The situation demanded documentation, so a door at the hotel was removed from its hinges, and the stiffened bodies—with Tom's gloved hand raised, Jimmy's legs drawn up—were tied to it. Then the door was held upright for a photograph.[13]

Once again, evidence that crime doesn't pay was on display at the St. James.

Pancho Griego

The Maxwell Land Grant and Railway Company attempted to enforce its judgments against "squatters" on company land in 1873 but ran into a great deal of resistance. Then in 1874 the secretary of the interior declared the grant lands to be public domain, throwing the whole situation into complete confusion. Prominent men in Santa Fe, known as the "Santa Fe Ring," took advantage of what can only be described as civil unrest in Colfax County to seek their own political and economic advantage.

One of the most outspoken critics of the Santa Fe politicians and the land-grant owners was a Methodist minister, the Reverend Thomas J. Tolby, who preached in Cimarron and E-town. He was mysteriously killed in September of 1875, the first in a series of linked murders. Cruz Vega, a man suspected of having knowledge of the minister's murderer, was next. He was tortured and then lynched. A relative of Vega, Francisco "Pancho" Griego, began threatening to avenge his death.

Griego had already proven himself hotheaded. Some months before he had been dealing *monte* in the St. James when someone disputed a bet. He knocked the money to the floor, drew a pistol and a bowie knife, and shot and stabbed to death three soldiers. When he was acquitted, it was said around town that the Santa Fe Ring got him off. By November he was back in Cimarron and in the St. James looking for trouble.

It quickly appeared in the person of Clay Allison. Allison, originally from Tennessee, had come out of the Confederate Army after the Civil War and made his way to the eastern plains of New Mexico, where he and his brother herded some cattle from Texas. They, like many others, liked the quality of the grass and perhaps of the sky and decided to stay, never asking permission of the land grant company. Allison was well respected for his skill with a gun, a fact Pancho Griego would have done well to consider.

On November 1, 1875, Griego made a few remarks in the St. James bar that implied Allison may have had something to do with Vega's death. Then, as if he were fidgety or overheated, he began to fan himself with his hat. Allison suspected the hat to be a cover for a draw, preempted it, fired two shots, and killed Griego. He then ran everybody out of the St. James bar and locked Griego's body inside until the next day. Allison turned himself in and was later acquitted on a plea of self-defense.[14]

Buffalo Soldiers

When Congress reorganized the U.S. Army after the Civil War, it authorized the formation of two cavalry regiments (the Ninth and Tenth) and four infantry regiments (the Thirty-eighth through the Forty-first) for African American soldiers. A few years later, in a reduction of the overall number of enlisted men, the four black infantry regiments shrank to two, the Twenty-fourth and Twenty-fifth. More than three thousand of these cavalrymen and infantrymen served at military installations in New Mexico between 1866 and 1900. They were known as "buffalo soldiers," a name given them by Native Americans who saw in them two resemblances to the revered buffalo: the texture and color of their hair and their boldness. From 1866 to 1869 black infantrymen were stationed at Fort Union, and from 1876 to 1881 five companies of the Ninth Cavalry served there.[15] Although the Ninth's primary assignment was to bring the Apaches under control, they became embroiled in the much murkier mission of maintaining order in Colfax County.

Territorial Governor Samuel B. Axtell had let it be known that he was displeased with the citizens of Colfax County, especially Clay Allison. In an effort to improve relations, some leading men in the county invited the governor to meet with them. The governor himself did not respond, but soon District Attorney Ben Stevens arrived in Cimarron on the instructions of the governor. Thirty men from the Ninth Cavalry arrived at the same time, under the command of Captain Francis Moore. They were apparently present to carry out the governor's instructions, later alleged to have been a plot to ambush Clay Allison and the other men who invited the governor.

The cavalrymen set up their headquarters in Cimarron near the St. James but were ordered to stay out of its saloon (and all the others in town). Captain Moore had also asked Henry Lambert not to sell liquor to the men. Despite these precautions, among the black troopers were three who managed to mire themselves in a predicament in the spring of 1876. The story varies somewhat from telling to telling.

Two of the soldiers disobeyed orders and made a visit to Schwenk's Saloon one afternoon, where they had the bad luck to meet up with three Texas cowboys—Gus Hefron, Henry Goodman, and David Crockett, said to have been a nephew of the popular hero Davy.[16] Crockett had apparently already made it known he didn't much like having black soldiers around town. After a few drinks and the bandying of threats, the soldiers, though they left the bar without a fight, felt sufficiently insulted to defy orders again later that evening and look further for trouble. Despite being told to stay in camp, Privates George Small, Anthony Harvey, and John Hanson found Hefron and Crockett continuing their drinking, by now having moved to the St. James bar.

At least two accounts hold that the soldiers ordered drinks themselves, were told by Lambert they could not buy liquor, insisted belligerently, and were then sold some with the understanding that they would leave the bar with it. Other accounts claim that Crockett and Hefron pulled their guns after insults were exchanged, but the three men in uniform could not draw their revolvers fast enough (they were wearing Civil War–era holsters with fastened-down leather flaps). This does not jibe, however, with reports that the five men traded fifteen or twenty shots. Whatever else happened, the three buffalo soldiers died in the shootout. Citizens apparently rendered no aid in the army's investigation because they objected to the black cavalrymen's presence, whether because of racism, or the soldiers' apparent connection with the hostile governor, or both.[17]

Well-Established House

The present St. James Hotel dates from 1880, and it has been generally believed that the St. James was a only a saloon before then. However, in accounts of the preceding stories, Lambert's place in the 1870s is almost always referred to as the St. James *Hotel*.

According to one writer well acquainted with the St. James in this century, Henry Lambert added four bedrooms onto the saloon as early as 1872.[18] It is certain that by 1875 the St. James was not just fueling the feuds of ruffians with liquor and gaming tables but also proffering Lambert's skill with food along with overnight lodging. The *Cimarron News and Press* ran advertisements in 1875 for:

SAINT JAMES HOTEL AND RESTAURANT
OLD AND WELL-ESTABLISHED HOUSE
NEAT, CLEAN, AND AIRY
FINE BILLIARD ROOM AND BAR

Lambert furnished his hotel with marble-topped tables, four-poster beds, velvet draperies, beveled glass mirrors, and English china, all jounced by ox cart over "Uncle Dick" Wootton's toll road over Raton Pass.[19] But the erstwhile White House chef had greater ambitions yet. The newspaper reported in November of 1879 that:

> Having made a satisfactory arrangement for the purchase of the building he is now occupying and for four lots adjoining each other on that block, Mr. Henry Lambert will proceed to erect a handsome building for a hotel. He informs us that as soon as spring opens he will raise the present building one story higher. It will have a north front 90 feet long, extending to the alley. . . . He will prob-

ably expend six or seven thousand dollars in improving his present property.[20]

When the territorial-style, two-story, adobe building celebrated its grand opening in 1881, the guest list featured people well-known in New Mexico and the region: Governor Lew Wallace (President Rutherford B. Hayes had removed Axtell from office in 1878); Frank Sherwin, a speculator and promoter who had become a director of what was now the Dutch-owned Maxwell Land Grant Company; Frank and Charles Springer and M. M. Chase, landowners and men of influence in the northeastern part of the state.[21]

Black Jack Ketchum and His Gang

The hotel was still frequented by prominent citizens when, at the end of the 1890s, the Black Jack Gang arrived, to close out an era in which so many bloody wrongs had lain open to view at the St. James.

Fred Lambert, Henry's son, a boy growing up in the hotel at the time, found it hard to believe that Thomas Edward "Black Jack" Ketchum and a fellow who went by the name of Bill McGinnis could deserve their reputations as brutal killers and thieves. According to Agnes Morley Cleaveland's portrayal of Fred Lambert's memories of his childhood at the hotel, Fred would recall later their friendliness to him. He remembered the way McGinnis could twirl his Colt .45 and drive a twenty-penny spike into a tree trunk with shot after perfectly aimed shot. Fred couldn't imagine why a man who could shoot that well would lower himself to rob trains.[22]

Black Jack's gang whiled away some of their time in the summers of 1897 and 1899 in the St. James at drink and cards. They spent some of it at their hideout cave in Turkey Canyon near Cimarron. And some brief but intense moments of it they spent holding up the Colorado and Southern near Folsom on a stretch where the train moved slowly around a double curve. The latter activity, repeated a couple of times, netted them some gain but also the attention of several determined men who formed a posse in the St. James saloon and rode out to Turkey Canyon.

From the fierce gun battle that ensued, Black Jack's brother Sam Ketchum did not escape. Shot in the arm, Sam was captured and brought back into Cimarron in a wagon en route to the territorial prison in Santa Fe. He is said to have told Henry Lambert, "Our next job was going to be to come and git us back all them nice shiny gold pieces you taken away from us!"[23] He never came back. He died of blood poisoning from his injury on July 24, 1899, a week after the battle. Black Jack himself happened not to be with the gang at the time of the posse's surprise attack.

About a month after the disastrous battle, Black Jack attempted a third hold-up of the same train on the same horseshoe curve—only this time he was alone. It was almost as if he wanted to die or couldn't muster the energy to conceive a fresh attempt. Frank Harrington, a conductor who had witnessed the earlier two successful robberies, was ready for him this time and shattered his arm with a shotgun blast. Too badly injured to resist arrest, Tom Ketchum was taken to the Folsom Hotel, a two-story stone building still standing in Folsom today, where a doctor administered first aid.[24] He was then moved to Trinidad, Colorado, where his arm was amputated (his brother had reportedly refused such treatment).

A big, handsome man with an exceptionally fine mustache, a man Fred Lambert remembered as willing to talk to a boy as if he were a man, "Black Jack" Ketchum was hanged in Clayton, New Mexico, in 1901. The hanging proved as sensational and gory as his last years had been. The headline read "Black Jack Decapitated on the Gallows, Tom Ketchum Hurls Himself Downward as Trap Falls and Bloody Head Flies From Body."[25]

The Don Diego Hotel

When F. W. "Will" Haegler bought the St. James from Henry Lambert's heirs in the early 1930s, he must have wanted to eradicate the bad memories stamped on the building. He intended to clean it up and make it a home for his four children as well as a hotel; he didn't want them to grow up encountering the occasional corpse in the saloon as Fred Lambert had. So he removed and sold off some original furnishings, including mantels, light fixtures, and maybe even the notorious bar. He converted the saloon into a dining room, and he even changed the hotel's name to Don Diego (*Diego* means James in Spanish). But the building continued in its long-time role as a community center. Because the town didn't have a bank in the depression years, Haegler had a safe put in the hotel and became an unofficial banker.[26]

Haegler sold the hotel in the late 1940s to members of the wealthy William J. Gourley family of Fort Worth. Gourley's stepdaughter and her husband, Mr. and Mrs. Henry Abernathy, managed it for a few years before selling it to another member of the family, Vera Gourley, W. J. Gourley's niece-in-law.

Gourley had founded the American Manufacturing Company, a producer of oil-field pumping equipment and, during World War II, munitions. He began purchasing ranch properties near Cimarron in 1945 and eventually amassed 480,000 acres.

The Gourley family's ties to the Don Diego Hotel have not been mentioned in any of the sources I have studied,[27] but they deserve attention because Mr. and Mrs. W. J. Gourley's land holdings eventually became consolidated into the WS/Vermejo Park Ranch, a huge guest ranch near Cimarron and Raton (whose complex history is the subject of chapter 8.) Members of this family from Texas became the owners and managers of two of New Mexico's most valuable historic lodgings, one of them a small hotel later widely publicized and the other a resort scarcely known even within the state despite its extraordinary size and beauty.

A Native Son Returns Home

During a visit to Cimarron to see his ninety-year-old father, Ed Sitzberger and his wife Pat

(*top*) The St. James Hotel ca. 1915–1920. *Courtesy of the Museum of New Mexico, Santa Fe, New Mexico. Neg. No. 49157.*

(*bottom*) The St. James renamed the Don Diego Hotel, 1935. *Courtesy of the Alpers Collection, Cimarron, New Mexico.*

Loree paused at the Don Diego Hotel and peered in the windows. It was easy to stop by—Sitzberger's father still lived where Sitzberger was born in 1931, in an old adobe right across the alley from the hotel. Sitzberger says, "We looked in the windows and said, wow, look at what's here!"[28]

In 1985 the couple worked for Los Alamos National Laboratory, Sitzberger as a mechanical engineer and Loree as an assistant to the lab director. They had been searching without success for an opportunity to build or renovate a lodging near Los Alamos with the idea of hosting high-level visitors to the lab. Suddenly, here it was, in the very hotel where Sitzberger had once played with the Haegler children, but too far in miles and in mind-set from Los Alamos to be the situation they had envisioned. Yet Sitzberger knew there was a summertime market in Cimarron and had family in town who could help out. And then there was just the nostalgia of it. So he walked in and asked Vera Gourley if she wanted to sell.

The answer was yes, and then no, and then yes again. In October 1985 Sitzberger and Loree got the keys to the hostelry they would restore to its original name.

Back in the 1950s Agnes Morley Cleaveland had mused about the expectancy of the Don Diego, "Drowsing in the sun . . . waiting for the stagecoach to round its corner. The twenty-six bullets buried in its ceiling are hidden under embossed tin, but at any moment will they be joined by others?"[29] By 1985 the hotel had been dozing for twenty-five years—only a bar and pool room remained open—but it was about to awaken.

Sitzberger wanted to start up his new business with a bar and restaurant. Renovating the bar, he thought, would be no problem, as it had been in use, but the kitchen had been out of commission for about thirty years: "My brother and I were walking around in the kitchen, and he fell through the floor. That gave us a clue what we were in for. So we stripped everything back to the walls and ceiling and started over. . . . We put in new electrical, new floor, new equipment."

Sitzberger and Loree soon discovered that everything in the building needed work, especially the roof. The renovation requirements proved to be extensive and expensive. But they also found that some of the original furniture from the 1880s still remained in the hotel and could be repaired and used. They also gradually acquired items that just seemed to belong, from some of Fred Lambert's paintings to old photographs that people would unearth in their homes and donate because they were glad to see the hotel coming to life again.

Sitzberger began making other discoveries as well, not so easy to explain: "There's a lot of history in my background associated with [renovating the hotel and getting it ready to open for guests]. It's really interesting to me. As we go through this . . . you'll find there's a lot more and wonder about the historical circle that's gathering around me. I'm not sure what's happening, but it's kind of fun."

Sitzberger and Loree separated, and it happened that he was able to move across the street into a home that had belonged to close friends, the Leitzells. It occupied the site of Lucien Maxwell's mansion, which had burned almost exactly a century before. Sitzberger was beginning to feel that his life was focusing on the intergenerational connections between his own personal history and that of the hotel and the larger community of Cimarron.

Later, after he remarried and sold the St. James, he and his wife Sandra moved into another house located a block east of the St. James—right across the old Santa Fe Trail, in fact. It's a house that deserves mention here for its own history as a hotel. When Miguel Otero, later to be territorial governor, visited his father there in 1874, it went by the name of the National Hotel. The senior Otero had contracted pneumonia while traveling and had to bed down in the National for a while to convalesce. His family learned of his illness and hired passage to Cimarron to be with him, in spite of Indian trouble along the trail at the time.

The adobe building, sometimes used as a private residence and sometimes as a lodging for travelers, served in the 1890s as a regular stage stop and in the early 1990s as a bed-and-breakfast called the Santa Fe Trail Inn. It is currently home to the Sitzbergers, who enjoy living in a house that possesses strong ties to both of their personal family histories.[30]

Unsubstantiated Roomers[31]

While some of the most compelling apparitions came from his own memories, Ed Sitzberger, along with his former wife Pat Loree, also found that in the St. James they had to cope with some contentious prior inhabitants. Loree told a reporter from the *Albuquerque Journal* writing a Halloween story that, from the beginning, every time she entered room 18, the hair on the back of her neck stood up. Then a doctor from California came to the St. James in 1987. The owners did not know him or anything about him, and no one said anything to him about room 18, but not long after he checked in he came to Loree and said, "You have a real problem upstairs."

He persuaded her to unlock room 18. Loree recounted, "There was a presence whirling in the corner near the ceiling, and it came down and knocked me to my knees. I got up and it came back and knocked me down again." She backed out of the room and fled, but the doctor stayed for awhile to get acquainted with the presence. Then he told Loree that the spirit should not be challenged. The room was kept locked and unavailable to guests.[32]

The St. James proved convenient not only for travelers but also for reporters seeking Halloween material. According to another such story a year later, a self-proclaimed witch visited the hotel and identified the occupant of room 18 as the ghost of someone named James or Jesse Wright. Sitzberger said, "The next day my former wife Pat went back into the hotel registers and found the name T. J. Wright three different times in 1881." The witch told him Wright had won the hotel in a poker game and was killed when he tried to collect.[33]

Would Henry Lambert have done such a thing?

Sitzberger, though an engineer schooled in the laws of physics, came to feel that some other laws must be operating in the St. James. He believes that the malevolent fellow in room 18 killed some of the birds in his aviary, a conspicuous feature of the hotel during Sitzberger's tenure as owner. Other spirits made themselves known to him and to others as well: a four-foot-tall imp nicknamed "Woody" who would break glassware, snitch toast, and make a mess of table settings; Mary Lambert, Henry's wife, who slipped from room to room, detectable only by the fragrance of her perfume.

All this supernatural activity has attracted plenty of publicity from journalists, both

Its haunted history: Halloween at the St. James Hotel in 1905. Henri Lambert in center. *Courtesy of the Alpers Collection, Cimarron, New Mexico.*

newspaper and television, and from various psychics. No doubt some guests who hear tell of the bullet holes in the pressed tin ceiling and the unhappy phantom in room 18 check in just to check them out. But not all guests come for the tales of gore or the ghosts.

Though many of the St. James' earliest guests in the 1870s proved to be unsavory, even murderous, many of its present guests are Boy Scouts. Waite Phillips, a wealthy oilman from Oklahoma, acquired a large piece of what had been the Maxwell Land Grant and then donated 127,395 acres of it to the Boy Scouts of America. Thousands of young men from all over the United States and other nations come to the Philmont Scout Ranch near Cimarron every summer to hike and camp in the shadow of a rock formation called the Tooth of Time. Coming from or going to Philmont, they often stop by the St. James. In addition to the scouts, Philmont provides other customers to the hotel and restaurant in the form of staff members—hundreds of them during the summer months— adult trainees, inspection teams, and so on. When Sitzberger was considering the market in Cimarron, he questioned some people at Philmont about whether the nearby St. James would fill a need. It would indeed. At that time they were driving guests forty miles to Raton and the historic Palace Hotel just for dinner.

Cimarron and the St. James Tamed

Walking through the St. James on the first floor, I pass several examples of the taxidermist's chilling craft—a mountain lion, a wapiti, and a pronghorn. Room 1 bears the name of Pancho Griego and a photo. The caption reads, "The night he decided to challenge Clay Allison was the last act of his life, except dying from a .44 slug." A sign near the room that houses the gift shop informs me that here two men died. Fred, and wife Katie, Lambert are observing guests going in and out the front door from their now inaccessible position within a photograph. Old guest registers with their blotted and curliqued signatures reside under glass; those who signed them reside under sod.

For a moment's diversion from intimations of mortality, I eavesdrop on a conversation in the lobby. A man is on the phone to his office: "Not much snow up here. We've been looking for snow and ended up in this very quaint little town with an old hotel." He misspells Cimarron for his listener. "We think it's so interesting, we'll just stay."

His wife, standing off to the side, asks no one in particular, "Is this the same Cimarron you always hear about in the western movies?"

Yes, ma'am, it is.

CHAPTER FOUR

The Stratford Hotel in Shakespeare

If this were played upon a stage now, I could condemn it as an improbable fiction.
—*William Shakespeare, from Twelfth Night*

The Town

"Just follow that road out of town till you come to a fork at the cemetery. It's back in those hills." The man at the Lordsburg KOA campground gestured toward stark, triangular hills not far away.

At the cemetery a sign with an arrow pointed toward "Shakespeare." The dirt road bent around a hillside until a few time-worn buildings came into view behind a fence that meant business. I could see adobe walls, metal roofs glaring in the July sun, a windmill, and what was once the main street, now occupied by a few of the battalions of army-green creosote bushes that hold sway everywhere in this desert.

Certainly not a fiction, but improbable? Yes. That this ghost town still hangs on. That out here in this bare-bones, inland landscape of sky and dry earth the town bears the name of an incomparable poet and playwright from damp, green, island England.

But it didn't always. It began more plausibly as a small oasis called Mexican Spring. In the desert, a spring in an arroyo provided ample reason for cross-country travelers to stop. According to Rita Hill, who owned this ghost town for half a century, by the late 1850s a few of those who stopped at Mexican Spring had decided for some reason to stay.[1]

When stagecoaches of the Butterfield Overland Mail route began traveling from St. Louis to the Pacific Coast in 1858, the route passed a few miles from Mexican Spring, eventually with a stop at a station called Barney's. Since water there could not always be depended upon, Mexican Spring probably became an alternate stop, Janaloo Hill believes. She is Rita Hill's daughter and the present owner of the town of Shakespeare. In any case, the Civil War soon halted travel over this southern Butterfield route.

After the war a Norwegian immigrant by the name of John Evensen arrived in Mexican Spring from San Diego to reopen a stage station for the Kearns and Mitchell line, which intended to make use of prewar stagecoach routes and stations. He found there three buildings that had been used as stage stations or commissaries, including what is now the back room of a building still standing in Shakespeare known as Grant House. Its roof needed repair, the door was off, and the oiled paper covering a small window was torn. Evensen did what had to be done to get the station operating again, and he would continue as its stage-keeper for many years.[2]

The Building

According to various oral accounts, another building in town was a one-story structure of tamped mud and rock that had been built during the Civil War to garrison soldiers. Evensen called it "the fort."[3]

The Town

Mexican Spring was renamed for Ulysses S. Grant after the war. Then silver was discovered nearby, and soon Grant's name was changed again, this time to Ralston, after William C. Ralston, the founder of the Bank of California. Ralston formed a company to exploit the silver discovery, staked a general claim, sold stock, and a boomtown was underway. Before long, so was conflict over claims, and the silver itself proved to be uncooperatively located in pockets. It wasn't the bonanza that had been sold to investors. But conveniently, just about the time disgruntlement might set in, reports began to circulate that a fabulous diamond field had been found somewhere in the Southwest, possibly at Ralston. William Ralston had diamonds that were brought to him appraised and began selling stock in prospective diamond mines. Despite confusion about just where the diamond field was located, investors still risked their money on it.

When it was finally learned that diamonds had been planted near Ralston and in Utah and the diamond prospectus was a swindle, the town of Ralston cleared out. Once booming with businesses, miners' tents, and stagecoach traffic, it turned into a near ghost town by 1874. A few persistent residents like John Evensen remained, though there was no longer much demand for his beans and biscuits and antelope steaks.

The Building

It is likely that "the fort" was transformed into a hotel during the Ralston years, between 1870 and 1873. It was remodeled, with a half-story of adobe added on top, perhaps by a man who would later remodel the town's history as well, Colonel William Boyle. Guests stopping at the small hotel would have found two large downstairs bedrooms, a dining room and kitchen, and four upstairs bedrooms. Nothing more substantial than muslin partitions separated the second-story rooms. When Emma Marble, whose family later managed the hotel, was told this, she was properly shocked: Why, a lady occupant of one of those rooms would have had to blow out her candle before undressing! This may have been more tease than truth, however, for few ladies traveled to Ralston.

The Town

In 1879 Colonel Boyle, an Irish-born mining engineer, and John Boyle, a well-to-do American who was apparently not related to him,[4] together breathed new life into moribund Ralston. They filed on old claims and started the Shakespeare Gold and Silver Mining and Milling Company. To banish the bitter aftertaste of the diamond hoax with the

The Stratford Hotel sometime between 1879 and 1893.
Original photograph from Emma M. Muir Collection. Copy by Ralph Looney and used with his permission.

sweetness of culture, they dubbed the town Shakespeare, named its main thoroughfare Avon Avenue, and its hotel the Stratford. They advertised as if it were a new mining camp, not a recycled one, and sure enough, the prospectors for sudden wealth arrived, lamps were lit in deserted buildings, and saloon doors swung open again.

The Building, now The Stratford Hotel

Mrs. Anna Woods arrived in Shakespeare in 1879 to manage the Stratford Hotel, bringing with her two sons, Ross and Tom, and two daughters, Lizzie and Jessie. Mrs. Woods may have learned of the hotel's need for a manager from Judge Hamilton McComas. She was from St. Louis and acquainted with Judge McComas, who was employed by a mining syndicate in St. Louis to represent its interests in New Mexico.[5] Janaloo Hill says of the new arrival's contribution to the civility of the town:

> Mrs. Woods ran this hotel very efficiently. She was of [the] sternest respectability. It was considered the nicest place in town to eat. . . . They had checked tablecloths in the morning and in the evening, [and] white table covers at noon for dinner. . . . They even had saucers under their cups, which was quite something for that day.

But Mrs. Woods' civilized efficiency at the Stratford could not save her family from tragedy that arose from an ordinary frontier circumstance—a shortage of eggs.

The Woods family's trouble began when Bean Belly Smith walked into the Stratford Hotel for his breakfast one morning in 1879 and was served, say, oatmeal or sourdough biscuits and bacon. Then Ross Woods came in and sat down, a good-looking young man suspected of indulging in a flirtation with Mrs. B. B. Smith. Ross's breakfast was also served, maybe the same thing Bean Belly was eating, except for one item—an egg.

Bean Belly sized up the situation and decided that he had been slighted. Why wasn't he served an egg, he demanded to know. The answer, provided by the waiter, or by Ross's mother herself, was simple: There was only one egg on hand that morning.

Smith did not take kindly to such favoritism and made insulting remarks to Ross, who quickly left. He went to his room, got his gun, returned to the dining room, and fired at Smith. He missed; Bean Belly did not.

Ross was buried in the Shakespeare cemetery, and his grave is distinguished by being the first one there to be graced by a marble marker, rarer even than eggs on the New Mexico frontier. Such markers were not available until the railroad came through. After placing the new marker on her son's grave a few years after his death, Mrs. Woods didn't remain in Shakespeare much longer.

The man who may have encouraged Mrs. Woods to come to New Mexico, her acquaintance Judge McComas, took his wife and six-year-old son with him on a business trip from their home in Silver City to Lordsburg in March of 1883. Though on a frequently-traveled road, they were attacked by Chiricahua Apaches. Both adults were murdered, and little Charley disappeared. Shakespeare's militia joined in the search for the boy, but he was never found.[6]

The Marble family fared better on the frontier than Mrs. Woods and her unfortunate son Ross or the McComases. William H. Marble, his wife Flora, and their two daughters settled into life in Shakespeare as they took over the management of Grant House, the stage station where John Evensen had tended to business since the end of the Civil War. One of the daughters, Emma, became fascinated by the town's history, learned much about it from Evensen and her own research, and would later pass on heirloom stories and details about Shakespeare's past to the Hill family.[7] The Marbles prospered at Grant House, where Mrs. Marble served meals in the dining room, and were able to take over the Stratford Hotel when Mrs. Woods decided to depart. They ran it until it closed in 1893.

In the Stratford Hotel's heyday, when it was successfully operated as a hostelry by Mrs. Woods and then the Marbles, it provided hospitality and even a job to men of gubernatorial stature. George Hunt, later governor of Arizona, worked as a waiter in the dining room, and two governors of New Mexico—Edmund Ross and Lew Wallace—stayed in the hotel.[8]

The Town

The demonetization of silver in the United States, Europe, and India, and the depression of 1893 eventually brought an end to silver mining in Shakespeare. Many residents moved away, taking even the timber and other reusable parts of their homes with them and leaving the adobe walls to melt back into the ground.[9] But not everyone left, and a few buildings remained intact, such as the General Merchandise building, where Janaloo Hill and her husband Manny Hough lived until it burned in the spring of 1997, the old mail station (a portion of it is the oldest structure in town), Grant House, and the Stratford Hotel.

Shakespeare had led several lives, weathered two mining booms and busts, and it wasn't over yet. In 1907 a mine near Shakespeare called the Eighty-five Mine went into operation and began to hire employees, this time to mine copper. A few other mines reopened as well. Like a cat claiming its allotted lives, the town shook itself into another resurgence.

The Stratford Hotel

The struggle to survive dominated the next era in the life of the Stratford. It had become a rental residence after it closed as a hotel, but with the startup of the Eighty-five Mine, a woman (said to be the sort who watered her soup) leased the hotel from Matthew Doyle as a boarding house for miners. Doyle had managed to acquire ownership of the Stratford and other buildings in town both by purchase and by virtue of being its last permanent resident.[10]

During the twenty-five years of the third mining boom, the old hotel building served not only as a boarding house, but also for a time as a brothel and then as a cramped apartment house. Doyle wanted to wring as much rent as possible from the town's buildings, so he partitioned the Stratford into rental rooms or half-rooms. A woman who visited Shakespeare in recent years told Janaloo Hill that she had lived in the Stratford during that period. Her family shared it with two others, all recently from Mexico.

One winter day the adults all left for Silver City to take care of some business, leaving the children alone, including this woman and her brother. When a sudden snowstorm delayed the return of the parents, the children ran out of firewood and started prying boards loose from the stair bannister and cupboards to burn instead.[11]

The Town

The copper mining ceased in 1932. When Matthew Doyle died he willed Shakespeare to Bob Reynolds, who had an idea the town could become a tourist attraction but didn't have the wherewithal to make that happen. So he sold it in 1935 to Frank and Rita Hill. They had lost a ranch through foreclosure in the Depression and were seeking another place to buy. Reynolds decided to sell it to them because he thought they'd take care of it. He was more right than he knew.

It was the town that proved to be the owner. It especially claimed Rita, who turned into a rapt student of its history. She listened for hours to stories of its past from the people that she, and later her only child Janaloo, called "the old-timers." Rita inculcated

Frank, Janaloo, and Rita Hill in Shakespeare in the 1960s. Grant House is seen immediately behind Janaloo and the Stratford Hotel beyond. *Photo by Ralph Looney and used with his permission.*

a devotion to the town and its past in her daughter, who grew up there wishing she could meet one of its ghosts, one who would talk to her and answer her questions about Shakespeare.

Janaloo left the family ghost town for a while, to live in Denver, Los Angeles, and New York. We can catch a glimpse of that former Janaloo—who pursued modeling, acting, and dancing in the big cities—in a photograph of her as a young woman with her parents. The three of them are pictured by the porch of the General Merchandise building, which burned in a tragic fire in 1997, with Grant House and the Stratford looming behind them. Frank Hill looks very much the range-rider he was, but his clothes hang loose on him, as if the desert winds had been slowly wearing him away over the years. His face is bronzed by decades in the sun. Rita sits on the edge of the plank porch and seems to be musing, perhaps a little tired. Her hat is tied under her chin, secured against that same wind, and she is wearing a shirt that looks big and durable, meant to work in. Between the two stands Janaloo, tall, trim, dramatically beautiful, dressed in stylish shirt and pants, poised, posed. It is almost as if her photo had been cut out of a western-wear catalog and inserted in this one, as if her clothes fit perfectly though she didn't.

But Janaloo Hill does fit, as few people at the end of the twentieth century ever do. She has shaped her life to the remnants of the town seen behind her, a bonding to place that most not only would not choose but might not even understand. The buildings seen in the photograph are no mere backdrop but form the core of a life decision:

> In the late 1960s it became obvious that if I wanted to keep Shakespeare I had to return to help my parents. My father's health was getting worse and the burden was too much for my mother alone. I had to make a choice and while the theater would most probably rock along perfectly well without my presence, Shakespeare just might not.[12]

She returned to make her contribution to the preservation of Shakespeare and in 1984 married a man, Manny Hough, who shared her passion for the caretaking of history. Besides ranching for a living, they repair and restore Shakespeare's buildings and artifacts, greet its visitors, research and tell its stories, even recreate them in song, dance and drama. Theirs is quite a story in its own right.

The Stratford Hotel

> All the world's a stage,
> And all the men and women merely players:
> They have their exits and their entrances . . .
> —*William Shakespeare, from As You Like It*

Janaloo and Manny and the folks who volunteer to help them have taken good care of the Stratford Hotel. In recent years it has acquired new corrugated metal roofing to replace the old that leaked badly, repairs to upstairs flooring and to tongue-and-groove ceilings, new muslin to cover ceiling and walls, and a few simple furnishings for the upstairs rooms appropriate to successive eras in the building's past.

The long dining room, originally the fort, has served lately as a theater for what Janaloo and Manny call "reenactments," dramatizations of stories from the town's history. "Death Over an Egg" must, of course, be performed there where the actual event took place. Janaloo writes the scripts for these reenactments and acts in them; Manny and neighbors from Lordsburg and other communities in the region also play roles. They bring to life again the characters who arrived by stagecoach or train, lived for a while, and sometimes died in Shakespeare. The dining room now offers new tables and benches, lined up as Emma Marble Muir had remembered them, for the spectators who come to watch Ross Woods meet again his untimely end.

The front room downstairs was once used as a parlor, so when I first saw it, it was set up that way for display with some pieces of furniture upholstered in dust and disintegrating fabric, a picture frame, a mirror. Stains streaked the whitewashed walls. Here was no period room with elegant furnishings, restored to some former splendor. Both the austerity of life in this unvarnished frontier town and the passage of time remained palpable.

The Stratford Hotel is as honest as bones.

The unprettified condition of its rooms, of the building itself, and of the town reveal the central fact of their history—change and decay. Mines and miners come and go, owners and renters build and destroy, adobe walls crumble, floor boards rot and splinter, dust sifts down from mud plaster and settles over everything. But, thanks to Janaloo Hill and Manny Hough, the stories and the physical presence of the improbable Shakespeare linger.

CHAPTER FIVE

The Montezuma Hotel, Plaza Hotel, and Castañeda Hotel at Las Vegas

The Montezuma Hotel

In October of 1882 a group of freight agents and managers for several eastern railroads were invited to take an excursion west and south into the wilds of Colorado, New Mexico Territory, and beyond—all the way into Mexico to La Ciudad de Chihuahua.

These men already knew one another; they gathered monthly to audit the accounts of express freight lines. The proposed trip sounded like a well-earned junket in congenial company.

Their tour took them first to Denver, El Paso, and Chihuahua City. On the return leg it brought them to Las Vegas, New Mexico, and, via a spur line of about six miles, out to Las Vegas Hot Springs and the splendid new Montezuma Hotel. Early on the morning after their arrival, George Street, who had been anointed as the trip historian, and his companions set out to discover firsthand the reason for the existence of the Montezuma Hotel. About its mineral baths he wrote:

> A Russian bath is a big thing. After disrobing in the quarters assigned to you, a clear-skinned but rather scantily attired attendant makes his appearance, covers you with a sheet, and leads you to a marble-floored room in which a row of cupboards runs along on one side, from which steam emerges at every chink. . . . You take your chances, enter an adjoining cupboard, and seating yourself on a small stool, the doors are closed and you are in the stocks. A thousand jets of hot water suddenly strike you like needles, and the boiling process begins. You gradually feel yourself melting away, and wonder how much of you will be left to take home to your family; but before you are entirely evaporated, the attendant makes his appearance, asks you how you feel, just to see whether you can speak yet, opens the prison door and leads you to the next room. There you are put through a course of spouts. Hot and cold water are fired at you alternately; you are laid on a marble slab, drenched with soap suds, scrubbed with a brush till you think the able-bodied attendant has mistaken you for a pine floor, shampooed till your skin is as smooth as the marble slab you are lying on, spanked with a paddle . . . till you are sore.[1]

The result of all this punishment, however, was that "you feel like a bird, fly across the bridge, prance around the balcony, and then enjoy the best and biggest breakfast that you have ever had."[2]

In 1882 the Montezuma Hotel at Las Vegas Hot Springs seemed destined to be one of the grandest of the grand resorts, brand new and blessed by mineral waters, dry climate, mountain scenery, and a wealth of amenities.

In October of 1982, exactly one hundred years after the railroad excursionists discovered the Montezuma, Charles, Prince of Wales, made his own discovery of it. His plane landed in Las Vegas in a thirty-mile-an-hour wind as two high school bands struck up "La Bamba." The thirty-three-year-old heir to the British throne descended the red carpet, his brown hair flying in the gusts, to the cheers of a crowd and banners that read "Viva Prince Charles—Armand Hammer." After being greeted by Armand Hammer, the chairman of Occidental Petroleum, and the mayor and city chamber president of Las Vegas, Prince Charles disappeared into a red limousine headed for the Montezuma Hotel. But he would not be sleeping there or lolling about in the bathhouse the next morning as George Street once had. The Prince, serving as president of the United World College International Council, stayed in the home of Dr. Theodore Lockwood, director of the United World College, and both had work to do the next day. They, along with about 850 other people, would dedicate the Montezuma Hotel, the Stone Hotel, and other buildings on a 110-acre campus as the Armand Hammer United World College of the American West. The prince and other speakers would offer inspirational words about promoting international understanding and healing a world wounded by war.[3]

The former Montezuma Hotel, known as The Castle, welcomed the prince, guests, and students. From her vantage above the Gallinas River Valley, she still looked almost as impressive as she had to those who had come a century earlier for soaking in the hot baths and streams of New Mexico sunlight. But these recent arrivals came for education and international ideals, not for the Montezuma. She was not what she had once been, and perhaps few in the crowd that day even knew her story.

THE FIRST MONTEZUMA HOTEL, 1882

> . . . so constructed that the sunlight shines through nearly every window, and through which the tourist or invalid can beguile his lonely hours, if he has any, with views of interesting points, precipitous stone walls, and smoking streams running irregularly down the rugged sides of the mountain.[4]

The resort hotel that welcomed George Street and his colleagues had opened its doors on April 17, 1882, only six months before their arrival, and had stirred flurries of praise. It was said to be the largest frame building in the country at the time, its furnishings rivaling those of its eastern forebears, the famed resorts at Saratoga Springs, New York.[5] The four-story, E-shaped Montezuma contained 250 rooms and was described as Queen Anne in style.

Despite its steep-roofed, medieval look,

the hotel was all spiff and polish and state-of-the-art technology inside: gaslights, steam heat, water piped to every floor, ranges, broilers, furnaces, and an electric annunciator. The first electric gadget patented for use solely in hotels, the annunciator allowed guests to ring for room service or assistance with luggage. The guest pushed a button in her room that buzzed in the office, where a metal disk revealed the room number from whence came the call. A popular saying went, "One ring for ice-water, two for bellboy, three for porter, four for chambermaid, and not a darned one of them will come."[6]

THE AGE OF RESORTS

In 1882 and 1883, when the first Montezuma Hotel gleamed in gaslit splendor on the Rio Gallinas, it was fulfilling a need of the era. Upper-class Americans had acquired the time and money to travel to resorts. These magnificent hotels in natural surroundings were intended to provide relief for those beset by bodily ills—or for those merely beset by the longing to bide their leisure in remote stylishness. No one could have predicted that the Montezuma's destiny would be so different from its companions being built from Nantasket Beach in Massachusetts to Monterey, California.

While the first skyscraper was under construction in 1883 in Chicago, soaring toward the future at ten stories tall, the Montezuma and other resorts were welcoming tourists into rambling, earth-bound structures set in the past. The Queen Anne style blended Gothic and Elizabethan elements and became characteristic of American resorts being established at mineral springs and seashores around the country. They often had extensive verandas, steeply pitched roofs, towers, lattice-work balustrades, and dormer windows.[7]

Despite the emphasis on closeness to nature, such a hotel would offer the latest comforts. It was required that the enjoyment of leisure take place in a building resembling a palace or in a dining hall sumptuous enough for a lord. This signified one's arrival at a certain status, even if only for a week or two in July.[8]

Though resorts of the 1870s and 1880s were built in proximity to beaches, springs, and mountains, much of what the guests did to amuse themselves had little to do with the natural environment. In addition to doing needlework and bowling, guests danced, played croquet, gambled, drank sherry cobblers, and participated in that most sacred threefold ritual of the day—dining. William H. Carruth, the author of a promotional booklet about Las Vegas Hot Springs, closes—and undercuts—his praise of the pleasures of the resort with this:

> One wonders why, in this country, it is necessary to pay so much attention to the conveniences and luxuries of a mere hotel. The joy of living is out of doors. But people do not live by this rule, and "mine ease in mine inn" has been so well provided for that one need not necessarily go out of doors at all.[9]

Historian Earl Pomeroy quotes a French traveler in the United States in 1887, "In

Europe . . . the hotel is a means to an end. In America it is the end. . . . Hotels are for [Americans] what cathedrals, monuments, and the beauties of nature are for us."[10] Resort hotels provided guests with access to the natural world in the form of vistas to be enjoyed from the ease of the porch or dining room or lawn. The hotel's purpose was primarily social. Tourists came to mingle with other tourists in socially acceptable places. This contrasts sharply with contemporary resort guests' longing for retreat and privacy.

The resort catered to women, providing an environment where they and their children could feel comfortable, unlike commercial hotels in cities and towns, designed for and populated by businessmen. Men labored in stuffy downtown offices to provide the kind of income that allowed their wives and children to escape into the crisp air of the mountains for a summer. In the evenings men without their families would dine in a city hotel restaurant and join their fellows in the bar or the lobby for smoking and talk. However, single young men would travel to the resorts to seek young ladies to court, albeit under their mothers' observant gaze.[11]

As was the accepted practice of the time, the Montezuma provided separate spaces for ladies and gentlemen. While the gentlemen whiled away their time in the basement billiard rooms, the ladies gathered upstairs in sewing rooms or sat on the veranda, keeping an eye on the children and moving their chairs as necessary to follow the sun, which "falls in wide sheets there all day."[12]

THE BEGINNINGS OF A GRAND RESORT

Gallinas Canyon and its hot springs were known to the people of Pecos Pueblo and to the Jicarilla Apaches as well. Since several Spanish expeditions marched through the area between the passage of Francisco Vasquez de Coronado in 1541 and the first decade of the nineteenth century, Spaniards must surely have found and used the forty springs.

About 1840, the property encompassing the hot springs was granted to Julian and Antonio Donaldson by the *alcalde*, head of the local community. Most of the springs they acquired have temperatures of 110 to 140 degrees. It would later be ascertained by a medical doctor and professor of chemistry that the chief constituents of the mineral springs are sodium sulphate and sodium chloride, but without possessing yet a precise chemical analysis, the Donaldsons understood that the springs had medicinal value from which they hoped to benefit commercially. According to Las Vegas historian Lynn I. Perrigo, they constructed the first building there in 1846, to be used as a bathhouse. Other sources maintain that the first building was a hospital built by the United States Army. In any case, all sources agree that the army had, at some point, possession of a building located at the springs and used it for the recuperation of soldiers from Fort Union, but abandoned it during the Civil War.[13]

According to Clarence Pullen writing in 1890 for *Harper's Weekly*, the hospital was converted after 1862 into a hotel called the Adobe Hotel. But according to several other sources, Winfield Scott Moore and his wife Minnie bought the property and built the Adobe Hotel in 1879. A guest recalled of Mrs. Moore, "the rustle of silk, a flash of diamonds, clean beds, and food, so appetizing, that I blush now to remember the size of the meals that I ate at Minnie Moore's table."[14]

We don't know how much they ate, but two guests at Mrs. Moore's for Sunday dinner on July 27, 1879, turned out to be—however improbable it sounds—Jesse James, traveling under the name Thomas Howard, and Billy the Kid. The Kid had ventured from Lincoln to Las Vegas for a stay of several weeks, probably drawn by the general boisterousness accompanying the recent arrival of the railroad. He was acquainted with the Moores. "Mr. Howard" also knew the hosts, having grown up in Missouri with W. Scott Moore. The Moores supposedly introduced these two guests; we can imagine that they talked shop. Miguel A. Otero, later territorial governor of New Mexico, often visited the Moores' Adobe Hotel for a weekend and recollected being introduced to Jesse James on that particular one. He described James as pleasant, reserved, looking like an ordinary businessman but with an unusual alertness and piercing blue eyes.[15]

However it originated, the Adobe Hotel, the first hostelry at the hot springs, no longer exists.[16] But the next hotel built after it, now called the Stone Hotel, still stands. By the time it opened in early 1880 with a grand ball, the railroad had arrived and changed everything for the hot springs and for Las Vegas.

Just a few miles away from the springs, Las Vegas, a town founded in 1835 and sitting astride the Santa Fe Trail, had already become a commercial center for the region. Now a steady stream of potential customers for hotels and bathhouses regularly rolled through town on the steel rails. Seizing the opportunity, a Boston capitalist, Alden Speare, organized the Las Vegas Hot Springs Company, in which the Santa Fe Railroad was the controlling shareholder, and purchased the springs and surrounding property in 1879. First the company built a new bathhouse and walled up the springs so that the water could be pumped into the baths. Then with local contractor F. C. Martsolf, they built the seventy-five-room Hot Springs Hotel, later called the Stone Hotel. So named because it is constructed of native sandstone, the Stone Hotel originally possessed a tower with a mansard roof and a two-story veranda with a balustrade. But even when new, it was not an elegant building and was completely outclassed by the Montezuma Hotel when it opened in 1882.[17]

The Stone Hotel charged only $2 to $3 a day, while the Montezuma asked $3 to $4 a day for a typical room. But with amenities added to the room charge, a couple could run up even bigger bills at the Montezuma. Charlie Dambmann, the playboy son of a wealthy silk importer in New York, was sent west by his parents in the hopes of bridling his habit of squandering money. However, Dambmann persuaded a Russian diva,

Madame Nixau, to abandon her contract with an opera company and elope with him to New Mexico. They settled into the Montezuma's bridal suite, at a cost (with all the extras) of $100 a day. But never mind, the talented prima donna won $21,000 in one night at baccarat.[18]

LEGENDS AND LORE

At the grand opening of the Montezuma Hotel, Don Miguel A. Otero (father of the Miguel Otero who later became governor) described how the Aztec monarch, Montezuma, had "disappeared from view amid the clouds" with a messianic promise that he would return "in glory from the east." Otero concluded that "tonight we hail his coming in the new and splendid halls of the Montezuma!"[19]

According to legend, Montezuma was born in Pecos Pueblo, situated at the passage through the mountains now named Glorieta Pass, west of Las Vegas. He departed from the pueblo, urging its inhabitants to keep a fire burning until his return, and flew to Mexico City on the back of an eagle. He vowed to reappear in the pueblo someday and save its despairing, and vanishing, people from their conquerors. This lore was known to early visitors to the area around Glorieta Pass and Pecos and is the source of the grand resort's name. Often mentioned, the legend appealed to tourists seeking in New Mexico what they deemed picturesque, exotic, even bizarre.[20]

The Aztec chieftain Montezuma was viewed as a savior, and so, in his own way, was Fred Harvey. At the time Fred Harvey arranged for the banquet of blue point oysters and spring lamb to be served at the opening of the first Montezuma Hotel, he was just hitting his stride. He was perfecting the food service that, by the mid-1880s, became "the subject of song, poetry, and legend."[21] He had assured the management of the Santa Fe Railroad that he would institute high quality and had emphatically, even heroically, done so.

For instance, Harvey dispatched his assistant Charles Brant to Guaymas, Mexico, to arrange for fresh produce for the Montezuma during the winter, as no canned foods would be acceptable. Brant also managed to get fresh shellfish, sea bass, and sea celery shipped over the Sonora and the Santa Fe lines back to the hotel. The sea bass were accompanied by four live green turtles supplied by Yaqui Indians. Each of the turtles weighed about two hundred pounds, but Harvey paid less than a penny a pound for them. A small pool in the Gallinas River could serve as a holding tank, so the turtle shipments continued. The Montezuma dining room always listed fresh green turtle soup and steak served with sea celery salad.[22]

THE MONTEZUMA HOTEL AT THE HOT SPRINGS BURNS TO THE GROUND

The Montezuma's Axminster carpets, stained glass, soup cauldrons for cooking green turtles, even its fireplugs, hoses and reels—all, within forty minutes from the first alarm, "remained to the eye only as a smouldering pile of ruins."[23] On a mid-January day in 1884 a fire destroyed the hotel. At first suspected of igniting in the gasoline room in the basement, it was later reported to have resulted from clogged gas mains. At the time only sixty-two guests were rattling about in the huge hotel, and they were gathering in the dining room for the noon meal when the alarm sounded, so all were evacuated.

The hotel was not even two years old when it burned. The Santa Fe Railroad, having invested so much already at the hot springs in an effort to increase passenger traffic on the line, lost no time in announcing plans to rebuild.

The first Montezuma hotel had been designed by the Kansas firm of Jerome, Rice, Moore & Emory.[24] But the second Montezuma Hotel would be designed by the Chicago firm of Daniel Burnham and John Wellborn Root, a partnership of national reputation. Within the month that the Montezuma burned, Daniel Burnham arrived at the hot springs, decided that the first hotel had never been sited properly and promised to rebuild on higher ground. The first hotel had stood with its back to the river and the landscaped grounds and central fountain in front and to the north of it. According to Mr. Burnham, this location did not display the building to advantage nor allow the sun to fall upon it generously enough. The new Montezuma would be situated on a hill well above the bathhouses and landscaped area and would command ample sunlight and a splendid view of the valley opening out onto the plains.

SINGING TO THE BLUE SKY IN 1885

In his partnership with John Wellborn Root, Daniel Burnham served as the executive, the planner, the one who sought out the jobs and then laid out the floor plans, at least in rough sketches. Root would then continue the process by working out the detailed designs, though not always following the initial plan closely. In the case of the Montezuma Hotel design, Burnham claimed that the resemblance between his original suggestion and the final design was slight.[25]

About the time the second Montezuma was built, Root satirized in an essay the Queen Anne style of architecture, and yet the Montezuma Hotel is a fine example of that style. The hotel's design exemplifies his concern, more often applied to tall city structures, with fitness to purpose and unity of elements. Root's biographer wrote that his "best buildings have a way of 'singing to the blue sky,' which proves the genius of the man." The Montezuma, she wrote, "seems to grow out of the very rocks. . . . [T]he absolute fitness of every line and feature of it make this far-away inn one of the most exquisite idyls its author ever dreamed."[26] A scholar of Daniel Burnham's work described the hotel as a "sumptuous, oversized country residence."[27]

The basement and first two stories of the second Montezuma Hotel were constructed, not of frame as the first had been, but of native sandstone, quarry-faced. The frame upper story and towers were sheathed with red shingles, the roof with gray slate. The hotel possessed three towers, each of a different profile and height, the most prominent being the one at the southeast corner roofed with what architectural historians call by a wonderful name—an ogee cap. It simply means that the pointed roof is composed of two curves, con-

The Montezuma Hotel from Fountain Park, ca. 1888. Photo by Dana B. Chase. *Courtesy of the Museum of New Mexico, Santa Fe, New Mexico. Neg. No. 56980.*

cave and convex. An observation deck projected beyond the wall of this tower, supported by curving brackets. The energetic could attain this observation deck by a winding staircase, and one described the high perch as resembling a "mammoth bandstand" that offered a "bewitching" view of the meadows, or "*las vegas*," for which the town was named, and the town itself.[28] Guests might also take in the views on three sides of the first floor from the vantage of a very long veranda.

IN ASHES AGAIN

The magnificent new Montezuma Hotel lasted not quite four months. Though it had been declared fireproof, with an alarm system that reached into every room, insulated wiring, and fireproof plaster, a blaze originated on the top floor under the roof of the largest tower and burned the frame upper portion of the building. This time, however, the stone walls of the lower two floors were left intact and much of the furniture saved.

Still unwilling to give up, the Santa Fe Railroad declared it would rebuild again, this time essentially duplicating the second version of the resort.[29]

The third, and present, Montezuma Hotel opened to the public one year later, on August 16, 1886. Having arisen for the second time from its ashes, it was called the Phoenix Hotel. But its customary name, the Montezuma, quickly regained sway.

LIFE AND LEISURE IN THE THIRD (1886) MONTEZUMA HOTEL

The Montezuma was designed with the health, comfort, tastes, and preferred activities of guests clearly in mind. The arriving guest entered the lobby on the east side of the building, greeted not only by the usual desk, vault, and key and mail rack, but also by a huge, maroon, terra-cotta fireplace in a "cathedral design." It and the ash-paneled ceiling and walls, large and elaborate furnishings, and flowerlike chandeliers must have reassured the new arrivals that this resort would host them with appropriate extravagance.

Guest rooms were arranged so that none would be deprived of windows to let in warm sun and cool mountain air, the drawing cards of New Mexico. The importance of mealtimes as a primary social occasion is indicated by the size and elegance of the dining room, almost one hundred feet long, sixty feet wide, finished in ash, and adorned with stained glass and what the *Las Vegas Daily Optic* called a "mammoth boufet" sixteen feet high.[30] Adjacent to the main dining room was a smaller one for the children; the first time I heard of it, as the mother of a twelve-year-old son, I was struck by the wisdom of it.

As soon as guests had settled in, they could begin the regimen of baths and treatments prescribed by their physicians. A patient drinking the mineral waters, said to be of the alkaline saline type, could, according to medical reports, relieve chronic rheumatism, gout, and dyspepsia. Baths in the same waters were supposed to have a wonderful effect upon the skin and could be used to alleviate rheumatism and blood poisoning. Baths and massages cost fifty cents or a dollar. The facilities could accommodate five hundred to a thousand bathers a day.[31]

A special offering at Las Vegas Hot Springs was the "mud bath." In a section of the springs along the bank of the Rio Gallinas, the water had percolated through the soil, creating a thick, black, chemical mud. Clarence Pullen, writing in *Harper's Weekly*, allowed as how one might shudder thinking of being immersed in it but "once in . . . finds the experiment not unpleasant." The tub was filled with mud ("first freed from all foreign substances") and then mixed with warm spring water to the consistency of "thin mortar."[32] The patient (if he or she was not disturbed by the notion of lingering too long in something resembling mortar) wallowed, piglike, for a time and then emerged from the tub sleek with black mud and ready to be washed and dried. The mud bath was thought to act like a poultice in relieving pain or as a soothing counterirritant.

After a bath a guest might feel invigorated enough for a walk about the grounds and over lawns so green that, to writer William Carruth, they instantly revealed their foreignness to this arid climate. Thirty carloads of bluegrass sod had been brought all the way from Kansas for the lawns and terraces. Carruth noted that despite its emerald color, bluegrass "cannot excel in gracefulness the plumed tufts of the native mountain gramma." More appreciative of the resort's original natural and cultural setting, Carruth commented that the lawns, flowerbeds, gravel paths, statuary, and a large fountain served as "a sure reminder that the Saxon has come."[33]

THE STRUGGLE TO SURVIVE

"The Montezuma was never more delightfully gay than now. Every evening there is dancing, and once a week a german is given, to which are invited the dancing people of the county and city."[34] The *Las Vegas Optic* of July 28, 1893, described the corridors of the hotel as "cool with the balsamic air from the pine-covered hillsides." The "little flirtation nooks" were dimly lit, and "the very air seemed fraught with tenderness."

The air was fraught as well with impending trouble. While local fancy dancers were joining hotel guests to show off their footwork in cotillions at the Montezuma, executives of the Santa Fe Railroad were more concerned about their necks and the expensive albatross hanging around them. Never profitable from the beginning, the Montezuma was running an annual deficit of $40,000. Even as the newspaper extolled Clark D. Frost's management of the resort and the excellent condition of the grounds, General Manager J. J. Frey of the Santa Fe Railroad was preparing to break the bad news to Las Vegans: the hotel would shut its doors by the end of August 1893. The company could no longer subsidize the continual losses.[35]

The Montezuma Hotel was important to Las Vegas. Eighteen thousand guests had visited in the past year, spending money locally. Manager Frost had spent $19,000 in improvements on the buildings and grounds, providing jobs in addition to those of regular employees of the hotel and bathhouses. The Santa Fe Railroad had promoted the resort nationally, and every advertisement carried the name of Las Vegas, fixing it in the public mind as a desirable destination.

But those eighteen thousand guests translated into an average of only about fifty a day, far fewer than the enormous hotel could accommodate. Why so few? What had gone wrong? Some blamed the continuing deficits on ineffective advertising or management that could not revive an ailing business. But Manager Frost had made strides in correcting those problems and predicted that the Montezuma would have become self-sustaining, for the first time, were it not for the Panic of 1893.

Disastrous economic conditions were sweeping the nation into a gutter. Mills, factories, and mines closed. Railroad after railroad failed—the Erie, the Northern Pacific, the Union Pacific, and the Santa Fe, which went into receivership in 1893. The railroad was struggling for its own survival and could no longer prop up the Montezuma.

The Santa Fe promised to keep everything about the hotel in "perfect shape, ready for reopening on short notice."[36] The Montezuma did reopen in July of 1895, and Las Vegas was touting itself in advertisements as a "Land of Innumerable Attractions." But then the hotel quickly closed again in August. The railroad tried to operate it in the summer, or for special occasions, from 1895 until 1903 but never succeeded for any length of time. Other resorts on the Santa Fe line, especially those being developed at the Grand Canyon, competed with the Montezuma, and travelers were beginning to prefer activities other than drinking prodigious amounts of mineral water and lying in tubs swathed in mud.[37]

The Montezuma Hotel seemed star-crossed. Two fires in quick succession and a national depression had cut short her career as a world-class grand resort. That phase of the Montezuma's life came to a close in October, 1903.

A NEW CAREER

The Las Vegas Commercial Club negotiated the transfer of the vacant Montezuma Hotel and its surrounding property in 1920 to the Southern Baptist Convention with the stipulation that it be used as a college. The grand resort, designed for dalliance, was about to be hitched to a new star—church-sponsored education.

The Baptists inaugurated the new college in 1922. By 1925, 255 students were enrolled, taught by twenty-nine faculty members. Monte Montgomery, a graduate of Des Moines, New Mexico's high school, entered as a freshman in the fall of 1928 and attended classes through the summer of 1929.

The students' lives revolved around the Montezuma. They lived, attended class, and ate their meals in the hotel. Before 1928 the men had lived in the Stone Hotel and the women in the Montezuma, but the 1880 Stone Hotel was in such poor condition by the time Montgomery arrived on campus that he and the other men were moved into the first-floor rooms of the Montezuma. Women were housed on the second and third floors. Rooms above the dining room served as the library and classrooms. Students had to leave the comfortably large confines of the hotel only to go to the bathhouses or a gymnasium.

Though Montgomery liked the small student body and the beauty of the canyon surrounding the campus, he remained at the Baptist College only a year because he began hearing rumors that it might lose its accreditation.[38] The numbers of graduates began to decline after 1926, and by 1930 the college closed, a victim of the depression that had already begun to rout prosperity in Las Vegas in the early twenties, long before the stock market crash of 1929.

HOME OF THEOLOGIANS

Montezuma, the Aztec monarch, never returned from Mexico to his legendary birthplace, but in the 1930s some young men fled from Mexico to refuge in the hotel that bore his name. They were aspiring priests, unable to pursue that vocation because, in all the revolutionary turmoil after 1914, the Mexican government had banned the training of clerics. Catholic bishops of the United States, concerned that young priests could not be educated in Mexico to carry on the faith, met in 1936 to decide a course of action. They appointed a committee to secure a location for the establishment of a seminary, which resulted in the purchase of the once-again-vacant Montezuma Hotel from the Baptist Convention in 1937 for $19,000.[39] In September of that year the grand resort opened once more. Who could ever have predicted she would now be officially named the Pontifical National Seminary of Our Lady of Guadalupe and would be a significant item of business on the agenda of the Holy Father in Rome? The Pope selected the Jesuits to staff the new institution.

One of the students must have been homesick, for he constructed at the end of a path east of the Montezuma a replica of a pilgrimage shrine in Jalisco, Mexico—Nuestra Señora de San Juan de Los Lagos. Perhaps all were homesick, for the seminarians packed up and departed from the hot springs in 1972 when it became possible to move to Tula, near Mexico City, and continue their studies. The Montezuma sat empty again.

Armand Hammer came to New Mexico to see the Montezuma in 1981. He (and Neil Lyndon, the writer who worked with him on one of his autobiographies) wrote:

> I had been immediately enchanted with the place but daunted by its dereliction. The buildings were almost in ruins. Every window was broken. The castle's roof was a maze of holes. The grounds were completely overgrown, and we walked around them through mud up to our ankles. Nonetheless, my mind was made up immediately. This was the place.[40]

When Hammer slogged through mud to look at the Montezuma, he was internationally known as a tycoon, philanthropist, art collector, self-styled diplomat in U.S.–Soviet relations, and adept businessman who had turned a nearly bankrupt Occidental Petroleum into one of the world's great energy companies. He described himself as a catalyst who brought people and situations together, and he succeeded in bringing together the Montezuma Hotel and the United World College movement, an effort urged on him by Charles, Prince of Wales.[41]

Hammer had met Prince Charles in 1977 and had become a friend, someone the prince could call on:

> As I came to know Prince Charles well, he inspired me with his enthusiasm for a multitude of projects. One night I was sitting next to Princess Diana at dinner and said, "You know, I can't say no to him, whatever he asks me to do. I have so much confidence in him that if he asked me to jump through that window there, I think I'd jump through the window." She smiled and replied, "Well, I'd jump right after you."[42]

While the princess's willingness to jump at the prince's bidding faltered in subsequent years, Armand Hammer's did not. One of Prince Charles's favorite causes was an international education movement dedicated to bringing together young people from different nationalities to live, learn, and work together—the United World Colleges. It was an endeavor espoused in the interest of world peace by the prince's admired great-uncle, Lord Louis, Earl Mountbatten of Burma. Mountbatten helped create the first World College in Wales and hoped for the establishment of a campus in the United States. But he didn't live to see it happen. He was assassinated in 1979 by Irish Republican Army terrorists. When the prince asked Dr. Hammer for assistance with fulfilling Mountbatten's dream, Hammer could not say no.[43]

The Catholic bishops had been approached by a buyer interested in developing the Montezuma into a resort hotel again, but they hesitated and then decided to sell to Hammer for the World College instead, at least in part because of the proposed philanthropic use. But buying the Montezuma and its associated grounds and structures for a million dollars in 1981 was only the beginning: Hammer then faced the daunting and expensive task of converting badly deteriorated buildings into usable residences, a dining room, a library, and classrooms, in very short order—the college was supposed to open in 1982. The grounds that had long ago been known as Fountain Park had to be re-landscaped as a college campus. Millions of dollars had to be found for all these projects as well as for the operation of the college and tuition subsidies.[44]

Hammer's original intention for the Montezuma was to rehabilitate it for use as the heart of the campus, not to leave it as a castle figurehead of symbolic value only. But the work required to bring the hotel into conformance with current standards, such as fire codes, not to mention restoration to its former glory, would prove to be costlier than Hammer had expected. So the decision was made to limit the immediate effort to making it weathertight, replacing broken windows, repairing the roof, and sprucing up the lobby for the dedication ceremonies.

George Clayton Pearl, an architect with the firm of Stevens, Mallory, Pearl & Campbell in Albuquerque, was asked to consult with Hammer and his associates after the purchase of the Montezuma property, to advise them about readying the existing buildings for occupation in a very short time. Long active in historic preservation, Pearl had admired the Montezuma and researched its history years before. He was of the opinion initially that portions of the Montezuma should be put into use by the college as quickly as possible. But in the weeks before the college's official dedication, Pearl changed his mind, as he learned more about the World College's financial situation. He visited the campus and then wrote to the construction manager:

> The greatest danger to that building [the Montezuma] is in having too much work done on it, too quickly, with very limited funds. Of all the buildings on campus, only the Montezuma warrants pedantic restoration, and such work is costly and time consuming. Now that the building has become so visible to so many people, I feel that it will eventually be restored and used optimally.[45]

The Armand Hammer United World College of the American West opened with one hundred students from thirty-nine countries and was dedicated, as the printed program put it, "In the Presence of the President of the International Council, H. R. H. The Prince of Wales." But within six years after the inspirational speeches and all the publicity surrounding the school's plans, including promise of the eventual restoration of the Montezuma Hotel, the hotel was put up for sale for $500,000.

By the spring of 1990, the United World College backtracked again and removed the Montezuma Hotel from the market. They had needed to find a buyer with millions of dollars to invest in restoration and a plan for the building's use acceptable to the college, as the Montezuma remains an integral part of the campus. It hadn't happened. So when Armand Hammer jetted into New Mexico to attend graduation ceremonies at the college,

Fireplace in the lobby of the Montezuma Hotel, 1880s. *University of Arizona Library, Special Collections, General Photograph Files, "Las Vegas, NM," folder 2. Neg. No. 10907.*

he had to assure questioners at a press conference that renewed plans to restore the hotel "won't cost that much. Our architects estimate $4 million or so. . . . I'd like to rebuild the hot baths, too. . . . It's one of the projects in the back of my mind."[46]

By the end of that year the projects in the back of Dr. Armand Hammer's mind would no longer have his extraordinary energy and abilities to push them toward realization. After a long and very active life, the catalyst died.[47]

PRESENT AND FUTURE

The Castle stands on her hill above the Gallinas River and the hot springs along its banks. Despite her age she remains magnificent. The unexpected sight of her from the road still elicits gasps.

The stained glass windows in the tall dining room buffet still sparkle in the late afternoon light. I imagine the clink of spoons in cups, the scraping of chairs on the floor, the dinner table laughter of guests. The grandiose fireplace and coffered ceilings in the lobby still look as though they belong in a castle on the crest of a storybook summit. From the windows of the upper stories, I can trace the old gardens, a palimpsest beneath the overgrowth. But a sudden summer shower brings water pouring through the veranda roof, and the grand lady's hallways smell of bats.

What of her future? Phillip Geier, president of the United World College, refers to "strategic plans to restore and adaptively reuse the hotel," not as a luxurious resort but as an "international center" located at a crossroads between the United States and Latin America and between the Atlantic and Pacific Coasts.[48] Recent state-funded studies have estimated the cost of restoring the

Montezuma to full use at $10 million and researched the possibilities for financing such restoration.[49] But in 1997 the National Trust for Historic Preservation assigned the hotel to its annual listing of America's "Eleven Most Endangered" historic places.

The Montezuma Hotel's story is that of a renowned beauty who, in her youth, entertained, charmed, and promised too much to her admirers. After surviving great setbacks, she passed into an unanticipated maturity, turning serious, contemplative, devoted to learning and international ideals. She has suffered repeated periods of abandonment and neglect, but they have never reduced those who care about her to despair.

The Plaza Hotel

Byron T. Mills—attorney, abstracter, and owner of the Plaza Hotel in Las Vegas—closed his 1882-vintage hotel and began to sell off its contents in the mid-1940s. He intended to raze the three-story brick structure that he had owned for twenty years, but somehow his plans didn't quite materialize. Instead he found himself telling stories about the building to a magazine writer. He related how men of various stripes of notoriety had come to the Plaza: Edmund Ross, the territorial governor whose vote as a U.S. senator from Kansas had prevented the impeachment of Andrew Johnson and cost him his senatorial career; and Bob Ford, the man who killed Jesse James.

Mills grew expansive. Officers at Fort Union had once frequented the Plaza's lobby, and then there were the days when it was dubbed the Hotel Romaine because Romaine Fielding had taken it over as a movie studio. But such an engaging past apparently did not convince Mills to give up the idea of demolishing the building, for he was quoted as saying, "I almost feel guilty. It certainly is an old landmark."[50]

Little did Byron T. Mills suspect that the Plaza would have the last laugh. He would later be described as a fuzzy shape haunting the staircase of the hotel that outlived him.[51]

SAVED BY AN IRONY

As the Plaza succeeded in evading Mills' plans for flattening it, so have many other historic buildings in Las Vegas survived over the decades through a kind of historical irony.

Early on, Las Vegas prospered as a commercial center, and after the railroad arrived in July of 1879, the town (two towns, actually, the old town centered on its plaza and a new one that sprang up around the tracks) continued to grow in mercantile importance. But after 1900, Albuquerque's designation as the new distribution center for the Santa Fe Railway and the construction of a new line, the Belen Cutoff, left Las Vegas in fact cut off. Less freight moving through town, fewer railroad employees, droughts and overgrazing, bank failures—all these brought hard times to the once-thriving town. But economic stagnation proved to be the salvation of many historic buildings. Las Vegas escaped the ravenous suburban growth, urban renewal, and wholesale demolition of old

The Plaza Hotel just after it was built is the the grandest structure on the Las Vegas plaza. The Exchange Hotel can also be seen near the left edge of the photo. *Photo by James N. Furlong. Courtesy Museum of New Mexico, Santa Fe, New Mexico. Neg. No. 67923.*

buildings to make way for parking lots that plagued so many more affluent communities in New Mexico and elsewhere. Frontier Las Vegas remained intact.

DESPERADOS AND DRUMMERS

Its boom days had begun with the Santa Fe Trail. In the 1840s, trade along the trail burgeoned and Las Vegas enjoyed the results: merchandise to sell in stores, employment with freighters, and opportunities for entrepreneurs. Among these, of course, were hotels, such as the Exchange Hotel (1852), which included a bawdy barroom known as Buffalo Hall. Dr. Henry Connelly, a trader who became a territorial governor, was an early proprietor. In fact, he removed the governor's quarters to his Exchange Hotel in Las Vegas when he withdrew from Santa Fe in 1862 just ahead of advancing Confederate troops.

The Exchange was not particularly comfortable, with guest rooms separated only by partitions that did not reach the ceiling and the back lot used as a noisy and dusty livery stable, but its patrons didn't mind so long as it remained a popular place for high-stakes poker and burlesque shows. The editor of the *Daily Optic* described one such show as "one of the naughtiest acts we have ever seen."[52]

As the railroad steamed into town, so did men who traveled under monikers like Rattlesnake Sam, Scar-Face Charlie, and Cold-Deck George. According to all reports they arrived in such numbers and with such fondness for cards and dice, lawlessness, and violence, that Las Vegas developed a reputation for twenty-four-hour-a-day gambling houses, robberies, shootings, and frequent hangings from the windmill on the plaza.[53]

The coming of the railroad also brought more traveling businessmen or drummers to town, and perhaps the rowdy old Exchange would not suit these "Knights of the Grip," with their fancy vests and stiff-fronted shirts. When the American Hotel facing onto the old plaza burned, a committee of local business leaders formed an association to fund the construction of a new one, to be the Plaza Hotel.

The Plaza illustrates two trends common in the eastern United States by the 1850s (it took awhile for the latest styles to drift westward to the hinterlands). The hotel's architecture was inspired by the Italian villa or *palazzo*, a style widely used in the United States for commercial buildings. Second, its first-floor facade featured large plate-glass windows and cast-iron columns manufactured in St. Louis and shipped by rail to Las Vegas. The technology for using large panes of glass supported by columns for storefronts had existed since the 1840s and 1850s but became much easier to obtain in New Mexico with the advance of the railroad.[54]

To Las Vegans the new Plaza must have appeared quite splendid and up-to-date, though even the classy Plaza had its occasional brush with the violent element. Robert "Bob" Ford and his partner Dick Liddil arrived in Las Vegas in 1884. By then Ford had become the subject of derision in a popular ballad as "The dirty little coward who shot Mr. Howard and laid poor Jesse in his grave." Ford had shot Jesse James—then living in St. Joseph, Missouri, under the alias of Thomas Howard—two years before in order to collect the reward on his head. Ford, who had been a recruit to the infamous James gang of train and bank robbers, was staying in James's home at the time. He claimed he shot the unarmed James at close range from in front. However, the generally accepted version of the murder has it that he shot the outlaw in the back of the head as he stood on a chair attending to the orderliness of his parlor by straightening a picture on the wall.

Ford showed up in Las Vegas with the intention of opening a saloon with Liddil, also a former member of the James gang. For a very brief period, Liddil leased the bar and billiard tables in the Plaza Hotel. Neither man stayed in that business for long, nor did either enjoy a long life.[55]

MOVIES

Las Vegas, so long dominated by guns, gambling and gangs, finally calmed down. Its economy slowed down too, and community leaders thought up schemes to lure new enterprises to town, including inviting motion picture star Romaine Fielding to take a look at Las Vegas in 1913. He did, liked what he saw of the scenery and stage-set old buildings, and ended up leasing the Plaza Hotel, renamed the Hotel Romaine, to use as a movie studio. The benefits to Las Vegas from Romaine's studio turned out to be both money and thrills. The filming of a lengthy movie about a labor uprising set in the far distant future—1950—involved hiring thousands of local extras and spending thousands more on a staged cavalry charge. But Fielding decided the edge of the plains at the foot of the Rockies was too cold in the winter and departed for the Texas Gulf Coast.

Byron T. Mills, the man who now haunts the Plaza Hotel, owned and managed it for about twenty years, from soon after the end of one world war to the end of the next. During Mills' tenure the Plaza provided jobs for students from New Mexico Normal University (after 1941, New Mexico Highlands University) as night clerks. But after World War II, it provided, for a time, more than jobs. Suites carved out of guest rooms became off-campus housing for married students. Katherine Slick, one of the present owners of the building, says, "A number of people who are in their sixties and seventies now have come into the hotel and announced, 'My wife and I had that room right up there. That's where our first baby was born.'"[56]

In the 1950s the dowager Italianate hotel was subjected to "modernization." The old, high, tin ceilings were covered throughout the building, as the owner installed new, lowered ceilings. Fortunately, he did not alter the windows in that process. He also removed bannisters from the twin staircases and some original doors and transoms, which he later returned during restoration.

Over time, the rooms upstairs declined in functionality and appeal to the point that the second and third floor ceased to be used and were closed off. But during those same years the Plaza Hotel Coffee Shop downstairs, run by a woman affectionately known as "Mama Lucy" Lopez, buzzed with political deal making. She served up enchiladas with green or red chile and ample quantities of liberal politics on the side. A political writer for the *Albuquerque Journal* apparently coined the term, the "Mama Lucy Gang" to refer to politicos who met in Mama Lucy's cafe and also to a powerful coalition in the New Mexico House of Representatives. At one point the state legislators honored Mama Lucy in song, with Roberto Mondragon, then lieutenant governor, as song leader:

> This song will not last too long,
> for it could surely get juicy,
> certain deeds are not wrong,
> when done by Mama Lucy.[57]

New Life for a Centenarian

> The [original] windows and doors were completely gone from the front. . . . The ceiling was dropped. Both stairwells were closed off. . . . The walnut floor was covered with linoleum and then shag carpet. It had this feeling of a bowling alley—a long, low space.[58]

Katherine (known to many as Kak) Slick described how the lobby of the Plaza Hotel looked when the rehabilitation process began in early 1982. As she spoke, she sat in the present lobby. No longer much like a bowling alley, the room now brims with light from the front windows all the way up to the original, fifteen-foot-high, pressed tin ceiling. The stairwells have been opened and missing bannisters restored. To one side of the lobby is the bar named after the still-resident Byron T. Mills (in fact, on one of my visits, a guest in sync with the spirit world had just reported two encounters with Mr. Mills). On the other side is the dining room with its dark green and white frieze found when old wallboard was removed. The frieze suggested the idea for border friezes in the renovated guest rooms. Cast-iron, fluted columns uncovered in the old ballroom were moved into the present dining room.

The lobby, restaurant, and guest rooms have an 1880s feel, without the inconveniences of frontier accommodations. In the era when drummers stopped at the Plaza Hotel it had seventy-five rooms, now reduced to fewer than forty to satisfy contemporary travelers' needs for more space. In those days guests whiled away their leisure in the public spaces, not in rooms we would now consider cramped.

The rehabilitation of the Plaza Hotel was accomplished in a little over a year and at a cost of two million dollars by the Plaza Partnership Limited. The partnership purchased the building from Dana and Lonnie Lucero, who had run a restaurant and bar on the ground floor and lived in an apartment upstairs (it was not being used as a hotel at that time). The Luceros joined with Kak and her husband Wid Slick and other limited partners in the project, which involved the town's first major private investment for a certified historic rehabilitation. The financial arrangements were complex: a grant-in-aid from the New Mexico Historic Preservation Bureau, an Urban Development Action Grant from the Department of Housing and Urban Development, a tax syndication to take advantage of tax credits then available to encourage rehabilitation, and conventional bank financing.[59]

I asked Wid Slick why he came to Las Vegas from Dallas and bought into the Plaza Hotel. The first reason was personal: He had visited for awhile and thought Las Vegas looked like a better place to bring up his son. A second reason had to do with long-term investment, with Las Vegas being "still sort of pristine, still not commercialized so much . . . Santa Fe thirty years ago."

Kak added that they wanted to be in "a community that would take its historic past and try to work with that. And [here] you have a hundred years of very diverse, very rich architecture, which you don't find anywhere else in the state of New Mexico. Not the kind of diversity we have. We've got Greek Revival houses, we've got classic Victorian. . . . We've got bungalows."[60]

And an Italianate hotel. May the Plaza outlive us all.

The Castañeda Hotel

A visitor to northeastern New Mexico at the close of the 1890s might have business with one Melvin W. Mills and heads for Mills' ranch on the Canadian River.

He rides through miles and miles of unhindered wind and unchanging prairie. But as he approaches the river, without warning, the pale grassland splits open into a chasm. Its walls drop abruptly, one thousand feet in places. The shining Canadian winds far below, red from canyon rock and banked with emerald bottomlands. A treacherous stagecoach road twists down the canyon wall to Melvin Mills' Orchard Ranch stretching for ten miles along the river. The traveler has found Mills' Shangri-la.

Mills, who established this hideaway empire by building on land homesteaded by his father in the 1870s, loomed large in the history of this region. Some of his neighbors spoke ill of him, and it has been said that he "seems to have been personally involved in every business venture, political feud, and financial intrigue in northeastern New Mexico";[61] but certainly an undeniable achievement was what Mills rooted in the rich alluvial soil of the Canadian River. There, where the river cuts through a gorge sheltered from plains winds, using water from irrigation channels and cisterns, Mills nurtured thousands of fruit and nut trees. They included peach, pear, cherry, apricot, plum, mulberry, quince, walnut and a special almond, his own soft-shell hybrid. Folks have claimed the peaches grew big as grapefruits. A farm and vineyard also produced cabbages, tomatoes, cantaloupes, grapes.

Six draft horses hauled wagonloads of this produce up the precipitous road to the top and over the grassland to the town of Springer. From there, the wonders from Mills' sunken gardens were loaded onto the train and sent to Las Vegas, intended for the "Civilizer of the West," Fred Harvey. The grapes, quinces, and peaches found their way to the tables of those who stopped at Harvey's trackside hotel, the Castañeda in Las Vegas, the first built in a chain of luxury hotels.[62]

In 1899 when the Castañeda was new, not only did Mills' Orchard Ranch send it fine produce, but seven dairies supplied it with milk, butter, and cream; steak arrived by rail from California. The hotel maintained a $200,000 silver service that could be transported down the line to other Harvey establishments for entertaining visiting dignitaries. A former museum curator in Las Vegas, who first ate in the Castañeda in 1930 with a descendent of Fred Harvey himself seated at his table, recalled that cowboys said the hotel was "the finest watering hole and camping place this side of the pearly gates."[63] Much of the Orchard Ranch would be swept away by rampaging floods in 1904, and other luxury Harvey hotels are gone, but the Castañeda still stands in Las Vegas, though deteriorated.

In 1896 the Santa Fe Railway had emerged from economic crisis, recovered its momentum, and planned to build a series of station hotels featuring Harvey food and service to attract more passengers to the West. The first of these was named by the railroad's president, E. P. Ripley, after a member of Coronado's 1540 expedition, Pedro de Castañeda de Nagera. But its architectural pedigree derives from a different place and time in Spanish Colonial history. Designed by a California architect, Frederick Louis Roehrig, the hotel was built in the then-popular California Mission style. It surrounds three sides of a square, with the center an open courtyard. The wings and central facade face toward the railroad tracks through an embracing corridor of buff brick arches, as if part of a mission quadrangle. Other California Mission-style characteristics are the bell tower atop the central portion of the building, gracefully scrolling parapets, and a pitched roof covered with metal tiles.

Not a sprawling estate set in a mountain canyon like the Montezuma, the Castañeda was never meant for travelers who wished to linger on sunny verandas or soak in tubs of mineral water. Much of its downstairs space was devoted to eating. Diners, while they enjoyed Mills' fruits or bread hot out of the bakery ovens, sat in a large, cardinal-red dining room. Fishnet lace curtains hung at the windows and potted plants perched on the tables just as cozily as in their homes, but the elegant furnishings, ornamented with a twisted rope pattern, were described in the newspaper as "sixteenth century" style. Many guests probably stopped only for meals, though the hotel provided forty-five pleasant sleeping rooms on the second floor, some furnished in bird's eye maple.[64]

One of those rooms was reserved for Theodore Roosevelt in June of 1899, but he spent little time there, preferring to join "his boys" encamped in Las Vegas's Lincoln Park and swap war stories. The occasion was the first annual reunion of the Rough Riders.

When the United States entered into war with Spain in April of 1898, twenty-one volunteers from Las Vegas were accepted into the First Regiment of the United States Volunteer Cavalry, more often known as the Rough Riders. They were commanded by Colonel Leonard Wood and Lieutenant Colonel Theodore Roosevelt (later promoted to commanding colonel), but it was Roosevelt who would be touted by the press as their leader and whose name would be linked with theirs.

When the war was over in only a few months, they returned in triumph and decided to hold a reunion the following year in June. Since so many of the Rough Riders had come from Las Vegas, and it offered better hotel facilities than other towns in the territory, it was chosen as the site.

In the days when Rough Riders cheered Roosevelt as he arrived on the train, the Castañeda was a preeminent railroad hotel, but it made a graceful transition into the automobile age. After the Santa Fe Railway constructed the Belen Cutoff, a branch that avoided the steep grades through the mountains of northeastern New Mexico, Las Vegas rail traffic fell off substantially. Freight traveled via the cut-off, but passenger service through Las Vegas continued as tourists from the East increasingly sought out the curious landscapes and peoples of the Southwest. In 1926, when Fred Harvey began providing automobile sidetrips called Indian Detours to the pueblos, the first tours linked the Castañeda, the Alvarado in Albuquerque, and La Fonda in Santa Fe. Visitors braving the poor roads and frequent breakdowns of auto travel in northern New Mexico at least could trust their safe passage to experienced drivers and enjoy the company of well-trained, young women guides called couriers.

But as automobile tourism came to dominate American travel, the Castañeda, like other Harvey hotels, went into decline after World War II. The Santa Fe Railway closed the Mission-style hotel in 1948, and it was slated for demolition. Eventually, however, J. J. Lawson of Las Vegas purchased it and converted it into rental apartments. Don

Eldh, an interior decorator from California who could still appreciate the hotel's dignified beauty despite its decline, decided to buy it in 1973. Eldh has renovated the billiard room and opened it as a bar as well as toiled over the years at maintenance, repairs, and efforts to make commercial use of spaces within the building. He had hoped to restore the hotel by its centennial in 1998. However, as of this writing, Eldh has put the Castañeda Hotel up for sale, hoping for a buyer with the vision and financial resources to bring it to life again.[65]

Las Vegas has often suffered from economic deprivation in the twentieth century but has never suffered any lack in the riches of historic legacy. This chapter deals with only three of the area's historic hotels—a world-class grand resort, the first of the luxury Harvey Hotels, and a restored commercial hotel on the old plaza. Two of these—the Montezuma and Castañeda—are so linked to the town's identity that drawings of them comprise the Chamber of Commerce logo. Other lodgings of historic importance in Las Vegas also await the visitor's discovery, along with hundreds of buildings of all types from the town's past.

CHAPTER SIX

The Black Range Lodge, Victorio Hotel, and Ocean Grove Hotel at Kingston and Hillsboro

By Christmas of 1882, Kingston was booming. Silver prospectors crowded into town and swelled its population to 2,500, a mining metropolis tucked into the darkly wooded mountains in southwestern New Mexico known as the Sierra Diablo or the Black Range.

Pretty Sam was opening a new casino and had invited just about everybody. He was offering free food and drink—champagne, whiskey, wine, gin, and mescal—and the best orchestra El Paso had to offer. Holiday celebrants arrived in numbers, dressed fit to kill in fancy gowns, swallow tails and white shirt fronts. Some even squeezed into old officers' uniforms. They danced and drank and were having a mighty fine time when Johnny Roach, the gambler, arrived in the company of his Springfield rifle. Johnny, testy because his lady friend had come to the dance with someone else while he was sleeping off a drunk, fired into the crowd of merrymakers. Startled but quick on the draw, many returned fire while others dashed for the dance hall's bolted back door. The back of Pretty Sam's new place extended out over Percha Creek, so when unwitting guests fleeing Johnny's shots broke through the door, they fell in a heap in the dry creek bed thirty feet below. Prospector James McKenna, who had arrived in the Black Range in 1877, ended the story in his *Black Range Tales* with this: "And so it happened that Pretty Sam's dance went into history as the biggest bang-up in the annals of Kingston."[1]

The big holiday party tradition has continued in Kingston, minus guns and unexpected tumbles into the gulch, and Pretty Sam's itself. The casino, like almost everything else in Kingston, has disappeared into the years. Recent festivities have taken place in the Black Range Lodge, built in 1940 with stones salvaged from nearby ruins, likely from both Pretty Sam's Casino and the Monarch Saloon, where in the 1880s on New Year's Eve "big games of faro and poker were going on with coin stacked virtually to the ceiling."[2] Perhaps some spirit of winter revelry emanates from those old stones. Just as Pretty Sam did more than a hundred and fifteen years ago, Mike Sherlock and Catherine Wanek, owners of the Black Range Lodge in the early 1990s, opened their doors to friends and neighbors for an annual holiday bash.

For one such celebration, guests arriving at the lodge formed a crowd that could barely squeeze in among tables laden with salmon, black beans and rice, chips, and pies, among folding chairs, a makeshift stage for musicians, a video arcade, and pinball games.

Unlike Pretty Sam's partygoers, these, though invited to dress formally, had not. Most stayed comfortable in jeans, plaid flannel, and sweaters, with an occasional shaved head or crop of purple hair among the teens. One fellow in a red T-shirt and green pants stood out with a tie that doubled as a sequined Christmas tree. When I complimented his contribution to seasonal glitter, I learned he was from Albuquerque and drove down to Kingston to work on a movie script with Sherlock and Wanek. Ben Whiteman, a white-haired neighbor caretaking the old Victorio Hotel down the street, explained to me that only a few more than twenty-five people resided in Kingston, one hundredth of the number in 1882, so most of this crowd must have come from somewhere else. Many hailed from Albuquerque and Las Cruces, and others had arrived from California, where the hosts had friends and colleagues in the movie industry.

Once outside the lodge, the folk ballads and country music faded into crystalline night air. The Black Range itself could be discerned only because its shadowy peaks blotted out stars in a sky so bright with them that its light reflected off wind-swept tatters of snow.

A Millionaire in the Afternoon

Kingston, where it was said that the prospector sallied forth a poor man in the morning and returned a millionaire in the afternoon,[3] is often called a ghost town by writers and other such romantics, but the town never really died. Bursting into life after the discovery of a rich silver district in 1882, Kingston flourished for only about eleven years and, as the fabulous deposits neared depletion, straggled into the twentieth century. Over the years the mecca in the mountains for thousands became a haven for just a few, looking only for a quiet place to retire, to paint, to write.

Today the Black Range Lodge is the only functioning historic hostelry in town, but in the 1880s a newcomer could have chosen among several hotels. One of the earliest was a tent lodging with an aisle running down the center that separated two rows of bunks stacked four high. The bottom bunks proved safer (and thus more expensive) because in the wee hours wild shots from the dance halls and saloons would rip through the "hotel's" canvas walls.[4] Such tents were called "mammoth lodgers." Sometimes the ubiquitous saloons in mining towns handed out blankets to patrons or hung canvas from the ceiling to create cubicles that could be advertised as "rooms,"[5] but Kingston provided better lodging than that early on. A town that soon boasted more than twenty-five mines—with names like Miner's Dream, Iron King, Grey Eagle, Black Colt, and Savage—spawned genuine hotels, places that could provide some comforts to men scrambling their way to fortunes. One of them—a large, white frame building named the Mountain Pride Hotel—served up oysters, shrimp, and stagecoach service from the railhead at Lake Valley twenty-seven miles away.[6] Across the street was the Victorio Hotel, probably built in 1884, and, oddly enough for a town harried by the Apaches, named for one of their fiercest and most elusive leaders, who had fought his last battle only a few years before.

Another of the hotels in town, the Occidental, a two-story frame building perhaps fifteen feet wide fronting Kingston's Main Street, was managed and later owned by

Mariah Brophy, the mother-in-law of a man who would feature prominently in Kingston's early history and later in the history of the nation in the twenties. Edward L. Doheny, a prospector who discovered a couple of the first mines upon which Kingston was built, married Carrie Wilkins, the daughter of the Occidental's manager, Mariah Brophy. He later bought the Occidental for $650 and then sold it to his mother-in-law for $350 in an apparent effort to provide her with a stable livelihood, hotelkeeping being one of the few ways a single woman could earn a living in a frontier town. Doheny and his wife struggled to make it themselves in Kingston but ended up having to leave for California, where another discovery, this time of oil, made him a wealthy man. Wealthy enough to be accused, though eventually acquitted, of bribery charges in the Teapot Dome Scandal with another New Mexican, Albert Bacon Fall, who served as secretary of the interior under Warren Harding.[7]

By the latter 1880s, Kingston, despite its location in the remote heart of Apache country, must have been a cosmopolitan place. Front page stories from the *Kingston Weekly Shaft* in 1889 reflect at the very least an editor's belief in, or hope for, a sophisticated audience interested in Chinese theater in New York, Oliver Wendell Holmes' views on "versemakers," "Lady Novelists" "Female Duelists," and a detailed guide to traveling to Paris. Such readers must not all have been grizzled sourdoughs tugging burros through the muddy streets of Bonanzaville.

And in fact, the register of the Victorio Hotel provides evidence of an international clientele. In the few months between October of 1886 and February of 1887, guests signed in from Canada, Greece, Egypt, and the Sandwich Islands, as well as from Chicago, St. Louis, San Francisco, and Boston. James McKenna said the register contained the names of some of the "best-known mining men of the world."[8] But despite the fact that the *Kingston Weekly Shaft* prominently featured articles that might appeal to women, no women signed the register at the Victorio (nor at other hotels in 1887). If a woman traveling alone required a room at a hotel, the clerk would sign her in, though probably not listing her name but providing only a notation of the presence of a lady.[9]

The most notable signature during that time is Grover Cleveland's, dated January 24, 1887, during his first term as president.[10] Unfortunately, despite much searching for corroboration of a presidential visit to Kingston, I found none.[11] In fact the Washington correspondent for the region's *Sierra County Advocate* reported in a piece datelined January 24, 1887, that President Cleveland had just hosted the first state reception of the new year, and despite three hours of shaking hands with diplomats, had returned to work the next morning "with more vim than usual." [12] Apparently Cleveland was not journeying through the West in the days just before January 24th. So the signature remains a mystery.

New Mexico's Most Notorious Hotelkeeper

Among the international arrivals, and women, in Kingston was one Sarah Jane

Creech from England, who later became Sadie Orchard. It would be impossible to write about the hostelries of Kingston and its neighboring mining community Hillsboro without mentioning Sadie and equally impossible to tell her story in factual outline without the vivid colors of legend. Not only are the facts themselves hard to pin down, but Sadie likely embellished them during her lifetime, and others have enthusiastically elaborated on them since.

Sarah Jane Creech apparently arrived in Kingston in the mid-1880s and set up shop as a prostitute on a street aptly named Virtue Avenue. A young woman of about twenty (if you trust the birth date of 1865 on her tombstone in Truth or Consequences), Sadie is usually described as small and shapely with black hair, blue eyes, and a propensity for profanity. New Mexico writer Erna Fergusson pictured her as having "short feet in shorter shoes, tight spitcurls, and a wicked chuckle."[13] One of the tales about Sadie is that she and the other "soiled doves" of Kingston raised $1,500 to build a church in a town possessing more than twenty saloons but no house of worship. Indeed, she donated her own diamond lavaliere to the cause.

Although Sadie was known in Kingston for her civic-mindedness, her business dealings with the traveling public did not become respectable until she left Kingston and moved nine miles away to Hillsboro, a mining town five years older than Kingston and raking in profits from gold as well as silver.

The order and dates of Sadie's business and marital activities in Hillsboro are difficult to ascertain, but she did marry a man named Orchard (several first names or sets of initials show up in different sources),[14] who owned the Mountain Pride Line, a stagecoach company carrying passengers and mail on the route between Kingston, Hillsboro, and Lake Valley. In 1884 a spur line from the transcontinental railroad had been extended to Lake Valley, a fabulous mining district that included one of the richest pockets of pure silver in the world—a subterranean room known as the Bridal Chamber.

Stories abound of Sadie's exploits and kindnesses, but none has captured the public's imagination so much as her self-established reputation as a driver of the Mountain Pride coaches. Sadie made her often-quoted claims in interviews in her later years with an *El Paso Times* reporter and interviewers with the New Mexico Federal Writers Project. She told the writer from the *Times* that she sometimes drove the four-horse teams and never felt endangered because she "could kick the foot brake with the best of them." One of her interviewers with the NMFWP in 1937 reported that she "often drove the great Concord coach herself and many of the passengers said that they would rather ride with her than any of the drivers she employed. She also broke many of the stagecoach horses."[15]

Was it true? Historian William S. Wallace, in writing about the Mountain Pride Line, never mentioned Mrs. Orchard at all, though he discussed in detail the day-to-day operation of the line during the period when Sadie would have been driving.[16]

Did Sadie have to tout her skill as a driver herself because she was a woman? Or did she

Three women in front of the Ocean Grove Hotel in Hillsboro, probably Sadie Orchard on the right, between 1893 and 1902. *Photo by George T. Miller. Courtesy Museum of New Mexico, Santa Fe, New Mexico. Neg. No. 76560.*

simply, in later nostalgic years, gild her experiences with the Mountain Pride Line? No matter which is true, the stories of Sadie Orchard as dauntless stage driver have now become indelible in the lore of Kingston, Hillsboro, and Lake Valley.

About Mrs. Orchard's role as a hotelkeeper there is more certainty. She established at least two hotels in Hillsboro, the Ocean Grove and the Orchard, which secured names for themselves for hospitality and good food. The Ocean Grove Hotel on Hillsboro's Main Street was well-known to lawyers in the region, who stayed there during court terms at the Sierra County Courthouse. And the lawyers were well-known to Sadie. Erna Fergusson commented that, "her terse, unquotable comments on them were doubtless just."[17]

A dramatic event in the legal history of the New Mexico Territory proved to be a highlight as well of the history of Sadie's Ocean Grove Hotel. The 1899 trial of Oliver Lee and Jim Gililland for the murder of Judge Albert J. Fountain and his young son received that era's equivalent of a media blitz in the form of numerous newspaper reporters descending on Hillsboro. Western Union ran the first telegraph line into town just for the occasion, and tent communities sprang up for each side's supporters. The prosecuting attorney was the powerful Thomas Benton Catron of Santa Fe, and the defense attorney, Albert Bacon Fall of Las Cruces and later of Teapot Dome Scandal fame. Sadie's hotel reportedly became a headquarters for Fall's defense team.

In Fall's startling closing argument to the jury, he accused the prosecution and the judge himself of a conspiracy to hang an innocent man. The judge threatened to send Fall to jail for contempt but then looked around and realized the courtroom was jammed with Oliver Lee's cowboy friends, all armed.[18] The jury acquitted the defendants and Fall did not go to jail—not until 1929. He remained free to return to Sadie's place for the post-trial celebration.

Up the hill from the Ocean Grove, next to the stagecoach corral, Sadie later established the Orchard Hotel. Edward Tittman, a lawyer who strenuously fought the removal of the county seat from Hillsboro to Hot Springs (now Truth or Consequences), stayed in the Orchard with his family when they first arrived in town from New York. Later, in the 1920s, the Tittmans often ate dinner there on Sunday evenings. Tittman's daughter recalls that Sadie, by then grown older and stouter, was very kind to them. She would don a hat to call on Mrs. Tittman because, as Sadie put it in her broad Cockney accent, the lawyer's wife was "a laaady."[19]

Today you would not find a trace of the Orchard Hotel with its wooden porch and walk-through passageway that Edward Tittman's daughter remembers. The village fire station now occupies its site. Behind it an open space surrounded by old rock walls marks the location where teams of horses once kicked up dust in the corrals for the Orchards' stage line. During the 1890s the coaches stopped here for the night on the return run from Kingston to Lake Valley.

Sadie Orchard hired a Chinese cook named Tom Ying, who had run an eatery in Lake Valley. After she retired, Tom took over the old Ocean Grove Hotel as his restaurant, and it was known as "The Chinaman's Place." It was closed for years after his death, but when the Black Range Museum moved into the building in the 1960s it was as if Ying had just walked out the door. The wood box was stocked, and jars of canned fruit stood on the shelf.[20] The cook's small black skull cap awaited—and still awaits—his return to the kitchen. In the museum you can visit Ying's domain: a black Banquet stove that looks to be about a half acre across.

The Black Range Museum contains a number of items that once belonged to Sadie Orchard, one of the most telling her scrapbook filled with clipped newspaper verses and sentimental greeting cards carefully pasted in so as not to waste a scintilla of space. Sadie was a canny woman, but also a woman of feeling. Her notoriety as a prostitute, a hotel proprietor, and a stage driver is rivaled by her reputation as doer of good deeds in the community, including nursing the sick and burying the dead during the influenza epidemic of 1918. She died in 1943.

Kingston and Hillsboro Today—From Mining to Tourism to Movies

Of Kingston's boomtown hotels, the Mountain Pride has vanished, but the Victorio still stands. It was originally a three-story stone and wood structure with a flat roof, offering more than twenty rooms and water from its own spring as well as a bar for thirsty guests. The roof eventually deteriorated so much that the top floor of the building was removed.

When I visited, the hotel was used as a second home for an out-of-town owner, and its genial caretaker, Ben Whiteman, took me on a tour of it. The interior had been completely altered over the years, though a bit of the original wall stenciling remained in one room. Whiteman led me down to the basement to show me the date 1884 carved on a stone. He told me he had heard that its cool, dark space had been used as a morgue to hold corpses awaiting graves that had to be dynamited out of the rock-ribbed mountain cemetery.

An easy stroll up the street from the Victorio Hotel, past Virtue Avenue, is the Black Range Lodge, location of the holiday party. Its origins as a hostelry do not go back so far as the mining era. By the time it was built in 1940, few original buildings in Kingston still stood. Most had been torn down or had burned over the years since the town was deserted by its thousands of wealth seekers. Mary Jane Henderson, who came from El Paso to join a few others living in Kingston, built the Black Range Lodge in the hopes of attracting some tourists to the romance of the old mining camp and to the cool forests of conifers and oak. She had the lodge constructed onto an old building already on the site, using the stones from nearby ruins. So at least a portion of the lodge probably dates from the earliest days of Kingston, but different sources offer different views on its original use.[21]

The two-and-a-half-story lodge possesses many windows and sundry porches and balconies for visitors who like to gaze at the mountains rising all around the pine-scented town. In the 1990s the lodge doesn't look much different than it did in a 1940s postcard. At that time Mary Jane Henderson envisioned a stopover for tourists in what was then an almost empty town: she was counting on the appeal of the scenic drive from Hot Springs via Hillsboro and Kingston to Silver City that had recently become much easier than before.

In Sadie Orchard's day stagecoaches plied the winding, climbing mountain road, easing along the Percha Canyon cliffs and struggling through sand and over rock. Fifty years later, a brand new road smoothed the way. James McKenna lived long enough to see it and described it as "the fine new highway . . . carved out of solid rock . . . from which, on clear days, one can see mountain ridges three hundred miles away." He noted that the highway passed over the Box Canyon on a steel bridge, while stagecoach drivers and passengers had once had to pass through the canyon "in danger of being ambushed by Apaches, or swept away by the cloudbursts."[22]

When the $750,000 Black Range Highway officially opened on August 18, 1935, Kingston suddenly returned to its boomtown size—for a day. A crowd of 4,000 gathered for the ceremony. Governor Clyde Tingley assured them that prosperity would return to Kingston, this time brought by travelers, hunters, and fishermen. He said, "I expect tourists to spend forty million dollars in New Mexico this year."[23] Three years later no boom had occurred, but the observant folks in Silver City were counting license plates. A headline in the *Silver City Daily Press* noted at the start of vacation season that "Out of State Cars Total 32 in Single

Black Range Lodge, Kingston.
Postcard from author's collection.

Week,"[24] and the *Press* ran cheering editorials on increasing auto tourist travel.

While his projections may have been optimistic, Clyde Tingley had good reason to expect travelers and lovers of the outdoors to make use of the new road. Kingston and Silver City perch on the edges of a great wild region, within which lies the world's first officially designated "wilderness area," now the Gila Wilderness. It had been established eleven years before in 1924, largely through the efforts of forester and writer Aldo Leopold. The visitors would come to the wilderness to follow trails through the mountains and their stands of virgin ponderosa pine, to find the traces of human history left scattered through the Gila National Forest. They would discover cliff dwellings, abandoned cabins, battlegrounds where the U.S. Cavalry fought the Apaches, and remnants of mining camps like Kingston, a tiny island of private property just inside the forest's boundary.

Mary Jane Henderson's hopes for tourist traffic through Kingston did materialize on a small scale, though Tingley's promises of new prosperity did not. A resident of Kingston today, Margaret Vetter, whose family acquired the building next to the Black Range Lodge (the fine old Percha Bank), recalls that "ghost town" Kingston possessed a store and post office into the 1950s.[25] Mrs. Vetter and her husband Paul had been drawn to the mountains for the fishing. They came to like the way history remained visible and tangible in Kingston and settled there in the 1960s. They decided to refurbish the bank, one of the town's few standing original structures, and eventually turned it into a museum that hosted annual art exhibitions. Busloads of people would arrive for the exhibitions from as far away as El Paso and Fort Bliss—the long-awaited tourists.[26]

One of the artists who exhibited his work there was Joe Goforth, a retired businessman from Silver City. He enjoyed spending time in Kingston and met there someone else who did, Jewell Strickland. Joe and Jewell took an interest in the Black Range Lodge, which had had several owners after Mary Jane Henderson but by 1970 was closed, full of cobwebs, "spooky," as Jewell put it. The two acquired the building at an auction and began the process of restoring it to usefulness. They were married there at the end of 1970 and opened for business in 1971. They ran it as a restaurant, bar, and lodging for about two years, then closed it and just lived there for a while. They reopened a few years later to groups by reservation only.[27]

Still a few more owners later, in 1984, Mike Sherlock and Catherine Wanek happened upon the lodge on their honeymoon. For years the lodge had not been available to just any and all passersby, but Sherlock and Wanek managed to arrange to spend a night there. Before they left town to return to Los Angeles, where two houses and jobs in the movie industry awaited them, they had charged on their credit cards the earnest money to buy the Black Range Lodge.

Sherlock had worked as a film editor, a teacher of filmmaking, and, in the early 1980s, was raising money to make short films. Wanek was an assistant director for studio features. The couple met as a result of a mutual interest in screenwriting and a desire to make their own films from scratch, from script to edit. They thought of their newly acquired lodge as a place to write and perhaps to serve as a production set. For about four years they lived in the lodge and wrote part of each year, with Wanek going off to work on location the remaining months to earn enough to support that writing time. But then "after waking up in the woods for a few years," as Sherlock put it, they wanted to stay year-round, to be at the lodge when the corn ripened in the garden.

Opening the Black Range Lodge again to travelers seemed like a good way to use ten bedrooms, a dozen or so bathrooms, and the large common areas, such as the second-floor dining room. So in 1988 the Black Range Lodge became a bed-and-breakfast, and Wanek and Sherlock took on new roles as host and hostess—baking muffins, furnishing and refurbishing the guest rooms in the homey old building in "rustic splendor," and showing videos to guests on request from their extensive library.[28]

Movies were never far away in Kingston and Hillsboro in the early 1990s, from the Black Range Lodge's former dining room turned home theater to the making of feature films locally. Where once silver and gold strikes brought thousands from all over the world into the Victorio or the Mountain Pride or the Ocean Grove, the filming of Rod McCall's *Paper Hearts* in 1991 brought a crew of forty and several stars into the towns, putting a little strain on the available housing. One of those stars, Sally Kirkland, liked sleeping at night to the rippling of Percha Creek so well that she thought about buying herself a place in Kingston or Hillsboro. The movie's writer/director/producer, Rod McCall, told a newspaper reporter he wanted to make the film in Hillsboro because "the place itself is a character. . . . You hear it through the windows, you feel it in the scenes on the prairie, on the road. It's all-pervasive." [29]

What is the character of this place? According to Mike Sherlock, it is living where you really appreciate your neighbors and the volunteer fire department, where a fellow from southern California who once knew nothing of seasons can at last see snow and the sharpness of stars piercing a winter sky. According to Ben Whiteman, it is a place where a man who loves mountains can be happy. There they are, right outside the door, and the road turns into a trail and goes on for a hundred miles into the wilderness. It offers, according to Margaret Vetter, a feeling of peace. And, a visitor might add, even the stones in the walls have plenty of stories to tell.

CHAPTER SEVEN

The Lodge at Cloudcroft

In the summer of 1916, Major Ernest Calvin Lee, a physician from Detroit, went farther afield with the National Guard than usual, all the way to Fort Bliss near El Paso, Texas. Lee had done service every summer for years, but this year President Woodrow Wilson had called out the guard, including Lee's Thirty-second Michigan regiment, to reinforce what was labeled "the punitive expedition" under the command of General John J. Pershing.

Pershing and his forces had set out into Mexico in pursuit of Pancho Villa and his army of revolutionaries. *Villistas* had defied the power of the United States in a raid on the border village of Columbus, New Mexico, on March 9, 1916, and were to be tracked down and punished.

One day in September soldiers stationed at Fort Bliss marched to the plaza in El Paso. This military parade excited the interest of El Pasoans, including Mr. and Mrs. Alfred F. Fegan, who gathered with friends and family on their veranda to watch. When some marching officers paused for a lunch break in the street, the Fegans invited them to come have some lemonade. Major Ernest Lee, senior medical officer, a bachelor aged 51, was among them.

He soon noticed that one of the Fegan daughters, Luisa, was an especially lovely young woman, and he sought to attract her attention. He began courting her, and in November the physician from Detroit and the young lady from El Paso were married. But because a far greater threat than Pancho Villa loomed in Europe, Major Lee soon had to leave his new bride for France with the Red Arrow Division of the American Expeditionary Forces.

When he came home after the war, in July 1919, to his wife and a baby daughter, they and other family members were waiting for him in a small New Mexico resort town in the mountains north of El Paso. It was called Cloudcroft. A family photograph shows his father-in-law in a black touring car surrounded by women, their arms filled with wildflowers. The caption reads, "For Major Lee's reception."[1]

By 1919 well-to-do citizens of El Paso had been ascending the Sacramento Mountains for two decades, climbing the cool slopes to escape the border city's heat by train, wagon, on horseback or, more recently, in automobiles. Just as the Lee and Fegan families would do from 1919 until the mid-1930s, many returned year after year.

The Breathing Spot of the Southwest

Cloudcroft, then and now, is a small community nestled at about 9,000 feet in mountain forests, amid the dark greens and blue-grays of fir, pine, and spruce, flecked with the white of aspen trunks. Below Cloudcroft, and visible from lookout points, lie the town of Alamogordo and the White Sands, a snowy expanse of pure gypsum dunes, the largest in the world. In winter the mountains themselves are snowy; the village receives an average of eighty-nine inches.

Cloudcroft was a creation of the Alamogordo and Sacramento Mountain Railway Company, itself a creation of the El Paso and Northeastern Railroad Company. Colonel Charles B. Eddy was president and his brother, J. Arthur Eddy, general manager of the El Paso and Northeastern, which was laying new track from El Paso north through New Mexico Territory toward Tucumcari in 1897 and 1898. When the Eddy brothers' crew ran out of timber for crossties, the Eddys solved the problem by establishing a new company, the Alamogordo and Sacramento Mountain Railway, that climbed into the heavily wooded Sacramentos and transported more timber down to the construction crew.

Colonel Eddy and his attorney, William Ashton Hawkins, astute businessmen, recognized not only the value of the forested mountain slopes for crossties but also for a resort. The summit of the rail line, a place the surveying party had dubbed Cloudcroft, for the clouds wreathing mountain meadows, would be a fine retreat for mothers and children from the suffocating heat of summertime in El Paso, and fathers could join them on weekends to relax.[2] Eddy and Hawkins's view of the dual uses of the Cloudcroft area was typical of developers in that era of rail expansion across the West: the same places, and even the same forests, could, they imagined, supply the raw materials for industry and for the growing business of recreation.

They began construction of the resort by securing rights to spring water from a nearby canyon and by building the Pavilion, a long wood structure that included a kitchen and dining area, a reception room, and a ballroom twenty-eight by eighty feet. It became the center of activities such as meals, dances, and musical performances for the first vacationers, who set up tents around it. Within a few years lots were sold and summer cottages made available for rental. The first advertisement for Cloudcroft and its new Pavilion described the area as "sheltered by dense forests . . . carpeted with moss, ferns and wild flowers . . . 'The Breathing Spot of the Southwest.'"[3] It officially opened in June of 1899.

Set Down Here in One of the Aisles of Nature's Grandest Cathedral

In Cloudcroft today you can still visit the long Pavilion with its rustic veranda extending around three sides. Though it burned in 1919 and 1922 and has been rebuilt and remodeled, it continues to resemble its earliest photographs.

Near the Pavilion you will discover the same Lodge at Cloudcroft that Major Lee and his family saw in 1919, though altered by changing times and different owners. It is a stuccoed building, three stories, gray with burgundy trim and a tower in front with a gleaming copper-clad roof. From its observation room at the top, it is said you can peer into the distance 150 miles and then, right there in the room, view under a plastic protector the names Judy Garland and Clark Gable once scratched into the wall. You can also see a shining white river of sand flowing between the Sacramento and San Andres Mountain Ranges.

A former owner, Gerald R. "Jerry" Sanders, described the building's architectural style as "turn-of-the-century charm with a touch of Bavarian and Italian schmaltz."[4] However, a scholar has described it as more like Jacobean architecture, an early seventeenth-century English style—Elizabethan with Renaissance influences.[5] Whichever description is more suitable, a visitor's first impression of the Lodge is likely to be at least a mild sense of incongruity; it looks more like a European resort than the rugged western mountain lodge one might have expected.

But let's go back to the beginning. The present Lodge with the continental flair dates from 1911 and is not the first Lodge at Cloudcroft. The first Lodge was completed a decade earlier, a couple of years after the resort community opened for business. The Pavilion's popularity induced the Alamogordo Improvement Company to build something more elaborate, a resort hotel, yet one that would offer all the mountain camp rusticity anyone could have asked. It was a two-story, slab-sided building with a forest-green shingle roof, a veranda completely surrounding it, "an eighth of a mile in length" according to the *Albuquerque Journal-Democrat*. It was:

> built of material fitting in so harmoniously with the surrounding forest scenery that it will seem to be an integral part of it. . . . So symmetrical are its lines and so soft its color that, huge as the structure is, containing over seventy-five rooms, set down here in one of the aisles of nature's grandest cathedrals, it does not seem to mar the effect in the least.[6]

This first Lodge belonged to the Shingle Style, as it was called, often used for summer homes and resorts. It emphasized elements linking a building to its seaside or mountainside surroundings: horizontal massing, rough-surfaced materials, verandas, and, of course, shingles. Another style known as the Stick Style could be seen in the ornamentation of the veranda's roof support posts and railing with diagonal braces.

Photographs of the interior of the first Lodge show a continuation of the diagonal patterns in elaborate decoration with branches that appeared to have just been lopped off the trees, arranged in diamond and fan shapes. These gave the interior the look of the outdoors, of a building handcrafted with local materials. The Lodge resembled the "camps" (summer homes) in the Adirondack Mountains of upstate New York built for the very wealthy.

After the first summer the Lodge was open, in September of 1901, the *El Paso Journal* published a piece entitled "Cloudcroft—A Pen Picture," which was a letter from a passenger agent to the general superintendent of the El Paso and

Interior of the first Lodge. *Courtesy of Sacramento Mountains Historical Society, Cloudcroft, New Mexico. No. 981.9.60A in Dorothy Jensen Neal collection.*

Northeastern Railroad. The writer rhapsodized about the sunsets from Cloudcroft's Scenic Point and described the Lodge as a

> handsome hotel . . . with a small dining room, dancing pavilion, small theater, cottages, and tents for those who prefer them, golf links (probably the highest in America), lawn tennis courts, baseball grounds, and other forms of amusement. The water supply is pumped from pure mountain springs.[7]

It is important to note that the Pavilion and first Lodge were not the only places in town to accommodate seekers after mountain coolness, nor are they the only remaining historic lodgings. On a slope at the east end of Burro Avenue is a two-story frame building now used as a gifts and collectibles shop, Mar & Mar Colliques, that was once the Texas Hotel (formerly named The Virginia). It was built in the earliest years of the resort community and retains its original pressed tin ceiling, staircase, and second-story porch (now enclosed).

The Cloud-Climbing Route

Primary attractions of Cloudcroft and its hotels were certainly the invigorating temperatures along with vistas of forested slopes and the White Sands and distant blue mountains silhouetted against gold sunsets. Equally desirable were opportunities to waltz or play golf in the company of ladies and gentlemen of similar social status. But the rail trip up the mountain to Cloudcroft must also have ranked high on the list. The *El Paso Journal* announced at the very beginning of the resort's history that "the tourist who has not wended that tortuous route to the clouds is but a freshman in the college of scenic exploration."[8] The route offered thrills, but for some the blood ran cold and the stomach lurched.

When passengers boarded the Alamogordo-Sacramento Mountains branch line, they climbed into open tourist cars that one of them remembers as being painted yellow and black with roll-down, see-through window covers that could be lowered in case of rain. According to Ernest Rees, former Southern Pacific station agent, "They looked like boxcars with the sides cut out. They were called 'ballyclaires' and held forty to fifty passengers."[9]

It took two hours and twenty minutes for the train to snake up the mountainside at twelve miles per hour on a track with thirty-degree curves and about a 6 percent grade. The train crossed canyons on wooden trestles that creaked. Passengers remembered that sound of the wood beneath them shifting slightly as being as much a part of the experience of the ride as the vertigo of sheer drops. Even the bold Pancho Villa complained that the train ride up the mountain made him ill.[10]

The Mexican Canyon Trestle, completed in 1899, is still visible today from U.S. Highway 82.[11] It stands fifty-two feet above the canyon floor. From the trestle the train would blow its whistle to alert Cloudcroft to its approach. Major Lee's daughter Peggy Kuula recalls that she and her playmates would hear the whistle and run down to the station:

> It was so exciting to meet the train and see the people come off. . . . The engine seemed so huge to us, all shiny and clean. . . . Sometimes honeymooners would be getting off, and you could always tell they were honeymooners. At least we thought we knew. Sometimes older people would be red in the face, their blood pressure up, and they would pass out and have to be taken back down because the altitude was too much for them.

If the summer train trip up the mountain could be either exhilarating or unnerving, the first winter trip by automobile to the Lodge must have demanded the sangfroid of an adventurer. A dirt road wound tortuously up the mountain, crossing the train tracks seventeen times.[12] The *Cloudcroft Silver Lining* reported that on March 12, 1909, a four-cylinder Studebaker pulled into the grounds of the Lodge (closed for the winter). Forced to serve as a plow, the car was covered with black mud, ice, and snow.

Only a few months after that automobile achievement, on June 1, the Lodge opened for the regular summer season. It had been improved by the addition of more bathrooms, and the number of train trips had increased. But only two weeks later, on June 13 between 1:00 and 2:00 A.M., the hotel caught fire and burned so fast that guests and their servants were barely able to escape with their nightclothes and their lives. The building was completely destroyed. The newspaper speculated that the disaster was caused by "a defective flue, as there was a good fire in the fireplace up to midnight, being Saturday night and the guests having been assembled around the fire having a good time."[13]

The New Lodge in "Nature's Roof Garden"

Despite local worries that the Lodge would not be rebuilt, construction began early in the summer of 1910. While the first Lodge had blended with its mountain forest setting, the second Lodge was designed by Chicago architects, who perhaps had never seen the majestic mountains of the West. It was designed, as the Lodge's commissioned historian, Dorothy Jensen Neal, put it, "with apparent disregard for harmonization with its surroundings."[14]

A large, stuccoed main building housed the lobby, dining room, kitchen, and offices. Fifty guest rooms were all located in a wing on the north side. Below the main building a basement allowed space for a ballroom, barber shop, bar, bakery, game room, bathrooms, storeroom, and boiler room. Across the front of the main building ran a veranda. Its north portion was covered, the roof supported by paired Doric columns; the south end, adjacent to the dining room, was left open to the sky. Projecting out onto the open section of the veranda from the two-story dining room were three huge bay windows, the most prominent feature of the building except for an observatory tower.

The first Lodge had been built with its entrance facing Chipmunk Avenue, its dining and kitchen areas facing Possum Avenue (now U.S. 82). The new Lodge was on a different site, higher up than the first; guests would be able to look west from the veranda toward the approach of the towering, lightning-laced thunderheads common on summer afternoons and to the deep colors of desert sunsets. The new location also meant that passengers arriving at the depot would set foot in Cloudcroft several blocks below the Lodge, so the railroad ran a spur up to a boardwalk that allowed guests to walk about a thousand feet to the front door of the hotel.

The new Lodge was completed (though probably not yet furnished) by the end of the summer in 1910, but it did not officially open until the summer season of 1911. The railroad advertised that its new hotel in "Nature's Roof Garden" had cost $100,000 and came equipped with steam heat, baths, electric lights, telephones, a brand new golf course, and spectacular views of the White Sands, which, it declared, resembled "white capped billows rolling in from the sea."[15]

Visitors from Across the Border

If Pancho Villa did indeed visit the new Lodge at its opening in 1911, as Lodge historian Neal says, he did so at a time that was, in the words of one of his biographers, "among the happiest, most peaceful he would ever know."[16] The despot Porfirio Diaz had been ousted, the Madero revolution in Mexico had temporarily triumphed, and Villa's hero Francisco Madero was installed as Mexico's president. Villa thought he could return to private life. According to Neal, he visited the Lodge in the company of "Provisional Governor [of the Mexican state of Chihuahua] Abram Gonzalez."[17] What Villa himself said of this time period is simply, "I reported the distribution of supplies to the governor of the state, Don Abraham Gonzalez, and this ended my campaign from 1910 to 1911. I then devoted myself to private business."[18] His private business, which included some farming and opening a shop in La Ciudad de Chihuahua during this brief respite between campaigns, apparently also allowed for a trip to the Breathing Spot of the Southwest.

But President Madero's efforts toward reform in Mexico were to be short-lived. In 1913 he was murdered. General Victoriano Huerta seized power. The American consul general in Monterey, Mexico, wrote to Washington that Monterey was the home of the Madero family, who feared that "vengeance was [also] to be visited upon the other male members" and who therefore "deemed it best to go to the United States."[19] To the U.S. in this case meant just across the border; the families of Francisco Madero's brothers moved to El Paso. They and a nephew of Francisco Madero then leased the first floor of the Lodge at Cloudcroft during the summers of 1915 and 1916. Their presence must have added considerably to the pleasures of gossip and the display of finery at the resort, for the wife and daughter of the nephew, Alberto, were "considered among the outstanding beauties of the world" and wore Parisian gowns, feathered hats, and "fabulous jewelry."[20]

The story of Pancho Villa's visit to the Lodge in 1911 has been repeated a number of times, but Paul Hernandez, an employee of the Lodge for sixty-eight years, recalls meeting Villa several years later, during the time when the Madero family was in residence. Hernandez was taking out ashes from the boiler as he did every morning (he would have been twelve or thirteen), when Pancho Villa, accompanied by another man, approached him and inquired if the Madero family was staying there at the Lodge. Hernandez said yes. He did not know what business they may have had with the Maderos.[21]

Golf, Gambling, and the Good Life

An early advertisement for Cloudcroft attempted to appeal to ladies' vanity and practicality at the same time by encouraging them to go to the resort essentially *free* by taking the money they would have spent on a summer trousseau and going to Cloudcroft instead. There it was cool enough for them to continue to wear their winter wardrobes, and they could hope that not *everyone* indulging in the good life at the resort would have already seen their gowns.[22]

GOLF

The ladies played golf in those dresses (and high-necked, starched blouses and straw hats and plaid capes and jackets with leg-of-mutton sleeves).[23]

The first golf course in New Mexico was created amid the trees and meadows of Cloudcroft only a few years after the eastern resort areas such as Newport and Southampton had established links for their sophisticated guests. This first course, along with tennis courts, was located in an area called Zenith Park, which U.S. Highway 82 now crosses.

When the new Lodge was being constructed in 1910, a golf course was built for it at the same time, just thirteen years after the first hotel golf course in the nation.[24] A professional named Jack Adams was hired to design the course. He planned meadow grass on seven of the greens and sand on two, but the first season of play proved that neither was satisfactory. So the Lodge began to mix oil with fine sand for the "greens." The oil kept the sand in place despite wind and torrential summer rains, a solution also employed elsewhere in the Southwest.

On these sand greens, golfers used a tool called a rake or drag to smooth a pathway between ball and cup. According to Paul Hernandez, who became course superintendent in about 1920, they would also rake the sand into a kind of barrier so that the ball would stop if it missed the cup. He also remembers keeping water handy in a bucket to wet the sand and dealing with burrowing gophers (he finally resorted to poisoned carrots). Players learned the tricks for success on sand greens and were later reluctant to switch to grass greens.

The changeover to seeded grass greens occurred about 1938. Rufus Wallingford, then manager of the Lodge, had seen tobacco planters cover their seeds to speed germination, so he tried that with the greens, tacking a thin muslin over the seeded areas, and reportedly soon had greens "like velvet."[25] No more native meadow grass or sand on the mountain course.

On sand or grass the ladies played golf from the beginning, in the face of disdain from the gentlemen. When in the mid-1920s, the manager of the Lodge, M. B. Hutchins, decided to encourage the women, he instigated The Lodge Women's Annual Tournament. At first the women arranged all their matches so as not to interfere with the men's play, but in the second year of the tournament, Mr. Hutchins reserved starting times on the course for the women competitors. One woman is said to have exclaimed, "First the right to vote, and now *priority* on the golf course—our emancipation is complete!"[26]

The Lodge golf course is not only one of the oldest in the Southwest but one of the highest in the world at 9,200 feet. In the days before golf carts a burro was employed to haul the less vigorous up the steepest part of the course. Golfers today, as in the past, play on fairways whose slopes demand strategy and stamina, amid forests into which balls disappear. In addition to the influence of altitude on the choice of clubs (250 yards plays like 200 in the thinner air), the mountain environment also affects whom you may meet on the course. An occasional black bear ambles across the fairways, but course rules discourage friendly overtures with food.[27]

GAMBLING

Not all of the pleasures available at the Lodge were so wholesome and aboveboard as golf.

Despite efforts to regulate or prohibit it, gambling has enjoyed a long and robust career in New Mexico. It was commonplace in the social life of the Spanish province. Diego de Vargas, provincial governor, tried in 1703 to prevent his soldiers from going so far as to wager their horses and saddles in dice and card games. Gaming and gaming houses had been licensed by authorities before New Mexico became a territory of the United States in 1850 and continued to be licensed afterward. By 1907 gambling in Albuquerque was a fifteen-million-dollar-a-year business. But statewide gambling prohibitions passed in 1917 and 1921, and for the next sixty years, until passage of the Bingo and Raffle Act in 1981, gambling was illegal throughout the state (except for regulated pari-mutuel wagering on horse races). But this is not to say that gambling ceased. On the contrary, for much of its history the Lodge at Cloudcroft offered gambling, like golf, as a primary recreational activity for its guests. It just wasn't played outdoors.[28]

From 1915 to 1932, Mr. and Mrs. M. B. Hutchins managed the Lodge, well-regarded for their gracious hospitality. Mrs. Hutchins arranged card parties and introduced poker in a room with screens to shield the players from view. She was described as quite a gambler with "card sense." Mr. Hutchins provided ostensibly "legal" slot machines in the basement, just barely within the law at the time because the player was not merely gambling—he or she received a package of mints whenever the lever was pulled. The mints were tossed aside, and entrepreneurial children of guests would gather them up and sell them back to Hutchins. Eventually, though, some guests objected to the slot machines, especially their attraction for the caddies and other young people who came to the Lodge to dance.[29] Apparently local law officers became suspicious or energized from time to time: Paul Hernandez recalls that one of his duties was to help hide the evidence of gambling whenever "the law got after Mr. Hutchins."

In the depths of the Depression (and just after he had divorced his first wife), Conrad Hilton leased the Lodge, noting that "the national economy was in the same precarious state as my personal economy." He said he didn't make any money—too few guests in those hard times—but it was a good place for him and his family. His mother Mary Hilton could escape the "oppressive Texas summer."[30] Peggy Kuula remembers her as a "warm, wonderful, grandmotherly person" who made friends with all the guests. Conrad Hilton's sons enjoyed hunting and fishing, and Hilton played golf and mulled over his personal situation.

During Prohibition the Lodge also harbored illicit liquor. Some of it came from local bootleggers, and some, according to Peggy Kuula, arrived in the suitcases of husbands and fathers coming up from El Paso for the weekend with their families: "They would unpack their clothes and there would be, in between shirts and underwear, whiskey for parties."

By 1941 gambling had moved out of the Lodge and into a neighboring private home. The gaming tables could be stowed quickly when a telephone call announced the approach of the sheriff. But during the war years and after, gambling equipment was returned to the Lodge and occupied a room in the basement that had been the children's play area.

By the late 1940s word was getting around that gambling was flourishing in southern New Mexico, with profits on slot machines (recently reinstated in the game room at the Lodge) running 40 percent to the owner of the location, 40 percent to the owner of the machine, and 20 percent to politicians. Judge James McGhee of Roswell was designated to carry out a clean-up operation and did so with gusto. Many of those who organized gambling in the region cleared out.[31] (This was during Thomas J. Mabry's administration as governor, and Mabry had, like many other governors of New Mexico, visited the Lodge on several occasions.[32] Presumably he had never noticed the game room.)

Along about the time of the crackdown on gambling the slot machines at the Lodge must have been removed from action again because, during remodeling in 1960, workmen found seven old slot machines. When Lieutenant Hoover Wimberly of the state police was sent to investigate, he hit the jackpot in one with his second nickel. The coins in the machines dated from 1937 to 1948. "Wimberly took the machines to the Alamogordo city dump and, as prescribed by law, smashed each to bits with a sledge hammer." [33]

THE GOOD LIFE

From the very first train excursion to Cloudcroft—six coaches leaving the El Paso and Northeastern Railroad depot on the Fourth of July, 1899—the emphasis on group pleasures was typical of turn-of-the-century resort life. On that day the village of Cloudcroft greeted the excursionists both in person at the station and with a Grand Old Flag-draped town. A band stirred them with martial music, and then they danced the afternoon away at the Pavilion.[34]

Over the next several years as Cloudcroft and the Lodge grew and changed, the variety of group activities also increased. Toward the end of the season in 1905, some local thespians presented "As You Like It" outdoors under the pines. By 1907 guests were arriving not just from El Paso but from several states and territories. The Lodge hosted dancing every night, offered orchestral music daily, and, in addition to the golf links, a baseball diamond and a tennis court. The Pavilion opened new bowling alleys in 1912. More amateur dramatics took place in an outdoor amphitheater, though by 1915 they were rivaled by the Pavilion's moving picture show that changed daily, ticket prices five and ten cents.[35]

According to the *Weekly Cloudcrofter*, after the new Lodge opened, Sunday evening concerts became so popular there was hardly room to seat everyone. Eclectic programs included everything from classical to ragtime. Peggy Kuula recalls that she

> never missed a concert at the Lodge. . . . Inside the Lodge was very imposing to a

> youngster because it had a beautiful fireplace. . . . The evenings were cool enough that the fireplace was really needed. . . . The balcony that is still there opposite the fireplace was a wonderful place to stand and look down and watch people. It would be decorated with pine boughs and way too many wildflowers. (It's a wonder there are any wildflowers at all now because we all kept wildflowers on our porches and on the tables at suppertime.) . . . I got the impression that there were people who stayed there and sang for their supper. There was an Italian *basso profundo* who was there every summer for four or five years.

During the 1930s Cloudcroft and its "aristocratic old lodge" remained "a congenial spot for well-bred people who prefer the companionship of their own kind," said a writer for *New Mexico Magazine*.[36] Well-bred, no doubt, but when a new bar opened after drinking again became a legal pastime, Peggy Kuula remembers there was too much drinking among the teenagers.

Martha Wallingford West, whose father Rufus Wallingford operated the Lodge from 1936 to 1942, remembered that guests played the slots, bridge, poker, and the jukebox. They rolled back the Navajo rugs and danced and danced—the Lambeth Walk and the Dipsy Doodle. When they tired of being indoors they went on picnics. By that time, most people drove to the Lodge (train excursions ended in 1930, and the last passenger train ran in 1938). The road was still so scary that some of the women passengers would get down on the floorboards, or so Rufus Wallingford would say. But for a picnic, guests would climb into their cars or ride with the Wallingfords, and everybody, the chef included, would go. When the moon was full, they descended the mountain's twisting road to the White Sands to marvel at the glow of moonlight on the ghostly dunes. West went on to say that people stayed for two weeks to a month and would end up knowing everyone. They were like a family.[37]

Twenty years after the Wallingfords had enjoyed the summer house-party atmosphere of the Lodge, a major change occurred in the resort's activities. C. W. "Buddy" Ritter, who became co-owner and manager in 1959, decided to take advantage of another attribute of its mountain location besides the refreshing summer temperatures. In the spring of 1962, Ritter wrote a letter to Antarctica to C. C. "Bud" Skinner, assistant director of the United States Antarctic Expedition, proposing to him that he come to Cloudcroft to build and manage a downhill ski area. Skinner had been a professional ski instructor at Sun Valley, Idaho.

Ski Cloudcroft opened the following year on Thanksgiving Day with Skinner as manager. The new facility included five runs, a beginners' slope, a T-bar lift, and New Mexico's first night skiing.[38] By 1993, thirty years after it opened, Ski Cloudcroft had been renamed Snow Canyon, and Lodge owner Jerry Sanders had invested several hundred thousand dollars in improvements. Other winter activities, such as sleigh rides and snowmobiling, had been added. The golf course, sparkling with new snow, lured guests out the back door of the Lodge on cross-country skis.[39]

Changes

I first saw the Lodge in late autumn, a season when for much of its history it had always been closed. The cold air was tangy with pine scent. Children squatted at the edge of the pond in front of the entrance collecting broken pieces of its thin shell of ice. Inside a fire burned in the lobby's brick fireplace below a copper hood, a mounted moose head, and a massive iron chandelier. A stuffed brown bear kept the moose company. The room had the feel of a Teddy Roosevelt sort of hearty outdoorsiness combined with comfortable Victorian wealth. Through leaded glass windows I could see a covered swimming pool and a steaming hot tub. Beyond that lay the golf course, not yet cloaked in snow. On a wall near the staircase that led down to the Red Dog Saloon was displayed a romance by Parris Afton Bonds, open to the fictional version of Pancho Villa's stay at the Lodge. I chuckled, wondering how he could afford it on a revolutionary's salary. Around the lobby and elsewhere we were all haunted by a public relations image: Rebecca, a pretty, red-haired ghost.

Much of what I noticed on that initial visit reflected changes in the Lodge over time, but from the earliest days of the first wood Lodge, its ambience has added up to mountain retreat plus style. This combination became firmly established during the era of the Hutchins family (1915 to 1932), who emphasized a genteel hospitality.

When the Hutchinses departed during the Depression and Conrad Hilton leased the hotel, the atmosphere changed, became "more commercial," according to Peggy Kuula. But Hilton's influence was short-lived.

The Wallingfords managed the Lodge under the ownership of the Southwest Lumber Company controlled by Louis Carr. Their six-year tenure as managers, from 1936 to 1942, lasted longer than any others between the Hutchinses and the beginning of the Ritter era. The Wallingfords tried to attract families and Cloudcroft citizens, to create a cottage-in-the-woods atmosphere. When Dorothy Neal requested reminiscences from Ellen Wallingford, she replied with memories of wildflowers—lupine, lilies, elderberry. She mentioned that liquor was not sold in the Lodge during their time but that hot toddies on the house were served to chilled golfers caught in afternoon showers. She recalled the same people returning year after year and thought of them as good friends.[40]

The next major period in the history of the Lodge began in 1953 when John B. Ritter purchased it and began renovating and remodeling the building, which had deteriorated. He also made a drastic change by keeping the Lodge open and fully staffed all winter. Before his sudden death in a car accident, he added rooms on the third floor, which had originally been a large dormitory-like space, and five rooms on the mezzanine. The iron chandelier in the lobby dates from his refurbishing of that room. He had the exterior of the building painted what Dorothy Neal called "a soft Broadmoor pink," referring to the famous resort in Colorado Springs.[41] Apparently he wanted to suggest a resemblance between the two historic hotels, both enhanced by spectacular mountain locations and golf courses. He also had a well drilled, ensuring ample water. (Back during the Hutchins era, the water sometimes ran out early in the day and would have to be hauled in milk cans from a railroad tank car.)[42]

After Ritter's death his family enclosed the unroofed porch outside the original bay windows and added that space to the dining room. The Lodge thus lost a porch where, from the beginning, guests had sat under the trees and danced under the stars.

John Ritter's son Buddy took over in 1959. He undertook quite a bit more remodeling over the next decade, including creating the Red Dog Saloon out of a room that had been by turns a reducing salon, a gambling hideaway, and a place of worship for Cloudcroft Episcopalians. Perhaps Buddy Ritter's most important contribution was to develop the Lodge into a full-fledged winter, as well as summer, resort.

Jerry Sanders, who purchased the property in 1983, fully appreciated the wisdom of emphasizing the Lodge's long history to potential visitors. At the same time that he made many changes in the physical appearance of the building, Sanders also sought to capitalize on its 1911 ambience. He had the exterior painted in gray and burgundy, colors that to him suggested the Victorian era. He added a gazebo in back and a pond in front. Sanders, during his decade-long tenure, initiated a multi-million-dollar program of improvements and expansion of the Lodge and ski area, as well as the purchase and renovation of the 1923 incarnation of the Pavilion.[43] The Pavilion then became an adjunct bed-and-breakfast inn. The successful results could be seen in the Lodge's 1986 listing as one of the 400 "top performers" among the nation's lodgings.[44] The hotel that had once primarily been a retreat for well-heeled Texans, especially from El Paso, and Mexican visitors now appealed to guests from all over the United States, tour groups, and other international tourists.

By the 1980s Rebecca the sweet-faced ghost had assumed her place of prominence in the Lodge's decor and advertising. Said to have been a maid at the Lodge in the 1930s, she had a lumberjack boyfriend, who killed her after finding her with another man. Though not mentioned by Lodge historian Dorothy Neal, the red-haired apparition has been seen by various employees and guests over the years.

My favorite story is that of a skeptical guest in the dining room who complained that Rebecca was no more than a gimmick. He even called Judy Montoya, the restaurant manager, over to his table to emphasize his point. Suddenly an unused wine glass that had been sitting on his table exploded. Several guests whose plates were showered with slivers of glass had to have their meals replaced. The man jumped up from his table and accused the restaurant of staging the incident. Montoya tried to placate him by buying him a drink and assuring him that the restaurant staff was innocent and that she had no explanation for why the glass shattered from bowl to base (but she has a suspicion).[45]

Significance of the Lodge

The application for registry of the Lodge at Cloudcroft on the New Mexico State Register of Cultural Properties answers the question of why the building is significant: "[I]t is one of the oldest and most prominent of the resort hotels in New Mexico . . . also . . . a major resort hotel built by a railway company. Many of the railroad era hotels and resorts have been destroyed."[46]

In fact, I know of no other railroad-built, rural resort still functioning, much less flourishing, in New Mexico. The Lodge stands alone in that respect. Because of its unique longevity, its history provides glimpses into the lives of the well-to-do and the well-known on both sides of the border between the United States and Mexico early in this century. More importantly, it reveals changes in the way Americans have enjoyed themselves at their resorts.

Early in the nineteenth century, when resort life was just beginning in the United States, "mere pleasure did not count. Health was the all-important thing, and one had to be an invalid or pretend to be one, to qualify for a trip to the seashore or springs."[47] American resorts were also given to religious zeal, the singing of hymns, and Bible study.

Cloudcroft and The Lodge were developed at the end of the century, when resort life had already gone to the devil and guests were given over to blatant displays of wealth, to courting, gambling, dancing, and drinking. But even so, one can see that earlier history repeated in the Lodge.

In the first years the advertisements emphasized the bracing environment of the mountains. A week before the present Lodge was opened, the railroad company entertained a Texas nurses' convention with a Cloudcroft excursion that included a visit to the Baby Sanatorium (later known as the Baby San). This sanatorium was founded by Dr. Herbert Stevenson, whose own child had died in the summertime heat of El Paso. The Baby San was intended to provide care for infants suffering from dehydration.[48] The Lodge certainly offered the promise of a healthful climate to its guests, many of whom were women with children. And while the Pavilion and Lodge furnished dancing, musical, and theatrical entertainments, worship services and box-supper church benefits took place there as well. As a kind of precursor to the fame of Rebecca, one such Pavilion box supper in 1914 raised funds by auctioning off young ladies dressed as ghosts.[49]

Over the years golf, gambling, and good food came to outweigh the health advantages of Cloudcroft for most visitors (some, in fact, may have thought twice about the possible ill effects of the high altitude before ascending to Cloudcroft). But the pleasures of resort life were largely still group activities for a long time—dressing up for dinner in the dining room, playing games, picnics at White Sands, tournaments. Guests compared vacations at the Lodge to settling in for an extended stay with family or friends.

Resort life has changed substantially in the last fifty years. Guests are more rushed and more mobile. They come by car, not by train (the last train went down the mountain in September 1947, and then the tracks were pulled up; the last train carrying passengers had run years before that). Guests no longer typically arrive with the intention of staying for weeks, nor, if one can judge from the Lodge's promotional literature, do they just kick back, shuffle a deck of cards, and stay put on the mountaintop. The Lodge advertises all there is to do and see in the surrounding area, from Carlsbad Caverns National Park to Ruidoso Downs. In a time when everything from margarine to beer is described as "lite," these destinations are listed in a hotel brochure as offering "light adventures" (I assume this to mean witnessing the evening bat flight at Carlsbad, for instance, versus rappelling ninety feet into nearby Lechuguilla Cave, open only to the "heavy adventures" of bona fide spelunkers). If only those who dismantled the Alamogordo-Sacramento Mountain Railway could have envisioned future demand for "light adventure."

Group activities do continue—a Murder Mystery Weekend in which guests participated in the theatrics of a crime and its investigation was in progress on one of my visits—but they no longer dominate the resort experience. Guests stay briefly and may come and go without even meeting other guests.

A postcard depicting the first Lodge mailed on June 12, 1908, asked its recipient, Miss Daisy Dutton of El Paso, "How would you like to be in this spot? Cloudcroft seems more beautiful than ever, the weather is ideal." [50]

The beauty and the weather of the Sacramento Mountains and Cloudcroft drew the family of Dr. Ernest Lee to leave El Paso, and later their home in the Española Valley, to travel there year after year. Dr. Lee served as a lumber camp doctor in Cloudcroft for a few years, and during that time in the mid-1920s his family lived there year-round. His daughter Peggy recalls wild blue iris and harebells, Indian paintbrush, raspberry-picking, mist rising off cabin rooftops after an August shower, red maples in fall, and a tree-toppling blizzard in winter.

Whatever else has changed, all those things remain. Along with the Lodge itself.

CHAPTER EIGHT

Vermejo Park Ranch Near Raton

It was 1912, the year New Mexico and Arizona were at last admitted to the Union as states, the year the Titanic sank and took 1,513 passengers down with her, the year Woodrow Wilson won the presidential election. But none of that seemed as important to William H. Bartlett as the verdant Sangre de Cristo Mountains after the summer rains. He wrote in September from New Mexico to a Mr. Smith in Milford, Connecticut:

> [T]here is nothing that appeals to me so much and takes such a hold of me and is so altogether satisfying as this mountain land. The mountains on my Western boundary rise to about 14,000 feet and the whole range is as green as early spring. The cattle are fat, prices are going up, I don't care what the market does and I don't care who is elected president. . . . I have ten or twelve thousand books here in the house with me. I have horses to ride, streams and lakes to fish, a most glorious climate under heaven and scenery that the old world cannot more than equal.[1]

Bartlett was probably writing from a desk in his high-ceilinged, marble-pillared library in a grand residence he had built just for himself. Incongruously urban and Romanesque in its wild surroundings, the stone mansion was hidden in a valley—Vermejo Park—deep in the mountains of northeastern New Mexico. (The Spanish word *vermejo* means "vermillion," and the valley is drained by the Vermejo River, sometimes crimson with silt washed down in torrents from canyon walls.) Bartlett had purchased his property from the Maxwell Land Grant Company, little realizing its significance in the history of New Mexico or how the story of his remote, private guest ranch could be seen as the story in microcosm of the settlement of the American West.

Crucial elements of that larger western story enter into the account of Bartlett's domain: Native American residents exiled from lands they had considered their home for hundreds of years; exploitation of natural resources, especially logging and mining; a bitterly fought land grab, with the rich and powerful winning out; settlement by Hispanic homesteaders, who sometimes managed in spite of land grant litigation to hang on to their small farms and ranches; the appeal of the spectacular scenery and abundant game to visitors; the impacts on pristine land of tourism, cattle ranching, and human attitudes toward wild inhabitants. It's all there in the story of Vermejo Park Ranch.

Near the Center of the Earth

The Vermejo country that would be claimed by so many, that would beckon and betray, enrich and ensnarl, was claimed first by Native Americans who, like most everyone in its history, arrived there from elsewhere. It is as if this land were a receptacle. Various groups poured into it and spilled out of it again over the centuries.

People of Athabaskan origin, pressing southward from Canada through the Great Plains between 1300 and 1500, settled into what became Arizona, New Mexico, southeastern Colorado, and the Texas and Oklahoma panhandles. By 1700 a group known as the Jicarilla Apaches had emerged. Their name means "makers of little baskets." They had poured into the Cimarron and Vermejo country and chosen to stay there, weaving their baskets in the bountiful land they considered "near the center of the earth."[2]

The Jicarillas occupied the territory between two very different groups of Native Americans, so they borrowed from the agricultural pueblos to the west and from the buffalo-hunting plains tribes to the east. They were adaptable, and they prospered—until 1841, when the Mexican governor in Santa Fe gave their land away to two men of Taos named Guadalupe Miranda and Carlos Beaubien. Nearly two million acres of the Jicarillas' homeland were suddenly lost to them, though neither they nor the recipients comprehended the meaning or extent of what had been done.

In the late 1840s, when Carlos Beaubien's son-in-law, Lucien B. Maxwell, began to acquire the family holdings that became known as the Maxwell Land Grant, he made no effort to remove the Jicarillas. He maintained friendly relations with them. As Anglo-Americans poured into their former hunting ground and the buffalo herds were exterminated, as the Jicarillas were more and more constricted, they were less and less able to provide for themselves. When an Indian agency was set up at Cimarron to dole out rations to them, Maxwell contracted with the government to provide the food. Along with the rations he offered fairness and counsel, and they learned to trust him.[3]

But in 1870 their trust must have been shaken when the Jicarillas found out that Maxwell had sold the grant; they insisted that the land was theirs, that they had simply permitted Maxwell to live on it because he was their friend. They didn't understand that it had not been theirs since 1841.

In 1883 the Jicarillas' dispossession was complete when the United States government moved 442 of them to the Mescalero Apache reservation in southern New Mexico. Within only a few years the Jicarillas began to flee that reservation and appealed to Territorial Governor Edmund Ross to support their efforts to return to northern New Mexico to establish their own reservation. In 1887 they did obtain a permanent home, but it lay outside their traditional lands. The Jicarilla Apaches had been spilled out of Vermejo country forever.

Big Land Grant, Big Trouble

If the Jicarillas found it impossible to understand how a Mexican governor could simply sign away their ancestral lands, so many others, more schooled in the arcana of legal and political wrangling, also found it difficult to fathom Spanish and Mexican land grant complexities.

Mexican land-grant law allowed for the disposition of lands deemed available to promoters and to individuals, with the purposes being to foster colonization, establish a frontier line of defense against the Indians, and reward loyal supporters. When the Treaty of Guadalupe-Hidalgo was signed in 1848 at the end of the Mexican War, the United States assured citizens in territories formerly belonging to Mexico that their property rights would remain secure. But such assurances meant little unless the United States could ascertain which Spanish and Mexican land grant claims were legitimate, so Congress created the office of surveyor general to pass judgment on claims. Unfortunately, the process was fraught with errors, outright frauds, and long delays. The history of Vermejo Park Ranch, linked as it is with the history of the largest of these troublesome land grants, is burdened with conflicts that arose from the uncertain status of the land-grant claim.

Lucien Maxwell and his wife Luz, Carlos Beaubien's daughter, developed comfortable relationships not only with the Indians living on the grant lands but also with ranchers and farmers who had carved small homesteads for themselves out of Maxwell's property. Some were of Spanish or Mexican descent, originally from the Rio Grande area, who moved east in search of fresh grazing opportunities. Other settlers arrived from the United States, assuming that they could establish themselves on vacant land just as their counterparts were doing all over the West. Maxwell simply made verbal agreements with them that they pay rent in produce—stock, hay, or grain—to help fill his government contracts.[4]

In 1870 the Maxwells sold an option to the Maxwell Land Grant to three investors; the option was then taken up by a syndicate of British capitalists, who formed the Maxwell Land Grant and Railway Company. Within five years it was bankrupt. After several more years of financial turmoil and litigation, a new company, the Maxwell Land Grant Company, was formed in 1880 in the Netherlands, and a group described in the *Cimarron News and Press* as "a company of wealthy Hollanders & Americans"[5] took possession.

What they possessed—in addition to valuable land, timber, and mineral resources—was feuding on a scale to match the gigantic grant. The source of the difficulty lay in disputed title. Beaubien and Miranda had had no idea how much land was included within their grant. Surveyor General William Pelham had rendered a decision in 1857 that the Maxwell Land Grant was "good and valid." Congress acted upon that decision in 1860 by confirming the grant with so vague a description that it left plenty of room—almost two million acres—to disagree about the details. Maxwell Land Grant inhabitants disagreed over them with guns. The conflict between pro-grant and anti-grant factions generated so much violence it became known as the Colfax County War.

Finally, in 1887, the Supreme Court rendered a decision: it "confirmed in Miranda and Beaubien and their grantees, the tract of land described in the patent previously issued by the government of the United States for 1,714,764.93 acres" lying mostly in New Mexico but lapping over into Colorado.[6] At this time it was estimated that 600 settlers, which the land grant company viewed as "squatters," were grazing 65,000 head of cattle, 3,600 horses, 16,000 sheep, and 2,000 goats on the grant lands.[7]

Settlers Along the Vermejo River

After the Supreme Court decision, some of the anti-grant settlers began to make deals with the Maxwell Land Grant Company to buy, lease, or sell their buildings and cattle. But along the Vermejo River, settled for generations by Hispanic people and later by some "wild Missourians" (as they were known to the company officials who had to deal with them), anti-grant resistance remained stubborn. When company men tried to negotiate terms, they encountered refusals to talk and threats of violence.

However, one by one, the men (or sometimes their wives) on the Vermejo did agree to terms with the company they had cursed. Yet the hostility, bloodshed, and anti-grant meetings continued until the end of the century, and the taste of bitterness remained on the tongues of those living in Maxwell Grant country.

The next outsider to shape the history of what became Vermejo Park Ranch, William H. Bartlett, bought a large chunk of the Maxwell Land Grant about the time the company finally wrested most of its property from the clenched fists of the squatters. Bartlett found some Hispanic settlers still entrenched along the Vermejo, but he had no desire to fight them. He simply employed them, along with some Anglo veterans of the Colfax County War and their sons, to work on the ranch he was building. He allowed them to continue to farm their old homesteads for family food supplies.[8]

The campaign along the Vermejo was over.

William H. Bartlett and "A Palace in the Forest"

In 1900 letters had arrived in the Maxwell Land Grant Company office from William H. Bartlett, a grain speculator in Chicago, expressing an interest in purchasing land for ranching. H. W. Adams, his cattle business manager, told the company that Bartlett also wanted a place suitable for building a hunting and fishing resort.[9]

Bartlett was as American as apple pie, the Fourth of July, and capitalist ingenuity. He could, had he been so inclined, have boasted of his direct descent from Josiah Bartlett, a signer of the Declaration of Independence. He was born in the middle of the country in the middle of the century—Peoria, Illinois, 1850. He proved to be an innovative trader in the grain market, revolutionizing the way business was done. He initiated the practice of selling grain by wire each night for acceptance the following morning, thus eliminating the need for middlemen.[10] He married Mary Campbell from Woodstock, Vermont, and they had a daughter and two sons.

In August of 1898, when Bartlett was 48 years old, he wrote to a business associate:

> My boy Willie is in trouble with his left lung. . . . He was taken down at Woodstock a month ago and about a fifth of the left lung was apparently involved. Dr. Babcock expects the lung to clear pretty well, but of course says the boy must go West.[11]

A year after the doctor's instructions to head west, Bartlett received a letter recommending northern New Mexico as the place to take his son. "You cannot imagine a more lovely spot to live in than is this Maxwell Grant country," the writer asserted, praising its duck shooting, trout streams, and "no end of Turkey and Deer" in the mountains.[12]

Bartlett was intrigued. He already had a foothold in the West, having gotten into the cattle business with H. W. Adams of Glendale, Arizona, so he wrote to Adams straight away about the suggestion. Adams responded with skepticism about the wisdom of trying to raise stock in the hard winters of northeastern New Mexico, but allowed as how "you might find it just the place for Willie."[13]

The Maxwell Land Grant Company conveyed to Bartlett in 1902 two parcels of land, one to Bartlett himself consisting of 169,423.39 acres and another to his wife Mary of 36,005.69 acres. The cost to Bartlett of this property—better than 200,000 acres of Rocky Mountain crags and pinnacles, ponderosa forests, grazing land, lakes, with deer and wild turkey thrown in—was $195,000, far less than he would pay today for a house in Santa Fe.[14]

A man seeking work as a superintendent at the new ranch sent a clipping to Bartlett from "our daily paper here" (Santa Fe). The headline read: "A Palace in the Forest, A Chicago Millionaire is Erecting a Mansion on the Vermejo."

> A palace modern in every respect, surrounded by parks and driveways, is to be erected in Colfax county twenty miles from the nearest railroad. The location is on the Vermejo river, fifteen miles west of Catskill. W. H. Bartlett, senior member of the grain and commission firm of Bartlett, Frazer, and Company of Chicago, has planned this mansion. He has purchased from the Max[w]ell Grant Company 200,000 acres of mountain and valley land on the New Mexico-Colorado boundary. The tract has been fenced and is being stocked with high grade cattle. The buildings alone are to cost over $100,000. . . . A game preserve for buffalo and deer is to be set aside. The streams on the land have been stocked with 50,000 trout. The buildings are to be completed by September when a party of Chicago millionaires and their families will come for a hunting trip and will compose a house party to dedicate the mansion.[15]

(*top*) Bartlett homes, ca. 1915. *Photo by Thomas Fitzsimmons. Courtesy of the Museum of New Mexico, Santa Fe, New Mexico. Neg. No. 30522.*

(*bottom*) William H. Bartlett's library in Casa Grande, ca. 1915. *Photo by Thomas Fitzsimmons. Courtesy of the Museum of New Mexico, Santa Fe, New Mexico. Neg. No. 71263.*

Laborers hauled native stone by wagon over mountain trails to build Bartlett's first house at Vermejo Park, completed in 1903 or 1904 and now called Casa Minor. Bartlett was not too busy with cornering the market in wheat to involve himself long-distance in the minutiae of the construction process, discussing in correspondence with architects J. L. Silsbee and H. C. Rogers such matters as whether or not to use cement mortar or what sort of wood to put in the billiard room (weathered oak) or the need for screened porches.

Early in 1904, Bartlett's son Willie and his wife Virginia and their daughters moved into the first completed house and declared they were "tickled to death" to be there.[16] But later in that year Mary Bartlett suddenly died, leaving her husband disconsolate. For years afterward he had fresh flowers from the greenhouse placed every day beneath her portrait.

Construction began on the second and largest mansion soon after the first was completed. It was intended for Bartlett's older son Norman, who managed timber cutting for the ranch, and for the numerous guests they expected to entertain. In keeping with its role as a sort of hotel, this second house included a patio, a large kitchen, dining room, and twenty-seven bedrooms.[17]

After the first two houses were built for his sons and guests, Bartlett wanted one for himself, though he did not live full-time at the ranch until he retired from trade in 1910. The stone mansion today called Casa Grande contained no dining room, as Bartlett apparently intended to join his guests for meals or simply eat alone, but it did include a huge room to house his library consisting of more than ten thousand volumes, including a collection of erotica.[18] The large library room would be completely redecorated by later owners, but when Bartlett enjoyed it as a kind of bachelor retreat, it included a polar-bear-skin rug, reading lamps, comfortable chairs, and bookcases with leaded glass doors around the perimeter of the room.[19]

In the midst of all this erecting of magnificent homes, Adams wrote to Bartlett, "We really need about ten cheap frame buildings for our help." He lamented that he couldn't keep enough men around to harvest the hay he was growing for the 6,000 head of cattle, and he wanted to provide "two and three room box houses" with "some good Mexican furniture" so the laborers would stay year-round. He wrote that they also needed a schoolhouse, a house for a resident doctor, and a church.[20] Eventually, the school and a house for the doctor were built, as well as a fish hatchery, a ranch store, a power plant, and other structures. A village grew up at Bartlett's ranch headquarters.[21]

The Good Life and the Wildlife on Bartlett's Ranch

In response to a threatened increase in the valuation of the land for tax purposes in 1913, Adams wrote:

> About 70,000 acres of the Vermejo Ranch was considered so unsuitable for any purpose by the Maxwell Company that they sold it at 35 cents an acre and it was bought more as a refuge for game than for any other purpose. . . . [T]he whole Ranch has been declared a 'game preserve' under the laws of New Mexico and at the present time probably has more wild animals on it than any other similar area in the State.[22]

One of William Bartlett's strongest interests in his ranch lay in the opportunities it offered for excellent hunting and fishing. He delighted in being able to invite his friends

Headquarters of Adams Cattle Co. and company store, ca. 1915. *Photo by Thomas Fitzsimmons. Courtesy of the Museum of New Mexico, Santa Fe, New Mexico. Neg. No. 30541.*

to enjoy nature's largesse, and some of his most amusing letters relate to their outdoorsman exploits, real and imagined.

While Bartlett was pleased with the native game and fish, he sought to enhance the offerings. He stocked ranch lakes with eastern trout and tried other fishes, too, such as black bass, yellow perch, and walleyes, that proved unable to reproduce and died out.[23]

His tinkering turned out to be more successful with elk. They had been hunted to extinction in northeastern New Mexico by the late 1880s, so Bartlett imported elk—seventeen cows and one bull—to establish a herd once again for hunters. The elk thrived, increasing in numbers to form a significant percentage of all the elk in New Mexico, and eventually supplied enough trophy bulls to ensure what is said to be the finest elk hunting in the United States.[24]

Much of the good life on the ranch depended on the cooperation of the wildlife, but it depended as well on other stock. Bartlett wrote to a friend:

> I have been loading up 'till I have made this an oasis in the desert and if the Government does not seize my wine etc. I am good for ten years at least. I have 25 cases more coming up from Dawson tomorrow and 25 cases of Haig & Haig should be there this week.[25]

Bartlett's letters are filled with invitations to friends and business associates to visit him. Many of them must have done so, for in the same letter he speaks of "trying to keep the hotel running until the first of January. Then I shall resign." It was not unusual for him to be hosting as many as twenty-five house guests. His hospitality floated on freely flowing liquor, often referred to in correspondence and in the memories of former employees and ranch families. Mrs. Marie Haddon Riley, whose father worked for Adams and whose husband served as game manager for Bartlett, recalled in an oral history interview that one night her brother was delivering groceries, passed by the window of Casa Grande, and saw a guest inside without "a stitch of clothes on. They were all . . . drunk in there having a party, you know. And he tried to get this polar bear rug around him."[26] The drinking may have been quite entertaining for the guests, but according to many accounts, it turned into the curse of alcoholism for Bartlett's older son Norman.

The sense one gets of the man from William Bartlett's letters is that he was shrewd and hard-dealing in business matters, while witty, affectionate, and kind to employees, friends, and family. It was plain that he

Bartlett Ranch headquarters, ca. 1915. *Photo by Thomas Fitzsimmons. Courtesy of the Museum of New Mexico, Santa Fe, New Mexico. Neg. No. 71237.*

was passionately in love with Vermejo Park Ranch. He wrote to an associate still in business in Chicago in 1911 about being glad he was out of the grain market:

> I am glad I am a simple-minded cattleman in New Mexico, only intent on robbing my neighbors and getting the best of a trade. It's so much more simple and then it's the custom of the country, and the penitentiary don't yawn for you. . . . You ask me when I was coming to Chicago. Do you think that is a friendly question? Would you have me leave the comfort of heaven to descend to the discomforts of hell? I sleep under 2 blanket[s] every night, it rains almost every day, the country is as green as The Garden of Eden, the cattle don't dare fall down for fear of bursting, the fishing is good, and I can tell the Chicago Board of Trade to go hang.[27]

Bartlett and H. W. Adams worked together for years, but finally Adams, who had for some time tried to extricate himself from their business arrangements, convinced Bartlett to buy out his one-third interest in the Adams Cattle Company. Bartlett paid him $150,000 and asked Adams to train Norman to take over as general manager in 1918. But, though they did not know it, all the Bartlett men were about to be banished from the Garden of Eden.

In December of 1918, William H. Bartlett Sr. died in his sleep in Casa Grande. He had not been ill, and his death was unexpected. In less than a year (September 1919) his son Norman died, reportedly from alcoholism, and in January of 1920 his son William Jr. died of pneumonia. Within thirteen months the Bartlett men were all gone. The ranch was left to Virginia, Willie's widow. Bartlett's daughter, Mary Bartlett Deering, had been left only a small yearly allowance by her father, so she contested his will, and the fate of Vermejo Park Ranch remained uncertain during six years of litigation.

Out of the sadness of that time emerged a story that would be told and retold so that it became a bit of the folk history of the place. After the deaths in quick succession of her father-in-law, brother-in-law, and husband, Virginia Bartlett faced decisions about the ranch property. One troubling group of items proved to be a *very* large collection of liquor —"wines and high priced foreign-made stuff, you know," explained Ted Haddon, a cowboy on the ranch who had a lot to do with the telling and retelling.[28] No small part of her problem was that the items she needed to dispose of were illegal, but she finally located a wine company in California willing to purchase the stash, and she managed to make arrangements with the railroad to transport it. But all that fine booze had to be hauled by wagon to the town of Dawson, where it could be loaded onto the train. According to Haddon, who served in the escort party, it filled sixteen large wagons.

The wagon train had to make many river crossings en route, and the road was never graded in those days, so wagons got stuck. Every time one wagon had to stop to wait on one ahead, which happened often, the momentarily idle cowboys would extricate a bottle from one of the cases and stash it—in the brush, under a rock, in a culvert. Then, like Hansel and Gretel following a trail of crumbs, the cowboys followed their trail of bottles back home to Vermejo from Dawson, and a jolly return trip it was.

Haddon explained, in the lingo of a cowboy, how he remained above it all: "I never drank but I was helping the boys get it, you know. I don't think I drank anything but sampled one breed of wine."

Paying Guests—The Vermejo Clubs

The 1920s brought dry years to many ranchers in the West. The precariousness of the cattle business resulted in the failure of some ranches. But while cattlemen struggled with the high prices of hay for feed to replace the withered grama grass, a new kind of ranching business was beginning to enable some enterprising ranchers to stay solvent.

Since the 1870s, Easterners and Europeans fascinated with tales of the American West had headed for the Great Plains and the Rockies, to hunt buffalo and angle for trout, to explore mountains, and experience life on a ranch. Some were remittance men (and women), scions of wealthy families who came west, not to seek their fortune but rather to enjoy being supported by the fortune back home while they sought adventure (or escaped misadventure). They were funded by remittances sent from often-prominent families in England or the East and found homes with isolated ranchers possessing ample room and a hankering for interesting visitors. Also, hunters in search of the allegedly endless quantities of game learned of ranchers' open-door policy.

At first ranchers welcomed all these visitors as guests, providing lodging and food in exchange only for their companionship. But as the visitors' numbers increased, the demands on ranchers' traditional hospitality forced some to begin charging fees for room and board. Thus a new industry was born—dude ranching—and by the 1920s it was flourishing.

When the Dude Ranchers' Association formed in 1926, three general types of facilities were considered dude ranches: (1) the working stock ranch in the plains or foothills that took in guests interested in riding and scenery, (2) the mountain ranch that offered hunting and fishing and scenery, and (3) the hot springs resort that offered bathing and, of course, scenery.[29] Vermejo Park possessed ample scenery to qualify for any of the categories and fit the descriptions of two out of three. It had been catering to the Bartletts' guests in numbers since 1904. But it had never been a true dude ranch, as the guests had never paid.

After all three Bartlett men died, an effort was made to sell the ranch to a British group. They hired a graduate of the Colorado School of Mines and former captain in the Air Corps Reserve, Sterling Rohlfs, to appraise the ranch. When that deal fell through, Rohlfs apparently had liked what he appraised so much that he proposed to Virginia Bartlett's brother, Douglas Millard, that they set up a syndicate to purchase the place and turn it into an exclusive dude ranch. Rohlfs served as its president, director, chief adventurer, and prankster extraordinaire.

Rohlfs headed the ranch from 1921 to 1928 and set a lively pace, with polo matches, rodeos, hunting parties, and practical jokes. A former midshipman from the British Royal Navy turned cowboy, Brownlow Wilson, remembered him as "more fun to be with than any other man I ever knew."[30] For instance, Wilson recalled one holiday when he and Rohlfs found some servants' uniforms with yellow and black striped vests and blue coats with silver buttons, leftovers from the Bartlett era. With these on, they served the Thanksgiving platter, making one small substitution—a sleeping Labrador puppy for the turkey. Mrs. Rohlfs, who had enjoyed a few glasses of wine (also left over from the Bartlett era), was poised to begin carving before she realized with a scream that lying on the platter was a pup and not a bird, and then only when it awakened, shook itself, and began to lick the catsup with which it had been doused.[31]

Between 1921 and 1926, when the ranch was finally sold, some well-known people visited—among them General Billy Mitchell, court martialed for insubordination during that same period for his criticism of high-ranking military officers; Amon Carter, Texas newspaper publisher; movie stars Douglas Fairbanks and Mary Pickford; and Mrs. Frederick Guest, who enjoyed the distinction of shooting an elk said to be the ninth largest in the world. It weighed in, when dressed, at 950 pounds.[32]

This first Vermejo Park Club failed to raise the necessary $1,800,000 purchase price for the ranch and so had to disband. In 1926 Harrison Chandler of the Los Angeles Times Mirror Corporation, along with Frank Garbutt and Bernal Dyas, bought Vermejo Park and organized another membership club. Members included, again, Fairbanks and Pickford, and other well-known figures in politics, Hollywood, and business: Calvin Coolidge, Herbert Hoover, Cecil B. DeMille, Adolph Zukor, Harvey Firestone, Andrew Mellon, and F. W. Kellogg.

A guest account book for 1927 indicates that arriving guests were fetched from Trinidad, Colorado, in the Club's Lincoln or Cadillac. The Lincoln was also used to haul back hunters' deer, but a GMC truck was required for the bulkier elk. Although the guests were supposed to be taking a breather from the hectic business of making money, they ran up charges for cables to London, day letters to Chicago, and lengthy phone calls to Los Angeles.[33]

Director Sterling Rohlfs possessed a reputation for recklessness. In 1928 he took off in his own plane with two passengers headed for Mexico City. According to one account, he misjudged how much fuel he would need, ran out, and crashed while trying to land in Toluca. All three men died.[34] Within five years the Club he organized had also crashed—into the Depression. It looked as though it might all be over.

Then Jack Hauskins came along. Described in Vermejo Club promotional material as a cowpuncher, Hauskins already had experience with a guest ranch in Colorado. In 1933 Harrison Chandler sold him a twenty-five-year lease on the Vermejo Club with an option to buy it—lock, stock, and stone mansions—for a million dollars. Hauskins claimed to want to make it America's Guest Ranch Supreme. Instead of handing over $5,000 for the privilege of life membership, guests would pay nine to fifteen dollars per day for horses, pack trips, and all the excellent food that all the members of a guest's family plus servants could eat. Since Vermejo Park was only open from May 1 to November 1, Hauskins' plan was to link it with Rancho Esplendor at Nogales, Arizona, which would offer golf, tennis, and deep-sea fishing in the Gulf of California for winter dudes and dudeens (yes, ma'am, that term was used.)[35] This winning combination, called All-Year Guest Ranches, Inc., sounded too good to be true, and it was. The Depression scuttled it. When Hauskins was unable to maintain his lease or purchase the property, Chandler closed up Vermejo Park's fine houses and leased the land to Ira Aten for cattle ranching only. No more paying guests would arrive for nearly twenty years.

Vermejo Park Ranch was never, in its first or later careers as a guest ranch, the classic dude ranch, where the ranching family passes the sourdough biscuits and syrup to guests who help with the chores and pal around with the cowboys. While some of its cowboys served as hunting guides for guests and became friendly with them, Vermejo Park Ranch in the 1920s was much more an elite resort than many other guest ranches across the West.

Game and Predator Work

From April 1, 1930, to March 31, 1931, Elliott Barker was employed by the Vermejo Club to take charge of what he called its "game and predator work"[36] on the estate, by this time more than 300,000 acres. Barker had grown up near Las Vegas, New Mexico, had worked as a forest ranger for ten years, and then farmed and ranched in the mountains until it looked as if he would go broke. The job with the Vermejo Club presented him with an alternative. His duties included some farm supervision, serving as a hunting guide, preventing poaching, and, most important, killing mountain lions.

Barker was not only gifted as a hunter but also as a writer. He authored magazine articles and books, including one about his year at Vermejo Park Ranch, *When the Dogs Bark 'Treed'*. In it he described what he discovered on the ranch in the first few months of his year there.

In the broad valleys and side canyons beneath the 13,000-foot Costilla Peaks, Barker found elk, turkey, and cattle sharing the summer range. He thought the range too heavily stocked with cattle. He also learned that while he was encouraged to kill lions, he had no work to do with respect to coyotes or prairie dogs. The United States Biological Survey (precursor of the Fish and Wildlife Service) already had a crew on the ranch poisoning prairie dog burrows and setting poisoned traps for coyotes, though the latter was against Vermejo Club rules because of the danger to hunting dogs. He noted that a large grizzly still roamed the Vermejo area, for he spotted its tracks near ranch headquarters. Of that he wrote:

> At that time there were not over a half dozen grizzlies left in the state. Now [mid-1940s], perhaps there are none; possibly two or three. In the early days we killed a good many grizzlies in the Pecos, Las Vegas, and Taos ranges. . . . One of my greatest regrets, where wildlife is concerned, is to see the grizzly disappear from the Southwest. It seems inevitable, for, with his wide-ranging habits and persistent, stock-killing proclivities, it is doubtful that he can ever be harmonized with the economic development of the country. [37]

In the fall, elk hunting was the main sport, but some guests shot ducks landing on lakes named Adams, Bartlett, and Mary's. They even picked off a few wild turkeys from their boats. But by the tenth of November the guests had departed, and Barker's duties as a hunting guide ended. He was free to devote his time to the pursuit of lions. He regarded it as his business, "getting rid of predatory animals which are depleting a game supply and damaging livestock,"[38] but also as a thrill, especially hunting with dogs.

Barker departed from Vermejo because he was appointed New Mexico State Game Warden. He felt that Vermejo was extraordinary:

> No area . . . in the Southwest has such splendid possibilities for public ownership. . . . My fondest hopes are that at some time . . . the State Game Department will own and operate the Vermejo park as a model game-management area. . . . I know nothing I would like better than to spend the rest of my life making and executing a wildlife management program for Vermejo Park, with wildlife given prior-

ity over the livestock in the use of the range.[39]

Only a few years later no guests were arriving to pay for the privilege of elk hunting, and Ira Aten's livestock had the run of the range. During the Second World War the owners of the property and Aten decided that the elk should be killed and butchered so the meat could be contributed to the war effort. By the end of the war the elk population was quite reduced.[40]

Harry Chandler, who had advanced substantial sums of money over the years toward the Vermejo Club's expenses, was offered the deed to the property in 1939. He accepted through Southwest Land Company, a family corporation. After Chandler's death Southwest sold the ranch in 1948 to William J. Gourley, who intended to make his ranch a resort for hunters. He began to build up the elk herd again, buying elk from Yellowstone at five dollars a head. After they were trucked to the ranch he pastured them in the "Elk Trap," an enclosure with a high fence, and released them after they became acclimated.[41]

William J. Gourley

By all accounts, William J. Gourley, like that earlier William, Mr. Bartlett, loved Vermejo Park Ranch with a passion. His wife, named Mary just as Mrs. William Bartlett was, said of W. J., "He loved that land, it was his life."[42]

William H. Bartlett and William J. Gourley shared several characteristics that went deeper than names. Both men came to the natural splendor of Vermejo Park and fell under its spell in their middle years, after success in business ventures had made them able to spend money as they liked. And what they liked was being outdoors presiding over a kingdom that included numerous cattle and game. They enjoyed tending and improving and building. Bartlett stocked lakes for his fisherman friends, and Gourley purchased turkeys as well as elk to release for hunting. Bartlett built mansions, and the Gourleys remodeled them. Both men wanted the property for their own pleasure, but a big part of their pleasure resided in sharing it with guests who could properly appreciate the extraordinary scenery, hunting, fishing, and accommodations.

But Bartlett and Gourley did not arrive in this Rocky Mountain wilderness *cum* cattle kingdom from the same world. Bartlett came from a long line of Bartletts who attended Dartmouth, and his connections were with the East and Midwest and people of wealth. W. J. Gourley's mother had run a boardinghouse in an Oklahoma oil field, and Gourley had to make his own way by starting up a welding business.[43] He built it into the American Manufacturing Company of Fort Worth, Texas, which produced oil-field equipment and, during World War II, munitions. The war years must have added substantially to his means and also, apparently, to a longing to channel his energy into something new: in 1945 he started buying up chunks of the Maxwell Land Grant.

Gourley first purchased the WS Ranch—108,000 acres adjacent to Vermejo Park

Ranch and possessing an even longer history. It was founded about 1881 by Harold C. Wilson, whose son Brownlow said he was "born in Australia but he was really English."[44] When Wilson died, the WS Ranch had to be sold in order to settle his estate among his heirs, so W. J. Gourley bought it.[45]

Gourley then purchased Vermejo Park in 1948 from the Southwest Land Company. But the WS and Vermejo together still weren't enough for him, so Gourley continued to annex thousands of adjoining acres in New Mexico—in both Colfax and Taos Counties—as well as some in Colorado's Costilla County. He exercised an option to buy the Ponil Ranch in 1956. He acquired 480,000 acres, by far the largest single tract carved from the Maxwell Land Grant.[46]

When the Gourleys obtained Vermejo Park Ranch, the houses had been closed up for years. They opened up Casa Minor and remodeled it for their visits (they never moved to the ranch on a year-round basis but continued to live in Fort Worth, perhaps because Mrs. Gourley would not have agreed to leave her home there permanently).[47] Mary Gourley finally said to her husband, "Well, we will go into the guest business. . . . [I]nvite everybody to fish and hunt, but we are going to charge them money and I will hire help and restore the house [Casa Grande]."[48]

And restore the house she did. According to Lee Gourley Wootten, her niece-in-law, she spent ten years furnishing Casa Grande, buying antiques and having them refurbished. She completely changed the character of the room that William Bartlett had used for a bachelor retreat and library. It became an imposing room, with its high, arched ceiling, antiques, Steinway grand, and a Persian carpet said to have belonged to a deposed Turkish shah.[49] But despite the Gourleys' alterations to the house that Bartlett had built to suit himself, Bartlett's presence continues there. Portraits of him and his wife remain in a room adjoining the former library—she a sweet-faced woman, he a portly gentleman holding a cigar, with a thumb hooked in his pocket, wearing a boutonniere, the very picture of success.

Before the Casa Grande remodeling, the large middle house that had served as a guest house during the Bartlett era was remodeled to offer thirty-five guest rooms. But it burned to the ground in December of 1955. The Gourleys closed down the guest operation for a year while Mrs. Gourley had William Bartlett's stable converted into what became known as "the Stables," with a large kitchen, dining area, and bar, which one visitor described as being decorated with "lots of mounted cadavers of bygone triumphs over nature."[50] She also remodeled stone cottages into guest houses.[51]

Those who knew and worked for W. J. Gourley described him as a self-made man who, though he had never ranched before, rode and worked with his cowboys. And when he couldn't ride with them, "he would call every morning from Fort Worth and talk with us here at the ranch for an hour or so," his ranch business manager, Ken Orr, told a writer. "It was his ranch and he ran it. He loved it, the land, the cattle, his men."[52]

His land had been abused by overgrazing over the years, and he sought to bring it back to health by reducing the number of cattle by more than half and spending as much as $650,000 in one year on fertilizer. He was building his Charolais herd and had big plans for improving the ranch as a resort destination—plans for ski slopes, a golf course, an airstrip—when he died, as suddenly as the earlier William, of a heart attack at the age of 81 in 1970.

Up for Sale

Gourley's ranch and American Manufacturing Company, of which the ranch was a wholly-owned subsidiary, were left to Mary Gourley. She said of the ranch, "It was a fun place for us as well as a hard-working place. . . . But after Mr. Gourley's death all the romance was gone."[53] She chose to sell the WS Ranch (as it was still officially named, though it included much more than the original WS Ranch purchased in 1945). The asking price was $26,500,000. In cash. It wasn't snapped up right away.

It did, however, attract a number of wealthy prospective buyers who visited to survey the realm, among them actor John Wayne; oil magnate H. L. Hunt; Robert O. Anderson, president of the Atlantic Richfield Company; Malcolm Forbes of the business magazine *Forbes;* and an Egyptian sheik with ample cash.

Then everything got more complicated. Elliott Barker's hopes from forty years earlier that the ranch would someday become public property revived. Barker himself, now head of the New Mexico Wildlife and Conservation Association, again urged public ownership, and this time he had company with clout: the U.S. Forest Service, U.S. Representative Manuel Lujan Jr., Senator Clinton Anderson, and Governor Bruce King. Both the state of New Mexico and Congress considered the possibility of acquisition of the ranch, with support from conservation groups and, surprisingly—in a state where the federal government is not usually welcomed as a landowner—from livestock associations and county commissioners.[54] But despite all the discussion of making taxpayers the next owners of Vermejo Park Ranch and opening up access to its wealth of natural and cultural resources, it didn't happen.

According to the *Chicago Tribune,* the Nixon administration placed a low priority on the proposed Vermejo purchase because the ranch was "not located near any major population center."[55] One of its greatest virtues, its magnificent isolation, proved to be the fatal flaw in the effort in Congress to secure it for the public good. The New Mexico legislature also killed a bill to allow the state's voters to decide if they wanted to issue bonds to buy the ranch.

The *Raton Range* asserted that:

> In the opinion of many, most of the land . . . rightfully belongs to the public anyway . . . the boundaries of the [Maxwell] grant were greatly exaggerated by clever lawyers and . . . wrongly confirmed by Congress in the 1880s.[56]

But Congress in the 1970s again confirmed, as it had almost ninety years earlier, that Vermejo Park Ranch belongs to whoever can afford it.

The Challenge of Paradise[57]

At the time the WS Ranch was placed on the market, it was touted as the largest in the nation under private family ownership. The King Ranch in Texas was larger in terms of acreage but was owned by a corporation. When efforts to find a way to buy the ranch failed in Congress and in the New Mexico legislature, the WS/Vermejo Ranch also came under corporate ownership: the Pennzoil Company's offer to buy the ranch was accepted in 1973. A writer for *Audubon* magazine, John Neary, set out after the sale to learn why an oil company would buy a giant ranch and what they intended to do with it. He was told that he would have to ask Pennzoil's president, William C. Liedtke Jr. Liedtke had been fishing on the ranch for 14 years and had been the one who wanted to buy it. When questioned, Liedtke answered:

> It's a damned poor investment from the standpoint of oil and gas. I had hoped to come up with lots of reasons to convince the board, but what convinced them was the land value. And a chance to preserve a beautiful part of the country.[58]

The registered owner of the property was the Vermejo Park Corporation, headed from 1973 to 1980 by a Pennzoil vice president, Robert Haslanger. His wife Ann also envisioned at Vermejo a chance to preserve, not only a beautiful part of the country but its history as well. Fascinated with the ranch's past, she began to search out information on the Maxwell Land Grant squatters, the Bartletts, Vermejo Club days, the Gourleys. She conducted a number of oral history interviews with people who had some connection with the ranch, and the transcriptions of those interviews provide a rich source of details, spiced with gossip, of everyday life on the ranch for cowboys and other residents.

The Vermejo Park Corporation owned the ranch but not everything on it or under it. Forests covered about two-thirds of the land, and in 1960 W. J. Gourley had sold the timber rights on 337,000 acres to the Pacific Lumber Company, an agreement supposed to remain in effect until the year 2000. Kaiser Steel Corporation already held rights to the coal under 300,000 acres and was strip mining in the northeastern part of the property.

At first Pennzoil maintained that neither the timber cutting nor the coal mining would necessarily produce significant environmental damage. However, by 1979, when the U.S. Department of the Interior and the Department of Agriculture once again looked at the possibility of acquiring Vermejo Park Ranch for the public, logging had definitely become a problem. Pacific Lumber was clear-cutting—neither healthy for downstream ecosystems nor appealing to downstream fishermen. When Pacific Lumber refused to stop clear-cutting, Pennzoil resorted to buying out the company and its timber rights for fourteen million dollars.[59]

The strip mining in York Canyon had a less extensive effect than the timber cutting, but guests arriving via New Mexico Highway 555 from Raton had to pass through the mining area en route to ranch headquarters. A first impression of Vermejo Park Ranch was more likely to be one of jumbo orange machines toiling amid piles of black overburden than of its famed mountain grandeur.

In 1979 these and other factors were all taken into account by a team of experts from the Fish and Wildlife Service, the Geological Survey, the Heritage Conservation and Recreation Service, the National Park Service, the Forest Service, and the state of New Mexico. This study team again raised the question of whether Vermejo Park Ranch should remain one of the largest ranches in the United States in private ownership or be acquired as public land.

The team's report, issued in July of 1979, summarized what Vermejo Park Ranch could offer as a national park or publicly managed recreation area. Its 492,560 acres encompassed a portion of the Sangre de Cristo Mountain Range and a geologic dyke known as The Wall. The ranch was home to a large elk herd "of national significance" and provided a winter haven for bald eagles. A wildlife census revealed an unusually diverse 60 species of mammals, 200 species of birds, 33 species of reptiles and amphibians, and 15 species of fish (most interesting to visitors: rainbow, cutthroat, and brook trout). Some animals appeared on federal and state endangered species lists.[60] Vegetation ranged from prairie grasses through conifer forests on mountain slopes to alpine tundra on peaks.

Though the cultural and historic resources on the property had been little studied, it was known that Vermejo Park Ranch contained within its boundaries a number of structures reflecting the history of the Maxwell Land Grant and its own history as a guest ranch. They included a stage stop, old homesteads from the anti-grant days, the remnants of mining and logging towns, and two of William Bartlett's elaborate mansions as well as his outlying hunting and fishing lodges.

The study team pointed out that these extensive valuable resources, while being protected at that time by Pennzoil, could be sold to an owner less concerned with stewardship. The property could be subdivided into small tracts "with severe impacts on existing numbers, diversity, migration patterns, and interrelationships of wildlife and vegetation."[61] The team also stated that Pennzoil would consider selling the ranch and that, given the high cost of such a property, "it is unlikely that a single individual or U.S. corporation would purchase the entire Ranch."[62] Thus, the experts concluded, continuing private ownership almost ensured eventual destruction of its unique, large-scale combination of cultural and natural resources.

On the other hand, the team acknowledged the problems inherent in having the timber and mineral rights to the ranch being exploited by companies other than Pennzoil or potential public owners and thus not under their control. Furthermore, timber and coal were providing jobs important to the local economy, jobs in jeopardy if the ranch were to be managed as a national park.

By April 2, 1980, New Mexico's congressman Manuel Lujan and Senator Pete Domenici had met with Robert Herbst, assistant secretary of the Interior, and decided, yet again, to drop plans to acquire Vermejo Park Ranch. Local opposition had asserted itself, particularly anxieties about losing jobs and tax revenues. New Mexico's elected representatives at the state and national level had flirted off and on for years with the notion of a love match between the government and the demiparadise, but the two never made it to the altar.

Guests and the Legacy of the Grant Today

Most guests come in the summer months, about fifteen hundred of them, many from the region—the home states of New Mexico and Colorado, nearby Texas, Oklahoma, Kansas, and more distant California. They, like their predecessors in Bartlett's era or in Vermejo Club days, hope to pull fish out of glassy mountain lakes mirroring the peaks or snatch them from fast streams. Some feel the need to improve their chances and take group lessons first, practicing casting on the broad emerald lawns of the Bartlett mansions.

Contemporary anglers do not linger for weeks as Bartlett's friends did; summer visitors now tend to stay about three days, hardly long enough to really slow down. Hunters, on the other hand, are far fewer in number, come from farther away, and stay longer. They hail from all over the United States and Europe and tend to stalk their preferred game about five days, at considerable expense. An elk hunter may spend nearly $9,000 for a week, including license, skinning of the kill, guides, vehicles, lodging, and gourmet meals (but bucolically enough, not including a television in the guest room).

Unlike guests in earlier eras, today they eat their lamb chops or buffalo burgers in a sprawling log building whose only compatibility with the older structures is its vivid red roof and the fact that it was constructed on the foundation of the Bartlett guest house that burned in 1955. (The Stables remodeled by the Gourleys also burned, in 1983.)

Most visitors today drive to the ranch, but they also arrive by Learjet at Raton's Crews Field forty miles away. Since guests do not come, as they once did, by train from Trinidad to Tercio, Colorado, and then by wagon or carriage down the Spring Canyon road into the ranch, they have less time to readjust mind-sets from urban towers and traffic to woods and mountain waters.

Those who would seek out more than deer or trout may find hidden away in the far reaches of Vermejo the sites of historic towns. The townsite for the oldest of these, Catskill, was laid out in 1890 by the Maxwell Land Grant Company as a logging and sawmill community. During Catskill's most prosperous years, every day thirty to fifty flatcar loads of lumber were shipped and three thousand cords of wood burned in the large, brick, beehive charcoal ovens still standing there today. However, such production could not be sustained, and by 1901 so much Catskill timber had been cut that the railroad pulled out.[63]

The center of gold mining activity on the Maxwell Grant, around Baldy Mountain and the boomtown of Elizabethtown, lay outside the boundary of what would become Vermejo Park Ranch. But briefly, between 1894 and 1900, gold mining flourished at La Belle, whose remnants are now on ranch property. By mid-1895 La Belle boasted a population of more than 600, a school building under construction, a newspaper, a jail, stores, livery stables, saloons, and three hotels, one of which, the Nadock Hotel, occasionally hosted outlaw Tom "Black Jack" Ketchum and his brother Sam. But when the ore at La Belle proved to be low-grade, the town's citizenry packed up their hopes for a windfall and took them elsewhere.[64]

The closely associated communities of Brilliant (1906) and Swastika (1918) were organized as coal mining company towns by the St. Louis, Rocky Mountain, and Pacific Company. Little now remains of either town except foundations and mine dumps. Both ghosts were acquired by Vermejo Park Ranch in the 1980s along with acreage that had belonged to Kaiser Steel.[65]

THE GRANT—WHO WILL OWN IT?

The most salient and troubling theme running through the complex history of the Maxwell Land Grant and its offspring, Vermejo Park Ranch, is the question of who is to enjoy it. This astonishingly abundant land—should it belong to Hispanic homesteaders or Dutch investors or Missourians with a yen to pioneer? Should it be for William Bartlett's friends or Douglas Fairbanks and Mary Pickford or any guest who can afford the high-ticket elk hunting? Should it be for the public—to litter and destroy, as some have suggested would be the inevitable result?

Vermejo Park Ranch had been considered again and again as a prime prospect for public ownership, and the idea had been withdrawn each time. But finally it happened.

In 1982 Pennzoil gave what was termed the "largest and most valuable donation of private land ever made to the Forest Service"[66]: 100,000 acres of the western portion of the ranch, known as the Valle Vidal, rendering it, at least, public land. Wrapped up in this gift to the people of the United States were historic ranches that had been absorbed into Vermejo and remnants of a logging community dating back to the 1870s,[67] the world's largest bristlecone pine tree, a big portion of the resident elk herd, and a major tax break for Pennzoil, variously reported as being worth from $20 million to $48 million.

Candidate Ross Perot, in the 1992 presidential election, accused President George Bush, running for reelection, of having allowed his friends at Pennzoil too large a tax credit for the donation.[68] Perot claimed the land was not worth it. But then he, like those legislators before him who had rejected public ownership, had perhaps little use for venerable bristlecone pines and had never seen Valle Vidal's high country when the golden aspens razzledazzle and Wheeler Peak, New

Mexico's highest, stands powdered with the first snow.

Sold—One of the Most Extraordinary Properties Left in the West

By the time Ted Turner—founder of Cable News Network, vice chairman of Time Warner, and philanthropist extraordinaire—started flying into Crews Field, Vermejo Park Ranch added up to 588,000 acres. True, Pennzoil had given away 100,000 acres to Carson National Forest, but then had acquired about 200,000 more, including 30,000 in southern Colorado. A spokesman for Turner, who has collected ranches in Montana and Nebraska as well as two others in New Mexico, told reporters, "I think that, in his opinion, it [Vermejo Park Ranch] is one of the most extraordinary properties left in the West."[69]

In June of 1996 rumors that Turner was interested in buying the ranch were confirmed, despite the 1979 study team's prediction that it was unlikely any individual or corporate owner would step in to buy the ranch and keep it intact. Pennzoil agreed to sell but retained subsurface rights to gas and oil on the property (which the company has not yet chosen to exploit). The Pittsburg & Midway Coal Company, a subsidiary of Chevron, owns the coal rights bought from Kaiser Steel. Turner plans to continue operating Vermejo Park in its historic role as a guest ranch, and his record as a major contributor to environmental organizations and causes through the Turner Foundation bodes well for the future protection of Vermejo's natural heritage.

For more than 150 years Vermejo Park Ranch, the largest remaining parcel of the Maxwell Land Grant, has tempted with its riches—grazing and farming lands, forests, deposits of high-quality coal, game, fish, ruined towns evoking its past. But the riches have always belonged to the rich. Despite decades of controversy, conflict, and argument in favor of availability to all, the irony is that this quintessential Western land has been preserved by individual and corporate wealth from the fate of so much of the West—being carved up and used up.

Men of unusual power and means—from Lucien Maxwell to William Bartlett, William J. Gourley, and now Ted Turner—have wanted to claim this land and protect, at least to some extent, its special character. They—along with the Jicarilla Apaches, English and Dutch investors, miners and loggers, would-be homesteaders, Vermejo Club members, corporate owners, celebrities, and thousands of guests—arrived in Vermejo Park from somewhere else. They found there a paradisal piece of the West with "horses to ride, streams and lakes to fish, a most glorious climate under heaven and scenery that the old world cannot more than equal."

CHAPTER NINE

The Shaffer Hotel in Mountainair

On an April morning in 1942, while Pop warmed himself by the big stone fireplace in the lobby of his hotel, a stranger came in the front door and remarked, "Pretty cool this morning." Invited to have a seat, the visitor explained, "I'm looking for a man by the name of Pop Shaffer."

"You don't have to go any farther."

"I'm Ernie Pyle." They shook hands. "I've been hearing about you, reading in the newspapers and magazines about your hobby, so I came over to have a talk."

The two men started with where they came from, and Pop said he'd been in Mountainair since 1908 but his native state was Indiana. Pyle hailed from Indiana, too, from a "wide place in the road," he said, near Pop's hometown of Harmony. They even knew some of the same people.

Ernie took a look at Pop's "critters" carved out of wood, the hobby that he had come all the way from Albuquerque to see, and then walked into the hotel dining room. He stopped and looked from one side to the other, taking in the whole room. He stared at the ceiling and didn't say anything for about five minutes. Then he squinted at Pop as if to say, "You crazy bastard. What the hell else are you gonna do?" but only asked, "Who did the work in this dining room?"

"I did it."

"It looks as though you are an artist at most anything."

"I'm only a blacksmith by trade."

My Blueprint Is My Imagination

This story about the day journalist Ernie Pyle met the owner and builder of the Shaffer Hotel, Clem "Pop" Shaffer, comes from Pop's own handwritten memoir and from the typed manuscript version grandly titled "Trials and Tribulations and Glory of Clem 'Pop' Shaffer, The Village Blacksmith." At the bottom of the page in the original, probably in the typist's handwriting, these words have been added: "No blueprints—my blueprint is my imagination."[1]

When he came in the spring of 1942 to check out Pop Shaffer and his imagination, Ernie Pyle was already a well-known news correspondent and columnist who would win the Pulitzer Prize the following year. It was clear to him that the Shaffer Hotel and its dining room were not created by a man who was "only a blacksmith." Though the names of Bataan and Corregidor strode in black headlines across the front pages of the *Albuquerque Tribune*, on the inside pages Pyle's columns ambled through Mountainair and joked about his visits to Pop. He concluded with this:

> I remember saying in yesterday's column that Pop wasn't crazy. Maybe I was little too hasty in that remark. I'd like to see if he's got any papers to prove he isn't.[2]

The Shaffer Hotel could not prove to a jury's satisfaction that Pop was a sane man, but it does reveal that its builder was astute and practical as well as brazenly imaginative.

But let's start with the latter trait. The dining room that brought Ernie Pyle to a standstill half a century ago would slow anybody down. When Dewey Tidwell, a pharmacist, or "pill roller," as he called himself, first arrived in Mountainair in the early thirties, he spent his first night in the Shaffer Hotel. He described his reaction when he went downstairs for lunch the next day:

> My eyes ran out on a stem when I saw the decor of that dining room. I might have taken it to be an Indian museum. The tables and chairs, bar and bar stools, rafters and light fixtures all were hand hewn, carved and painted in traditional Indian colors. Huge Navajo rugs covered the floor. And more rugs hung on the walls, along with several large oil paintings of landscapes and Indian country. The whole layout was dazzling.[3]

The dining room is not merely a decorated space but is a multimedia celebration of Pop's free-wheeling originality. Almost everything it contains is incorporated into the composition: curtain rods, window and door trim, tables and chairs, bar, chandeliers, stained glass transoms, fireplace, and the extraordinary ceiling.

Painted panels spread across the ceiling, resembling Native American rugs and repeating such traditional patterns as the Zia sun symbol, New Mexico's insignia; the thunderbird; and the reversed swastika, symbolizing the four directions. Other designs are pure Pop, such as a geometric man in black tie and tails. In these panels and all over the room, colors vibrate—blue, orange-red, black, white, green, yellow. Even the brick fireplace is multicolored. A zigzag or lightning motif zaps across carved trim, down table legs, along open trusses and chairbacks, everywhere. Arrows zing around the room, come to rest on the trusses and stretch above the windows as curtain rods. Carved animals, similar to hundreds of others for which Pop achieved some national fame, hang by their tails in the four chandeliers, cheerfully balancing lanterns over their noses. Pop's daughter-in-law Pauline recalls painting the glass panels around the lanterns: "I'd say, 'Pop, what kind of design do you want on this?' He said, 'Oh, anything that looks kind of Indianish.'"[4]

Pueblo Deco

Outside, the hotel's appearance reveals that Pop Shaffer's flamboyance was balanced by another, more practical side.

(*top*) The Shaffer Hotel dining room, with several of Pop Shaffer's critters on display. In the foreground and to the left of the table, a gourd sewing basket resembling a duck, and to the right, an ash tray resembling a monkey. Both these items were presented to President and Mrs. Franklin D. Roosevelt in 1941. *Courtesy of the Harding Kayser Collection, Mountainair, New Mexico.*

(*bottom*) Pop Shaffer's critters, 1940s. *Courtesy of the Harding Kayser Collection, Mountainair, New Mexico.*

The two-story, white hotel sits on a quiet street one block south of the intersection of U.S. Highway 60 and New Mexico Highway 55. The older, unadorned part of the building now bears only the Shaffer name and the date 1923 above its storefront windows. Their painted panes and trim provide the only color on this functional west wing, which Pop built as a replacement for a frame building that burned in 1922.

His decisions about the new structure's use were pragmatic. He wanted the ready income from renting part of it as a Ford dealership and added hotel rooms in response to requests from traveling salesmen. He also possessed the foresight to realize that he would do well to shift his business from blacksmithing for people's horses to tending their new automobiles, so part of the first floor was intended as a garage. Today the 1923 wing houses offices and shops.

In contrast, the 1928–29 addition flaunts vividly painted ornamentation on its walls as if it were heirloom turquoise. Opalescent glass proclaims "Dining Room" in large letters above the entrance. Marcus Whiffen and Carla Breeze cite this east wing in their book *Pueblo Deco* as an example of Art Deco influenced by Southwestern Pueblo-style forms and Native American craft designs. They point out that the newer part of the building "is distinguished by its incised stucco work . . . a technique rarely employed elsewhere."[5]

Most people notice immediately the shapes on the east wing's facade: squares, long rectangles, and triangles, all recessed ("incised") and painted in bright colors, and the reversed swastikas. (Pop used these Native American symbols prominently at the hotel and at his nearby property called Rancho Bonito until 1937, when people associated them with the Nazis.) All these designs were skillfully built into the original forms for the wall.

To the west of the hotel, adjoining the 1923 wing, stands a fence that also attracts attention. Ernie Pyle wrote, "[Y]ou can find in that fence practically everything in the Western hemisphere or the Sears Roebuck catalog." All due respect to Ernie Pyle, but some of the shapes Pop created from stones inlaid in concrete couldn't be found in any catalog or elsewhere in either hemisphere. Besides a leering Satan, they include an array of two- and four-legged unclassifiables that sprang full-grown from Pop's fancy.

Rancho Bonito

The Shaffer Hotel is not the only repository of Pop Shaffer's art. Just a mile away on State Highway 55 several more of Pop's buildings stand like large-scale sculptures on his 240-acre Rancho Bonito, owned and maintained until recently by Jackie Hudgeons, Pop's granddaughter, and her husband Herman. The property now belongs to Dorothy Cole.

Rancho Bonito served as a kind of outdoor art supply store, studio, gallery, and playground, as well as a working farm. There Pop felt free to indulge himself, creating hundreds of his critters out of brush, stumps, and roots that piled up when the land was cleared. He also built three buildings, beginning with a barn in 1937, painted in farm implement colors (easily available to him) and alive with figures, faces, and eyes staring from their walls.

The beings who inhabit the barn's white exterior are easy to spot—a yellow demon's face in the midst of an orange Art Deco sunburst, black thunderbirds, other demons toting pails. The fiendish eyes below the words "Rancho Bonito" are so clearly watching you watching them that Jackie Hudgeons told me they discourage would-be vandals: "People are afraid, especially after dark, to come out here."[6]

The faces and forms are less obvious in the nearby rock cabin built to house Pop and Mom Shaffer's tenant farmer. Native stone flowers, a duck, and other, more mysterious profiles gradually emerge as you gaze, like those in children's find-the-shapes puzzles.

Red, white, and blue dominate a log cabin Pop built to display both his patriotism and his smaller animal sculptures. The windows of the cabin appear to have stained glass eyes and painted legs, as if they might stalk away toward the blue Manzano Mountains on the horizon. Inside the cabin a visitor today can see only a tantalizing few of Pop's small critter sculptures: a long, horned beast made of a highly polished cholla cactus skeleton and a slithery, gnarled snake casting a cold marble eye. Most of Pop's zoological garden was exiled to Arizona after his death, when his wife sold the sculptures to a tourist stop called The Thing near Benson. A few reside in museums, such as the Museum of International Folk Art in Santa Fe, and collections.

Pop transformed the materials of the land around him, twisted pieces of juniper and pine, uncut stone. That was his delight, to see things in the natural shapes that no one else could see until his hands allowed them to spring forth. Everything in his surroundings must have seemed full of emergent life to Pop, and he wanted to extend those eyes and mouths and limbs into walls and windows and fences.

Pop Shaffer has been described as a "folk environmentalist" and his work on the Shaffer Hotel and Rancho Bonito as a "folk art monument of major proportions."[7] The buildings and their surroundings do envelop the visitor in ingenious environments—an "Indianish" Southwest; a red, white, and blue log-cabin America; a remnant kingdom of unearthly animals and denizens of the underworld—all shaped by the eyes and hands, the "trials and tribulations and glory of . . . the village blacksmith."

Looking Back

Clem Shaffer was born in Harmony, Indiana, on July 26, 1880, the thirteenth child of a blacksmith. He learned his father's trade and made his way first to Oklahoma and then on to New Mexico and Mountainair, a brand new town in 1908.

It was growing into a community at the south end of the Manzano Mountains, in the dead center of what would become the state of New Mexico, where pale prairie spread like an open palm held out beyond the dark piñon and ponderosa pines, the big-tooth maples and Gambel oaks closely gathered in the foothills and canyons. The area was being homesteaded by sawmillers and farmers, mostly from the Midwest. They experimented with planting wheat, oats, rye, corn, and potatoes but by 1914 had decided that pinto beans made the most successful dryland crop. Thus they relearned what indigenous peoples had learned hundreds of years before: beans tolerate New Mexico's dry weather until the rains come in July. Other settlers ranched, grazing livestock on the native grama grass.

Mountainair was situated on the new Belen Cutoff route of the Atchison, Topeka, and Santa Fe Railway. The cutoff provided a more direct and economical route across New Mexico than the original main line over Raton and Glorieta Passes. From the second decade of the century until 1946, Mountainair farmers shipped carloads of pintos at forty thousand pounds of beans to the rail car.[8]

Before Clem Shaffer settled in Mountainair, he had married a milliner from his hometown, Pearl Brown, and had two children, Donald and Mildred. But Pearl died in 1911, and Clem remarried in 1912. He and his new wife, Lena Imboden, a local woman years younger than he, started out married life on ten dollars he got by selling his ticket to the Jim Flynn versus Jack Johnson prize fight in Las Vegas, New Mexico. When Pop wrote his memoir at the age of sixty, he said, "[W]e are still going I guess on the intrest of the $10.00."[9]

Shaffer's memoir is filled with the exact details of dollar transactions, of sales and swaps. Always "trading and traficing," the enterprising Shaffer recalled, "I have owned 20 farms 160 akers each sense I been in the country but traded and sold all of them but 4 places I still own." In 1916, Mountainair was prospering and Pop Shaffer along with it; he wrote, "[I]n 1916 we made one of the bigest crops of beans we ever made people had lots of mony." Always alert to opportunities, the year before he had begun selling John Deere and Moline farm implements in addition to blacksmithing. When his place of business burned down in 1922, he began to construct a new concrete building:

> I got the first story up and the traveling men got after me to put the second story on top of the concret and put a hotel up their my wife heard them talking to me about it and she wanted me to do that to she said I'll run it so she is sill runing it.

And so the Shaffer Hotel, though built by Pop, was really Mom's.

The walls of the first floor were constructed a foot thick, and each is a continuous pour of concrete—mixed by hand, hauled by burro up ramps, and tamped by hand. G. Harding Kayser, a former owner of the hotel, described this as "inconceivable in today's building procedures."[10] Shaffer, ever resourceful, filled the walls with pieces of burnt metal from his shop instead of rebar.[11]

When the Shaffer Hotel opened in 1923, the first floor was occupied by a Ford dealership that provided some rental income and a garage. The *United States Good Roads Bulletin* for 1923 announced, "There are now thirteen million automobiles . . . and new cars are being turned out at the rate of two millions annually. The people of the United States are on wheels."[12] And they were trying out their new wheels on the highways of New Mexico. In 1923, U.S. Highway 19 ran through Mountainair; it was surfaced near town, but to the east and west, portions were only graded or even unimproved. "Unimproved" might mean some adventurous going. For instance, in one section of state road northeast of Mountainair, dense stands of sunflowers overgrew the roadway. The *Automobile Blue Book's Standard Touring Guide* for 1925 described the road from Encino to Socorro through Mountainair as "gravel, dirt, and hard sand, some poor stretches."[13]

But after sturdy auto travelers struggled over the roads with stops for repairs and tire changes along the way, or alighted from the train as Dewey Tidwell had, to find only a path leading from the tracks into town, they finally arrived at the Shaffer Hotel. They found themselves in good hands.

Lena Shaffer, by all accounts, did the work of managing the hotel. According to Pauline Shaffer, she was a talented and able woman, who crocheted and embroidered bedspreads and tablecloths, canned fruits and vegetables, and made big yellow bars of laundry soap. "She knows she's gotta do it . . . or I'll quit her. I'll go out to Los Angeles and get me one of them redheads with lots of money. Somebody's got to keep me," Pop told Ernie Pyle.

Hard-working Mom Shaffer registered guests and tended her ferns and vines that reached from floor to ceiling in the lobby, the only part of the hotel originally on the ground floor. Then she hustled up and down stairs serving her clientele in twenty-five guest rooms on the second floor, which were arranged around a central dining room with a skylight.[14]

While Mom Shaffer stayed busy, Pop, by his own admission, "didn't do much from 1924 till in 1929 I built a dining room on the hotel also 8 more rooms the dining room is very unusal pice of work." Indeed.[15]

The new construction on the Shaffer Hotel wrought a mysterious transformation in Pop. The blacksmith, horse trader, and fellow who needed Mom to take care of him turned into an artist. In 1928–29, Pop built a two-story addition onto the original building, with rooms upstairs and the large dining room and kitchen downstairs. It is the design of this building that has attracted so much interest over the years for its "Pueblo Deco" style of ornamentation.

Pop added to the hotel the stone and concrete fence on the west side, which he described in his memoir as "a very unusal piece of work also." You can read on it his proud inscription, "Built by Pop Shaffer in 1931." Pop told Ernie Pyle, "And do you know, there are 931 rocks in the whole fence. And to use every number in the year, there are 131 rocks in that center panel. I didn't do it on purpose either, it just turned out that way."

Artists—lucky with numbers, crazy, or otherwise—were not common in Mountainair in those days, but business was good, and occasionally there would be a bit of accidental cultural excitement. When pharmacist Dewey Tidwell arrived from West Texas oil boom towns, Mountainair seemed easy-going by comparison. But he liked what he saw of the thriving main street, with a drugstore, hardware store, post office, five-and-ten, and Chevrolet dealership just a short distance from the hotel. In the hotel he could find entertainment—dances in the dining room. It rented for $2 an evening, including the use of a piano.

One rainy night in 1932, four drenched guests checked into the hotel, two ladies and two gentlemen. They had driven from Clovis and gotten stuck in wet sand a few times on the way. After changing into dry clothes, they came downstairs to a dance, and a couple of them offered renditions of the latest tunes, explaining that they were professional musicians. One turned out to be Harmon Oscar Nelson Jr., a bandleader, who was on his way from Boston to Hollywood to marry Bette Davis.[16]

The highway through town brought not only musicians headed for California but Okies as well, in weary old cars weighed down with worries, kids, chickens, and rag-tags of former lives. Occasional bank robbers passed through, too. One bunch drove a Hudson into town and treated bystanders to a chase and a shootout with the sheriff and deputies near the Shaffer.[17]

Pop, though newly turned to artistic pursuits, had not given up his propensity for buying, selling, and trading real estate. In 1930 he acquired 300 acres "of good farming land" just south of town which he called "Rancho Bonito" or "beautiful ranch." He wrote in his memoir:

> [I]n 1937 I started to build my tinant a house and barn on the ranch I also built a show house for my wooden animals I also built a work shop where I make all my woden animals when we had our dining room open to the public we raised the most of the stuff we served.

So Rancho Bonito furnished the hotel with fresh milk, butter, eggs, chickens, bacon, beef, and vegetables. It also became a tourist attraction in its own right. By this time U.S. Highway 60 passed through Mountainair bringing, according to Pop's count, twelve thousand tourists a year to Rancho Bonito to see his three hundred or so animals of all sizes and shapes. The cover of the January 15, 1943, issue of *The Family Circle* pictures the commandant of cadets at Randolph Field in Texas, Spencer Tracy and Katharine Hepburn in *Keeper of the Flame*, and a grizzled Pop Shaffer glaring into the toothy jaws of a lion with a tree burl mane. Other photos inside picture him in his overalls, working intently, a cigar jutting from his lips. The magazine reported that "strictly in his spare time, Pop engages in the hotel business with his wife, which is pretty small fry when compared with the amazing zoo that he has assembled."[18] Concerning the origins of his menagerie at Rancho Bonito Pop wrote simply, "I saw some things." Pyle called them "the craziest, weirdest, crippledest, laughingest herd of night-marish animals you could conjure up from your worst case of indigestion."

The hotel business and Pop's notorious hobby prospered in the late 1930s and into

(*top*) Clem and Lena, "Mom and Pop," Shaffer on their 50th wedding anniversary, 1962. *Courtesy of the Harding Kayser Collection, Mountainair, New Mexico.*

(*bottom*) The Shaffer Hotel, probably in the mid-1970s. *Courtesy of the Harding Kayser Collection, Mountainair, New Mexico.*

the 1940s. Mountainair's pinto beans and its population grew, the latter nearly tripling in size from 1920 to 1940, when the population stood at 1,477.[19] But World War II, followed by a drought in the late 1940s that devastated bean farming, brought change and decline to Mountainair and the Shaffer Hotel.

In the dining room guests had been able to eat a full order of hot cakes and eggs for a quarter or the Special Pinto Bean Dinner—pintos, bread, butter, and coffee—for fifteen cents while sitting below the local version of the ceiling of the Sistine Chapel.

Lena worked hard to ensure that the dining room ran smoothly. She was very particular about having a clean coffee pot and shiny silverware, but in the war years she was unable to hire the necessary help. In 1943 the Shaffers were forced to close the dining room, and it didn't reopen after the war, though Lena continued to run the hotel until 1970, six years after Pop died. Then she sold it, but the new owner couldn't make a go of it, and it reverted to the Shaffer family. The building remained vacant for several years.

A New Lease on Life

G. Harding Kayser recalled how the next period in the life of the Shaffer Hotel began. Kayser was a native whose grandmother homesteaded at the foot of the mountains in the 1880s. He graduated from Mountainair High School in 1941 and returned to the community in 1972 after retiring from a career with the Department of the Navy.

> In October of 1981, I was sitting in my little real estate office and a gentleman came in and introduced himself as the government representative for the General Services Administration. They were looking for a location in town to put the National Park Service headquarters. My first reaction was, 'Hey, I spent thirty years with the government; I don't want to get involved with them again.' But I took his information, and I talked to my son. He convinced me that we ought to take a close look at [restoring the hotel for the headquarters]. With the incentives that the government was offering, the tax advantages for restoration, it looked like it might be worthwhile.

The National Park Service was looking for a place to house administrative offices and a visitor center for the new Salinas National Monument, created in 1981 to protect and interpret for visitors three archeological sites—Abo, Gran Quivira, and Quarai. The three groups of Pueblo and Spanish mission ruins are located in a wide arc around Mountainair.

In the 1980s tens of thousands of visitors discovered these sites, but even so they remain uncrowded, hidden away in the rural heartland of New Mexico. Their ruined splendor surprises—the size and solemnity of church naves and sprawl of rock-walled rooms—yet remains quiet enough to hear the wind, the hum of bees in a transept, the distant crowing of a rooster.

In response to the need for a headquarters

for the Salinas National Monument, Harding Kayser, his son George, and Joe J. Brazil Jr. formed a company and bought the Shaffer Hotel. Harding Kayser remembered that the deteriorating building "was just on the verge of going ka-thunk." They received authorization for a ten-year lease with the National Park Service and began to ready Pop and Mom Shaffer's place for a resurrection.

Building codes, as well as requirements for wheelchair access to the second floor, dictated changes, including installing an elevator (the only one in Torrance County at the time) and a sprinkler system for the hallways. The latter met safety regulations and still allowed the owners to retain the original transoms over the doors. Rooms in the 1923 building were converted to offices, sometimes by removing partitions to create larger spaces.

The lobby, dining room, and second-story rooms in the 1928–29 wing were left much as when Pop Shaffer completed his handiwork, though the rooms were renovated recently for bed-and-breakfast guests. Except for one, they contain original furnishings and fixtures.

The dining room still amazes first-time visitors, just as it did in the days when the Shaffer Hotel's letterhead heralded it as "The Most Unique Dining Room in the World, Clem Shaffer, Prop." Paintings by Martin Shaffer—Clem and Lena's son, described by Jackie Hudgeons as the "only *professional* artist in the family"—continue to hang in the dining room, accompanying his father's brand of artistry. In the lobby the big stone fireplace, pressed metal ceiling, and the semicircular three-seater and unusual desk contrived by Pop remain there, just as they were when Ernie Pyle walked through the door one April morning.

After seven years as a tenant in the building rehabilitated for its use, the National Park Service, in 1990, moved its offices and the visitor center out of the Shaffer Hotel and into a nearby building. This left the Shaffer Company with a need to find new occupants. The rooms in the east wing were all made available for bed-and-breakfast guests, and a mix of businesses, agencies, and individuals rented space in the west wing. Thanks also to the restoration efforts of Donald Shaffer and to his daughter and son-in-law, the Hudgeons, Rancho Bonito remained open to visitors.

As we talked about Mountainair's future, Harding Kayser said he thought he detected a whiff of change in the wind. Mountainair voters had passed a school bond in 1991, the first one in more than a decade, but he also pointed out that "we will continue to have an employment problem here until we can get some small manufacturing concern that will create jobs." He leaned forward in his chair and looked at his hands, covered with dirt from the garden where Mom Shaffer once grew roses. He had been working to restore it. Then he turned toward the window of his second-floor office and looked at the reddening sky behind the silhouetted mountains. The stained glass mountains in Pop Shaffer's windows in the hotel dining room echo these Manzano, or Apple, Mountains, named for orchards planted in the early 1800s. Kayser mused: "When you hike right to the top of that mountain there, at 10,098 feet, and look around, it's an incomparable view, you know, 360 degrees, and it's beautiful all the way up. There's a spring about half way there where you can stop and get a drink of the freshest stream water."

The Cibola National Forest of the Manzanos, the Salinas National Monument, and the Shaffer Hotel and Rancho Bonito provide incentives for some travelers to stray from Interstate 25 about thirty-five miles east to Mountainair. But then there is the back way—the deliciously slow, winding route through the mining towns and old Hispanic villages south from Santa Fe and Albuquerque on State Highways 14, 337, and 55. The route itself offers wanderers the chances we look for, the deep breaths, the reaches of grassland opening up between mountain ranges, and the pleasure of places that will scarcely notice as we pass by. Then, at the end of the trip, we find the hotel and rancho, one man's unabashed expression of adaptation and originality next door to the ruined majesty of mission pueblos, expressions of mingling peoples and hallowed traditions.

Harding Kayser explained to a writer for the *Albuquerque Journal* in 1984, "What we are trying to do is to perpetuate something started long ago by Pop Shaffer. This hotel depicts a particular culture—of this area, of the Indians, and, I guess, of Pop Shaffer himself."[20] The hotel and Rancho Bonito were built in the prosperous years of a community of immigrant farmers and ranchers settling into a place haunted by reminders of long habitation. Through his prismatic vision of his adopted Southwest, Pop Shaffer "saw some things," even in the debris that accumulated as newcomers cleared the land. Like the Salinas pueblo dwellers before him, he created with what the earth gave. He was, as Ernie Pyle put it more than fifty years ago, "an artist at most anything."

CHAPTER TEN

La Posada de Albuquerque

Gus Hilton, known to the village of San Antonio as *El Coronel,* pioneer trader, founder of the Hilton Mercantile Company, lay dead and mourned. His son Conrad, just back from World War I and thirty-one years old, realized he could not fill his father's shoes. He possessed $5,011 and too many ideas, but he lamented to his mother, "I just can't seem to get started."

She answered, "You'll have to find your own frontier, Connie."[1]

He didn't venture far. Only as far as Albuquerque, which was not pleased to see him. Conrad Hilton, would-be banker and frustrated dreamer, was told his bankroll was too small and nobody wanted to move over and make room for him anyway, so goodbye. Years later, recalling that painful snub, Hilton took satisfaction in shaping his rebuttal—the Albuquerque Hilton Hotel, the tallest structure in New Mexico when it opened, ten stories and a sixty-foot sign on top bearing his name.

Symbol of Growth

On Friday morning, June 9, 1939, the *Albuquerque Journal* greeted the new hotel with an entire section of the paper playing up its symbolism for the community: Progress, Confidence, Growth.

Emerging from the Depression and still hesitating on the threshold of World War II, the citizens of Albuquerque were building homes, businesses, filling stations, a million-dollar municipal airport. The newspaper's advertisers apparently expected that hotel guests would cruise up to the entrance in brand-new Buick taxis, sip Dewar's White Label in the La Copita bar, and purchase orthopedic shoes from the hotel shop. In short, optimism blessed the city and its inhabitants.

The *Journal* recognized that:

> A hotel means more to a city than merely a place where travelers halt to rest on their journey. It is a place where . . . good fellowship prevails and the social and economic gossip of the four corners of the world is exchanged as one takes his ease in the inn.[2]

The new hotel's design and amenities were intended not just to please travelers, whose numbers were increasing, but also to proclaim the identity and vision of the city burgeoning on the banks of the muddy Rio Grande. Downtown Albuquerque had grown up in a lowland intimately associated with the river. Once its main channel, and later a swampy area threatened by flooding, the downtown district had finally staved off the river's encroachments by the 1930s. That the Hilton Hotel rose to new heights from a depression where water had once collected in ponds could have been, but was not, noted by the *Journal* as an example of Progress. The newspaper did, however, make much of the fact that the Hilton was erected on the site of Trimble's Livery Stables. In the 1880s and 1890s the stables had supplied transportation for all comers, from a tallyho for hauling pueblo-bound tourists to a rental hearse.[3] This historical link boded well for the new hotel at the corner of Copper Avenue and Second Street as a future community social center and hub for visitors.

The 135-foot-tall building constructed by J. E. Morgan & Sons of El Paso seemed the essence of modernity in 1939. Built of reinforced concrete with a stuccoed exterior, its height and clean, rectilinear lines exemplified business success and orderly technological progress.[4] The *Journal* announced in a headline—"10-Story Hostelry Here Cost More Than $700,000"—and portrayed for readers the financial clout required to erect such a structure.

While the building itself spoke for business acumen and state-of-the-art construction techniques, its interior called attention to the cultural milieu. Anton Korn, the architect, had designed an earlier Hilton hotel at Lubbock, Texas. Although from Dallas, Korn was said to have become enamored of New Mexico's architectural heritage. He and Conrad Hilton wanted the Albuquerque Hilton to represent southwestern craft traditions, particularly those of Hispanic woodworkers, furniture makers, and artisans in tin and wrought iron.

A typical guest, let's say a traveling businessman from Tulsa, entered the hotel from Copper Avenue and noticed a mural in the foyer, a tourist's map of the state listing Indian ceremonials such as the Corn Dance at Santo Domingo and the Apache Devil Dance at Mescalero. The gentleman then paused in the two-stories-high lobby for a few moments becoming aware of dark red tile floors, plump leather couches, and an abundance of carved wood in wainscoting, mezzanine railings, and corbeled ceiling beams. If it all looked somehow Spanish to this fellow from Tulsa, Conrad Hilton and Anton Korn would have achieved their aim.

After registering for a $2 room, the guest proceeded to the elevators, touted as the "latest in vertical transportation." But instead of sporting moderne chrome or steel interiors to match their speed, these elevators were lined with weighty wood panels depicting a mythical version of a New Mexico Hilton Inn. Near the inn lingered a carved friar, roadrunner, and burro, its rider hidden under a sombrero. When the businessman reached his room, he tossed his bag on a handcrafted cedar dowry chest from Taos or Española and opened the very latest in windows, "suspended on flexible springs" (no weights and ropes), in order to let in a cool high-desert breeze. The Hilton Hotel greeted travelers with its own special flavor—New Mexico blended, the brand new and the traditional.[5]

A visitor today also walks right by the original map mural painted by local artist Ben Turner, though its colors have faded and might not attract her attention. She may notice instead the dark wood panels along the wall across from the mural but not know that they once adorned the elevator. She too pauses in the lobby, drawn to the pattering of water on tile in a fountain. Made in Juarez, Mexico, it was added during restoration. The couches have been replaced with small round tables, chairs, and a bar, but the gleaming carved wood and floor tiles look almost the same as in early photographs. After registering at the desk, a slightly smaller reproduction of the original, the guest goes to her room, which doesn't much resemble its 1939 counterpart in price or appearance. She looks out the window at the city rising like a Rio Grande flood into the foothills of the Sandia Mountains. As she settles in, she thinks about the look of the building, now labeled as Territorial, and why she liked walking into La Posada for the first time. A relief from the intense high-elevation sunlight and glitter of metal and glass structures that tower over the hotel, its interior seems pleasantly out of step and built on a more comfortable scale. Now the emphasis is on the traditional.

Tradition And Opportunity

That emphasis would please the man who conceived the hotel. Conrad Hilton considered the pinnacle of his career to be the acquisition of the Waldorf-Astoria in New York. His purchase of the aristocratic hotel aroused fears that this Westerner from the uncouth lands of New Mexico and Texas would destroy certain of its "revered fixtures." Hilton said of those fears:

> I didn't come to New York to blow it up. I believe in tradition. I believe in preserving it. I once built a hotel in Albuquerque and the first thing I said to the architect was that I wanted it to stand for the Southwest.[6]

Hilton was brought up by his devoted Catholic mother Mary to believe in tradition, most importantly, the disciplines of the faith. His father Gus taught him to believe in another tradition, American business enterprise and resourcefulness. The *Journal*'s opening day coverage of the Hilton Hotel detailed the legendary origins of Conrad Hilton's quintessential American success story. Certainly there were Humble Beginnings. In the village of San Antonio near Socorro, Gus Hilton had saved his family from financial disaster by turning their sprawling adobe home into a railroad hotel. There were also Burning Ambitions. Connie's were fueled by his father's achievements in the mercantile business and other endeavors. But the story was not quite so simple.

Rebuffed by the Albuquerque business community when he tried to start a bank, Connie was advised by Emmett Vaughey, the father of a young woman he had escorted to dances, "Go to Texas, Connie, and you'll make your fortune." Vaughey was dying as he spoke, but his urgent words made Connie feel alive for the first time in months.[7]

Oil-boom Texas offered opportunities all right. Shortly after Hilton had followed Vaughey's counsel, and despite his intention to buy himself a bank, he ended up owning the Mobley Hotel in Cisco. It was doing a brisk business, and right away he gleaned two principles that became the basis for Hilton hotels. The first, he claimed, came to him from a nightmare. In the dream he saw Gus waving the twelve-gauge shotgun Connie had bought at age thirteen with his first salary increase. Gus was chiding him for a mistake, for not getting the most for his money, and saying, "'*You'll never get rich that way*.'"[8] When he awakened, Hilton knew he needed to maximize the use of space to squeeze even more earnings from the boomtown Mobley. The second lesson learned in Cisco was that success depended on developing an esprit de corps among the hotel staff, a principle later seen in action in the Albuquerque Hilton.

Texas provided Hilton the chance to make money and give free rein to his ambitions, but it exacted a price in bitter experience: violence (a valued partner was murdered in the Dallas Waldorf in 1922 by a former financial backer), failures, mistakes, and the struggle to survive the economic disaster of the Depression. Hilton gained, lost, and regained a number of hotels in Texas. By 1937 it looked as though he might be on his way up from rock bottom. He could consider expansion, so he set his sights on California.

Hilton bought the Sir Francis Drake in San Francisco and the Breakers in Los Angeles. Albuquerque was but a single melodic theme in the symphony of empire he was hearing in his head. Of the Albuquerque Hilton, he wrote:

> J. B. Herndon and I went on our single building spree. Both of us had long discussed an inner, quite unbusinesslike desire to make good in Albuquerque. Here, where I had once danced with Eleanor Vaughey, I had been told I couldn't make the grade with an original capital of $5,011. Here, J. B.'s father's bank had failed in the cattle collapse in the '20s.[9]

But Hilton was already in daydream pursuit of the largest hotel in the world, the Stevens in Chicago, and the "greatest of them all," New York's Waldorf Astoria. He was not spending much time, physically or mentally, in Albuquerque.

J. B. Herndon Jr. was. Though Herndon was eleven years younger than Hilton, they became friends in Albuquerque as young men. Herndon's father had been president of the State National Bank, and the bank's failure ruined the family financially but didn't stop young Herndon from going on to become a banker himself. He was managing a bank in Hollywood, California, in 1929, when Hilton offered him a job as secretary-treasurer of his growing hotel company.

Herndon took satisfaction in managing the new Albuquerque Hilton, where from the comfortable vantage point of success he could look across the street to the site of the bank whose demise had brought his father down. During the two years of preparation and construction before the opening of the Albuquerque Hilton, Herndon supervised the hiring of staff and purchase of furnishings. (As opening day approached, he told the *Journal* he hoped never again to see another furniture factory.)[10]

One of the employees Herndon interviewed was a bellman by the name of Tommy McMullan. McMullan was just passing through Albuquerque on his way from Phoenix to a job at the Hotel Clovis when he heard that the new Hilton Hotel was under construction and the man in charge, J. B. Herndon. McMullan had worked with Herndon before at the Lubbock Hilton, so he stopped to talk. Herndon said, "I'd give you a job here, but you won't stay. If you'll promise me you'll stay and work for two years, I'll give you the job."[11] McMullan was a man of his word. He worked as a bellman for the hotel from its opening in 1939 until he broke his hip in 1990, fifty-one years later. His popularity with guests and loyalty to the hotel exemplify the spirit Conrad Hilton hoped to engender in staff.

Over the years Tommy McMullan, a lively and sociable man with an eager grin, became a repository of the hotel's history, filed in his memory in the form of stories he delighted in telling and retelling. One of his favorites, and one that gives us a candid shot of Conrad Hilton, is told about opening day.[12]

On June 9 the bellmen on duty were arranged around the lobby garbed in the maroon and blue outfits that were supposed to make them look like Andalusian peasants on holiday.[13] McMullan noticed some people with luggage at the Second Street entrance trying to get in and realized the door was locked. He asked the desk clerk, "Did you know those doors were locked?"

"Yeah."

"Then why am I standing post here?"

"That's what I've been wondering for two hours."

Disgusted, McMullan started outside for a smoke when he spotted Hilton and a man walking toward the hotel. Hilton had not forgotten his early training hauling baggage for train passengers arriving at the station in San Antonio—he was carrying the man's valet pack. McMullan recalled jumping on that bag "like a chicken on a June bug." The Second Street door was promptly unlocked, and Hilton escorted the man up to the desk clerk and said, "This is a friend of mine from Texas. I want you to take good care of him." Then Hilton turned to the Texas drummer and said, as if conveying upon him a great honor, "You're the first paying guest to check in at this hotel."

Later, the desk clerk confided to McMullan that he was relieved Mr. Hilton had said that about paying because the hotel was filling up with numbers of Mr. Hilton's friends who were *not* paying guests. The clerk had been uncertain whether or not to charge this latest arrived "friend from Texas" for his room.

Stories From The War Years

Conrad Hilton remembered in his autobiography several events from December 1941.

Yes, of course, he recalled Pearl Harbor, but there was also the first invitation to come look over a New York hotel with an eye to acquisition. And there was the first meeting with Georgia "Zsa Zsa" Gabor. He called her the "Hungarian siren." She threatened to marry him, he laughed at such a ridiculous notion, and five months later they stood before New Mexico Supreme Court Justice A. L. Zinn and were wedded in a civil ceremony. Both were divorced, so their marriage could not be recognized by the Catholic Church, and this, Hilton later believed, doomed it from the start.[14]

Of course historic hotels advertise the celebrities who have slept, dined, or celebrated in them, thereby allowing all of us later and lesser guests to imaginatively share the spotlight. The unsanctified marriage between hotelier Hilton and the glamorous Georgia Gabor provided two New Mexico hotels with a certifiable claim. As befit a man more enamored of hotels than women, Hilton's nuptials took place in both the Albuquerque Hilton and La Fonda in Santa Fe.

Hilton and his bride-to-be arrived at the Albuquerque Hilton on Thursday, April 9, 1942, where their previously secret plans to marry were announced by manager Herndon and his wife at a dinner party. The next day in Santa Fe Hilton and Gabor said their vows in a suite at La Fonda filled with white Easter lilies, narcissus, and roses. They honeymooned at La Fonda. But they did not live happily ever after. Before the war was over, their marriage was.[15]

Tommy McMullan maintained a store of famous personage stories from the war years, including one about how Zsa Zsa Gabor planted a kiss on his cheek while a crowd of onlookers applauded. Whether for him or for her, he claimed to be unsure. He also enjoyed telling how Clyde Tingley, former governor of New Mexico and chairman of the Albuquerque City Commission during the war, ran city hall from his favorite chair in the lobby of the Hilton, his glasses shoved back on his forehead as he conferred with Democratic politicians (while the Republicans gathered at the venerable Alvarado Hotel a few blocks away).[16] Tommy recalled that Tingley's wife Carrie did not stay at home behind the scenes but was often present in the lobby observing her husband's exercise of civic power.

Tingley's Albuquerque was becoming a center for aviation and military training. Two months after the Hilton Hotel opened its doors, a municipal airport at the southeastern edge of Albuquerque inaugurated service, boasting one of the longest runways in the country and fine flying weather almost all year. In 1940 the United States Army Air Corps began servicing military planes at the new airport and then leased adjacent land for a flight school, to become Kirtland Field by 1942.[17]

Perhaps the story Tommy McMullan relished the most was one about movie star Jimmy Stewart, stationed at Kirtland Field during the war. He liked to spend his furloughs at the hotel. Manager Herndon had cautioned McMullan never to drink with guests, so Tommy assured him, "Mr. Stewart wants me to come by and have a drink with him in the evening after I get off. But I'm not going to do it."

Clyde Tingley addressing an audience at the groundbreaking for the Hilton Hotel in Albuquerque, July 1938. *From the Albuquerque Progress Collection, Gift of Sunwest Bank. Courtesy of The Albuquerque Museum. Neg. No. 80-184-458.*

"Jimmy Stewart wants you to come have a drink with him? What does he drink?"

"Good Scotch."

"Well, hell, I would do it."

McMullan just liked to listen to Jimmy Stewart talk. "I'd sit there, and he'd sound just like he does in the pictures, you know."

Stewart was sent overseas. McMullan recalled, "When he got back, he had a little chicken on each shoulder."

The Bomb, Espionage, And The Hilton

Albuquerque's population almost tripled in the decade of the 1940s.[18] In the early forties, while Colonel Jimmy Stewart's fellow servicemen and women and their families added their numbers to the city's growth, a laboratory on the Pajarito Plateau ninety-three miles away was drawing, like a hidden magnet, an international group of scientists. There an isolated boys' school named Los Alamos Ranch School and its surrounding acreage had been taken over by the Army for a secret project. Numbers of scientists quietly arrived—physicists, mathematicians, ordnance experts, chemists, radiologists, scientists from places like Berkeley, MIT, Columbia, and the Ballistics Research Laboratory in Maryland, émigrés from Italy, Austria, Denmark, Hungary, Germany. Among them were the world-renowned: J. Robert Oppenheimer, Emilio Segrè, Edward Teller, Enrico Fermi, Niels Bohr, John von Neumann and Hans Bethe.

Along with the illustrious scientists a young man by the name of David Greenglass arrived. A machinist in the Special Engineering Detachment, he was willing to share what he knew about the explosive lens he was working on with a chemist named

Harry Gold who, Greenglass said, showed up at his door in Albuquerque on June 3, 1945.[19]

Harry Gold arrived in Albuquerque, he would later testify, as an emissary from Greenglass's brother-in-law in New York, Julius Rosenberg. His purpose was to obtain and pay for information about the fabrication of the atomic bomb from the Los Alamos machinist and convey it to a Soviet agent. The events in Albuquerque on June 3 formed the core of the government's case against Julius Rosenberg and his wife Ethel, Greenglass's sister, who were tried in 1951, found guilty of espionage, and executed in 1953. The prosecution's two vital pieces of evidence of the transactions between Gold and Greenglass were a bank record showing the deposit said to be payment to Greenglass for information and an Albuquerque Hilton Hotel registration card. Without the Hilton registration card, the government had no proof that Harry Gold had been in Albuquerque that Sunday morning.[20]

The strange thing about it was that Gold did not spend the Saturday night before his alleged meeting with Greenglass in the Hilton. According to his own trial testimony, the only lodging he could find in crowded wartime Albuquerque was the hallway of a rooming house. He did not go to the Hilton until Sunday morning, when he registered in his own name. He met with Greenglass twice that day, obtained the handwritten information and sketches, paid him $500, and then departed by train for New York without ever spending the night in room 1001 at the Hilton. At the Rosenberg trial, the prosecution presented a photostat of the hotel registration card, providing the only documentary evidence that the espionage meetings could have taken place.

Years later, researchers Walter and Miriam Schneir, in their exhaustive study of the Rosenberg case, found that the registration card, which the defense had failed to examine at the trial, bore *two* dates, not one. The front of the card was dated 6–3–45, but the time stamp on the back read "Jun 4 12 36 PM '45," a time when Gold's testimony claimed he had already left Albuquerque. The two dates should have been the same, and when the Schneirs interviewed Hilton employees who had worked at the hotel in 1945, all agreed that standard procedure was for the clerk to date a registration card and then immediately insert it into the time stamp machine. This discrepancy, along with other oddities about the card and the FBI's handling of it, caused the Schneirs to submit the photostat of the card to a handwriting and document expert. She concluded that it had some of the earmarks of a forgery but could not say for certain without examining the original (not available to the Schneirs because never entered into trial evidence).[21]

The true story of Harry Gold and his registration card at the Hilton Hotel in June of 1945 will probably never be known. The man and woman it most concerned, Julius and Ethel Rosenberg, died in the electric chair at Sing Sing Prison without knowing it. The couple claimed all along their innocence of the charges of being a sort of criminal never known before—atomic spies.

Whether or not Harry Gold ever registered at the Hilton in June, government evidence and his testimony indicate that he came to New Mexico in September to obtain information from another spy from Los Alamos, physicist Klaus Fuchs. According to the photostat of a registration card, he stayed in the Hilton Hotel on September 19, 1945 in room 521. This time the clerk's date on the front and the time stamp on the back match.[22] And by this time, between June and September, the world had been utterly changed.

Almost six weeks after Harry Gold's alleged June meeting with Greenglass, on July 15, General Leslie Groves, chief of the secret Manhattan Project at Los Alamos, flew into Albuquerque just before air traffic shut down from Santa Fe to El Paso. It was the day before the first atomic bomb test at Trinity Site, and Groves intended to maintain tight security right up to the last moment. When he strode into the Hilton Hotel he found its lobby crawling with a crew of edgy scientists killing time before proceeding to base camp at Trinity. Groves ordered them to disperse and try to make themselves and their anxious wait less obvious.[23]

The next morning at 5:29, Captain Thomas O. Jones, local security chief for the bomb test, was awakened in his room on the fourth floor of the Hilton by a silent flash. He jumped up from the bed and gazed out the window to the south at the glow spreading across the sky. He wondered if anyone could be left alive at Trinity.[24]

The sudden, ghastly dawn of the atomic age was boiling upward from the desert floor, spotlighting not only the nearby Oscura, or Dark, Mountain Range but much of central New Mexico. Neither Jones nor anyone else knew yet what that dawn meant even for the moment, much less the future. Jones's presence at the Hilton, 110 miles from the blast, represented the scientists' uncertainty, for it was his job to evacuate New Mexico towns around the test site if the explosion were to engender an uncontrolled radioactive cataclysm. Almost as amazing as the results of the test itself was the stark fact that it was conducted in the face of such unknowns.

After the billowing, raging fireball had metamorphosed into a ring of ash and begun to drift away, the experience of witnessing what might have been Armageddon gave way to euphoria. General Groves announced to a colleague that "the war is over as soon as we drop two of these on Japan."[25]

The Fifties

Groves's prediction soon came true and the war ended, but the expansion it and atomic research had brought to Albuquerque did not. Kirtland Field became Kirtland Air Force Base, and nearby wartime support facilities turned into Sandia National Laboratories and storage depots for nuclear weapons. And despite the joke locals told on themselves about Juan who went to heaven and was refused admittance at the Pearly Gates because San Pedro never heard of anybody coming from Albuquerque,[26] tourists didn't care whether the city's citizens were heaven-bound or not. They somehow heard of Albuquerque and arrived.

Even Californians, those fortunate who had already staked out their claims in the Mecca on the Pacific for Route 66 travelers, cast a glance back over their shoulders. Journalist Harrison Mason wrote a long piece in the *San Diego Uptown Examiner* in May, 1950, describing the excitement of downtown "Albuquerque Atom City." With no hint of angst about Nuclear Doomsday and losing no opportunity to reiterate his point, Mason wrote, "Albuquerque is not only crowded, thronged, and busy daytimes but also far into the nights." He informed readers yearning to go places that the city had 65 fast buses, 150 restaurants, 75 taxicabs, 14 movie houses, and 1,200 hotel rooms—the principal hotels being the Alvarado, the El Fidel, the Franciscan, and the Hilton, all charging the same daily rate of $4.50 for a single.[27]

Some of the visitors streaming into the city were just getting their kicks on Route 66 and would pause for a night in the El Vado Motel or buy a burger and motor off into the sunset. Others arrived for longer stays on national defense business. Many traveled to the state's largest city to attend conventions. Tony Montoya, who began with the Hilton Hotel's building maintenance staff in 1948 and still works at La Posada in the 1990s, recalls the days before Albuquerque's convention center. Conventioneers held all their events at the hotel, so the high-ceilinged, spacious lobby was used for exhibits and displays—live cattle in pens for the cattlemen's association; coffins for a morticians' meeting; a small airplane to be suspended from the carved beams and an automobile, both troublesome to maneuver through the entrance doors; and tipis set up for a gathering of Native Americans.[28]

Occasionally visitors with national political agendas made their way to Albuquerque and the Hilton, remote though they were from the power centers of the country. On March 29, 1957, Pat Munroe of the *Albuquerque Journal*'s Washington bureau wrote, "New Mexicans of all political opinions will find Senator Jack Kennedy hard to resist on his maiden trip to the state for a speech tonight."[29]

In his speech that evening at a Democratic fundraising dinner at the Hilton, John F. Kennedy chose to honor the memory of a territorial governor of New Mexico (1885–1889) and former citizen of Albuquerque, Edmund G. Ross. Like Kennedy, Ross had served in the United States Senate. When Ross was sent from the frontier state of Kansas to Washington in 1866, he took his place in the camp of the Radical Republicans bent on punishing the former Confederate states and opposing President Andrew Johnson, Abraham Lincoln's successor. But as opposition turned into a frenzied effort to impeach Johnson, Edmund Ross did not do the expected and go along. Despite almost unbearable pressure from his fellow senators and constituents, Ross summoned the courage to speak the words "not guilty" and saved Johnson from impeachment by a single vote. Ross's refusal to be railroaded into a vote in favor of articles of impeachment, based on what he deemed inadequate evidence, halted his career in the Senate.

Ross later left behind the bitter reminders of failed ambitions in Kansas and moved to

Livestock display, Hilton Hotel lobby, c. 1945. *Courtesy of The Albuquerque Museum. Ward Hicks Advertising Collection, Gift of John Airy. Neg. No. 82-180-582.*

New Mexico to begin anew, little suspecting the political challenges awaiting him. President Grover Cleveland appointed him territorial governor of New Mexico, and he took up residence in the Palace of Governors in Santa Fe to face down the fierce depredations of both the legislative assembly and the Apaches.

Kennedy had extolled Ross's vote for Johnson and the independence of the presidency in his book *Profiles in Courage*, published in 1956, the year before Kennedy visited Albuquerque for the first time. A grandson of Edmund G. Ross, also named Edmund Ross, from Albuquerque, must have felt proud sitting in the audience at the dinner listening to the Senator from Massachusetts tell 500 Democrats that "America today needs the spirit of Senator Edmund G. Ross."[30]

Kennedy's profile of Ross's courage begins with the words, "In a lonely grave, forgotten and unknown, lies 'the man who saved a President.'"[31] The senator probably did not know it as he exhorted his audience that night, but Ross rested not far away from the Hilton Hotel and all the hubbub of a $25-a-plate Democratic dinner. His grave in Fairview Cemetery is neither forgotten nor unknown, thanks in good measure to John F. Kennedy's book. In May, after his speech at the Hilton in March, Kennedy was awarded the Pulitzer Prize for *Profiles in Courage*.

What *was* forgotten over the years was John F. Kennedy's visit to the Hilton and his tribute there to the valor of New Mexico's Edmund G. Ross. My search for the story of Kennedy's visit began with a remark in passing from La Posada's former manager, Theresa McFerrin, that she had heard from Tommy McMullan that Kennedy wrote some of *Profiles* in the Hilton. A perennial bit of hearsay about historic hotels is that some well-known writer has penned his or her immortal words in the comfort of a guest room, presumably during a short book or a long stay. But that hint about Kennedy set me on the trail of recovering the actual story.[32]

Long after this chapter was written, I had the unexpected pleasure, while leading a walking tour of the hotel, of having one of my listeners come up and introduce himself as the great grandson of Edmund G. Ross, who had also been present in the ballroom that evening in 1957 and met the future president. This unfolding Ross family story proved far more engaging than the original hearsay, but I was grateful to Tommy McMullan for remembering some link between the Hilton and *Profiles in Courage*.

The Hilton's accidental but significant role in the international drama of the Trinity test and the Rosenberg trial had slipped even farther from public recollection and also had to be reclaimed from obscurity. Odd how these small but revealing events, the connective tissues joining the life of Albuquerque and New Mexico with that of the nation and the world, wither away. Why is it that people recall of the Albuquerque Hilton's heyday nothing of the registration card that helped to destroy the Rosenbergs or Kennedy's speech that helped to revive a political reputation . . . but only that Zsa Zsa slept there?

Not everyone forgets. Howard Bryan, popular columnist with the *Albuquerque Tribune*, recalled on the forty-fifth anniversary of the hotel's opening that:

> As a young reporter I spent half my time pounding the sidewalks between *The Tribune* offices and the Hilton Hotel, as the Hilton seemed to generate more news than any other place in town. All the big conventions were there, all the big receptions, and most of the visiting celebrities stayed there.[33]

He remembered interviews in the Hilton with a diverse group of the famous, from Will Durant, the historian and philosopher, to Roy Rogers and Dale Evans, from the Archduke Otto of Austria to movie producer Mike Todd only three days before he was killed in a plane crash. Todd impressed Bryan with his unwillingness to be granted the "big shot" treatment while on his way to the Hilton to give a talk on "Showmanship in Business" and publicize his film *Around the World in Eighty Days*. When informed that he was to be driven in a motorcade to the Hilton behind a police escort with sirens screaming, he requested that they be silenced. "Sirens are undemocratic," he said, "and divide Americans into two classes."[34]

The not-so-famous gathered at the Hilton as well. Albuquerque high school students danced cheek to cheek at proms in the ballroom, and Chamber of Commerce and Kiwanis Club members shook hands and slapped shoulders at their regular meetings. It was at a Kiwanis Club meeting that Mike Todd spoke.

But much that had characterized the Albuquerque of earlier decades was, in the fifties and early sixties, starting to pass away. Albuquerque surged upward from the green cottonwood meanders of the Rio Grande into the brown and bouldered lower slopes of the Sandias, subdivision by subdivision and business by business, leaving the downtown core to decline. The railroad, crucial to Albuquerque's development after the 1880s, was losing out to highway construction and truck transport. Even Route 66, that highway of dreams, was eventually to be superseded by Interstate 40, stranding businesses on the old route's Central Avenue through town. The Hilton Hotel Company began building a new Hilton near the interstate in the early 1970s, and in 1974 the original Albuquerque Hilton became the Plaza Hotel.

The hotel lost its reputation as a social center but retained much of its charm. In 1977 Susan Dewitt lamented in *New Mexico Architecture* the fate of downtown Albuquerque, describing it as "currently a most unpromising place." But she added, "Downtown has the buildings best known and loved in the city for their beauty, familiarity, [and] scale," listing the Plaza Hotel among them.[35]

E. H. Goatley, president of the corporation that owned the hotel, claimed in 1979 an increase in business because more people were traveling by train or bus due to the energy crunch. A reporter who interviewed Goatley for the *Downtowner* admired the hotel's ambience, saying that it seemed to have been "overlooked by the last 40 years of modern 'advances.'" Goatley, however, inspired more by the spurt in business than by the vintage atmosphere, went on to say that he was planning to paint over the murals in the lobby to achieve a "clean" appearance.[36] More than murals would disappear before the Plaza Hotel reached its nadir.

Comeback

On Valentine's Day, 1982, the Plaza Hotel closed, its future in the hands of Kerr Companies of Minneapolis, a firm noted for renovating hotels down on their luck. Tommy McMullan helped permanent residents carry their belongings out of the hotel and wondered about his own future.

Kerr was supposed to spend two million dollars to refurbish the hotel, rename it the Bradford, and open it by the following Christmas. Norman Kerr, chairman of the board for Kerr Companies, announced, "When people come into our lobby it will *not* look like a New Mexico art shop,"[37] and his business acted on that threat by bringing in a hit man—National Content Liquidators Inc., of Ohio.

The wrought iron chandeliers made by craftsman Walter Gilbert (who also created wrought iron work for another beloved downtown landmark, the KiMo Theater) were up for sale for $75, definitely a bargain. The bed that Lyndon Johnson had slept in during the 1964 campaign was tagged at $155, not worth as much as the cigar humidor from the lobby going for $325. The liquidators priced all of the parquet flooring ripped up from the ballroom at $1,500. Clyde Tingley's heavy chair showing scrapes from his shoes, the wainscoting, corbels, railings and spindles, barbershop chairs, even the key rack from the registration desk were all carried off by buyers as if by a whirlwind. The building was gutted.[38]

But the Bradford Hotel did not open by Christmas. The stripped structure sat empty until September 1983, when Southwestern Resorts Associates bought it and tried to undo the damage wrought by Kerr. They advertised to buy back the sold-off furnishings and fixtures and thus reclaimed the key rack from the registration desk, Clyde Tingley's chair, some light fixtures and even some of the woodwork. Southwestern's restoration team then used reinstated items as models for replacements. Molding, wainscoting, and other woodwork sold by the liquidators had to be reproduced at the cost of a quarter of a million dollars.[39]

The 1939 beamed ceiling above the lobby was still there but had been painted yellow, so restorers repainted it to simulate the original appearance of the wood. With a few repairs the deep red tile floors remained the same. Peter Choate, the restoration designer, added the fountain and the bar to the lobby. Theresa McFerrin, who served as general manager from 1984 until 1989, credits Choate with being "responsible for the feel of this hotel." [40] McFerrin, the only woman managing a major hotel in Albuquerque at the time and one of only a few in the state, turned the newly restored lobby into a gathering place again, as people collected at small tables there in the evenings for drinks and music.

The 160 rooms of the Hilton became 114 rooms expanded to suit changes in the expectations of the traveling public. Conrad Hilton had assumed the hotel's clientele would include many traveling businessmen, and while they wanted a handy barbershop and an attractive mezzanine to set up sample tables for their wares, they did not demand much space for the night. In the 1980s traveling families and conference attendees wanted more room.

As for the businessmen's barbershop, Southwestern Resorts Associates, unable to reinstall its original chairs sold in 1982, acquired a couple that had done service in the barbershop of the Franciscan Hotel, an architectural landmark demolished in 1972. Perhaps this offered some symbolic though cold comfort to those who cared about historic preservation.

Of the four big hotels that had dominated the hustling downtown when Harrison Mason of San Diego visited Atom City in 1950, only two still stood their ground, and one of them, the El Fidel, no longer functioned as a hotel. The Hilton, now renamed La Posada de Albuquerque, remained as the sole representative of the hospitality of the past.

The restoration was considered a success. The year following its reopening in August of 1984, the hotel and the Boehning Partnership architectural firm received several awards, including the Governor's Award of Honor for Historic Preservation from the Cultural Properties Review Committee and the Bainbridge Bunting Award for outstanding effort in historic preservation from The Albuquerque Conservation Association.

La Posada now participates in what some call a renaissance in downtown Albuquerque. People drive down in the evening and then leave their cars, finding restaurants, bars, theatre, and music within easy walking distance and varied enough to suit a range of ages and tastes.

"An instant success." In looking back on the opening of the Albuquerque Hilton in 1939, that's how Conrad Hilton remembered it. Governor John E. Miles attended the opening ceremonies and named Hilton an honorary colonel. Connie confided to his old friend Will Keleher, "It was a nice try, that 'honorary colonel,' but it won't stick."

Keleher agreed, "In New Mexico they got used to one Colonel Hilton and I guess your dad will be *The* Colonel as long as our memories stretch back to the pioneers."[41]

But Connie Hilton did manage to find his own frontier.

OFFICIAL
AAA
HOTEL
AAA
MOTORISTS

CHAPTER ELEVEN

Hospitality Recycled

In our national passion for whatever is touted as the latest, the fastest, the easiest, Americans often demolish old structures that seem to have outlived their original purpose, reducing to rubble the energy and skills they represent as well as masonry, lumber, and plaster. And though some consider it less expensive to build anew than to restore or refurbish the old, the cultural and historical price of demolition can be beyond reckoning. Historic buildings offer not just a resource-conserving opportunity for reuse but, more important, continuity and tradition. Just as biological diversity sustains plant and animal communities, the chronological diversity of older structures mixed with new nourishes a human community's sense of its identity over time.

Old hostelries play a unique role in this diversity because they have served as public gathering places offering distinctive local varieties of welcome. Their architecture, furnishings, and stories may speak a community's true name. Across New Mexico, individuals and businesses have rescued old hotels from destruction and, when they could no longer serve as lodgings, have recycled them for new use, adding the texture of local history to banking or shopping.

The Amador Hotel in Las Cruces

In the harvest season of 1863, a team working for Martin Amador was cutting and hauling hay at the foot of the crags and spires of the Organ Mountains. A band of Mescalero Apaches attacked, stealing livestock and provisions and killing three men. Three decades later Amador would not have forgotten the incident and would be seeking recompense from the United States government for the attack.[1]

On August 15, 1869, a wagon train belonging to Amador was attacked near the Burro Mountains in Grant County by sixty Indians, and his teamster Esquino Lazar was killed.[2]

Martin Amador operated mercantile, farming, and freighting businesses out of the community on the Camino Real known as Las Cruces, whose name, The Crosses, has been attributed to a burial ground for travelers who perished. Perhaps it was Amador's troubling experience with the hazards of the road in southernmost New Mexico Territory that convinced him to establish safe quarters with thick adobe walls for his teamsters.[3] They used Amador's rooming house as a headquarters as they plied his trading routes from Santa Fe to Silver City and from forts in the region down into Chihuahua, Mexico.

The lobby of the Amador Hotel, Las Cruces. *Courtesy of the Rio Grande Historical Collections, New Mexico State University Library, Las Cruces, New Mexico. Ms 4/RG83-73.*

By the mid-1880s Amador, with his far-flung interests, decided to expand his original, one-story lodging known as Amador Hall into what the *Rio Grande Republican* described as a "first-class hotel."[4] Not only did the enlarged, two-story Amador Hotel possess thirty rooms, but it also added an important amenity to Las Cruces, a "perfect little gem" of a theater. It opened in March of 1886 with a performance of Gilbert and Sullivan's *H.M.S. Pinafore*.[5]

So in its early years the Amador Hotel provided soldiers garrisoned nearby, Las Cruces citizens, and travelers with opportunities to attend performances and *bailes* (dances) in its "Temple of Amusement." Eventually, it became a kind of museum, thanks to the Amador family's penchant for travel and collecting. This community cultural center remained in the family, passing from Martin Amador to his daughter Corina and her husband Frank Campbell and finally on to their son, Martin Amador Campbell. Each generation contributed to the antiques, paintings, and oddities accumulating in the space occupied first by the theater and later transmogrified into a most unusual lobby.

The national travel magazine, *Holiday*, ran an article in 1946 entitled "New Mexico's Slaphappy Hostelry" describing the lobby as "the size of a cow corral stuffed with Spanish, Indian, and pioneer American relics."[6] The "relics" so prodigally furnishing the hotel included, for starters, a painting of the Madonna dated 1722 by a Spaniard, Tomasso Martinez; a toreador's "suit of lights"; a painting of Las Cruces dated 1887 showing a pastoral view of the village and its fields spread below the Organ Mountains; an ornate bronze Japanese incense burner; Apache burden baskets with horsehair handles;

Pueblo pottery; and an autographed photo of a genial-looking Francisco "Pancho" Villa.

Today these and numerous other items from the Amador, insured for more than a million dollars, are displayed in the Citizens Bank of Las Cruces, which championed the eccentric and fondly regarded Amador when it could no longer sustain itself as a hotel. A group of Las Cruces businessmen chartering the bank in 1969 decided to buy the building and remodel it for the new bank's use. They called themselves the *Amadores* (Lovers), a name derived both from the object of their affections and their motivation to link the new bank with a symbol of community tradition.

Citizens Bank occupied the building until 1986, when it required a new structure with more space. At that time Doña Ana County bought the Amador, located conveniently just across the street from the courthouse, to use as the county manager's complex of offices. Beneath the white wooden balustrades of its galleries, which once rang with the applause of Las Cruces theatergoers for traveling players, now filing cabinets and desks perform their quiet duties. Offices occupy rooms still bearing the girls' names given them by Corina Amador Campbell, so the story goes, because she believed calling hotel rooms by names rather than numbers to be a charming foreign custom.

Among the offices is a spacious one occupied by New Mexico State Court of Appeals Judge Rudy S. Apodaca. On one of his shelves sits a photograph showing the Amador Hotel in the mid-1880s, with an "imitation mottled block stone"[7] exterior and a narrow wooden balcony. You'd never know it was the same building as the present, plain, pueblo-style one. Today's Amador, like its downtown surroundings, seems flavorless—until you go inside and see what remains of its guest rooms and its galleries with ornamental railings reminiscent of New Orleans (a city Don Martin admired).

Or until you listen to someone who knows it well, like Rudy Apodaca. He wrote a mystery, *The Waxen Image*, that was published in 1977. In it he included a description of the Amador Hotel as he remembered it from growing up nearby, though he provided it with a fictional name, the Sandoval Hotel, and located it in a town called Esperanza, or Hope. Apodaca is happy to recount his experiences with the Amador—applying for a job there when he was a kid, meeting there as a member of the Citizens Bank Board of Directors, and finally returning as a judge to a room coincidentally bearing the name Esperanza. Listening one day to Apodaca's recollections, Dan Trujillo, public information officer for Doña Ana County, remarked, "Judge, the Amador Hotel is in your destiny."

The Val Verde Hotel in Socorro

Socorro. Its name means "succor." And that's just what travelers needed in the summer of 1919 when the Val Verde Hotel opened its doors. They were not only the usual Santa Fe Railway passengers, accustomed by now to Fred Harvey's dining car food and taking their ease, but also included a hardier variety of vagabond. What was grandly titled the

Ocean-to-Ocean Highway brought motorists into this small town in New Mexico's Rio Grande midsection. They were valiant, ready to cope with a less-than-grand highway reality—numerous tire changes on roads cut into volcanic rock, on-the-spot repairs, and sandy gulches impassable after rainstorms.[8] Such motorists must have offered up thanks as they chugged into town and caught sight of the Val Verde Hotel's third-floor, mission-style parapet.

The hotel was designed by the well-known architectural firm of Trost & Trost in El Paso, responsible for several notable hotels in the Southwest, such as the Franciscan and the El Fidel in Albuquerque and the Paso del Norte in El Paso. The Val Verde, built in a U-shape around a courtyard, provided guest rooms, a dining room, lobby, and lounge. Future hotelier Conrad Hilton from the nearby village of San Antonio rented space in the new hotel, "a small $30 a month office," as he later described it, where he tried "to rebuild with the tag ends of my father's dream."[9] After his pioneer father's death, Hilton attempted to maintain the family's mercantile trade from the Val Verde but was growing restive and ready to seek out his own brand of success.

When the hotel was a decade old, in the summer of 1929, Margaret and Walter Paxton arrived to take over management of it. The Paxtons were experienced in the business of providing hospitality, Mr. Paxton as a hotel manager and Mrs. Paxton as superintendent of service with the Harvey Girls at Kansas City's Union Station. The new managers intended to reopen service in the dining room in mid-August. On August 13 the Rio Grande flooded, devastating the valley, and the Val Verde immediately became the headquarters for Red Cross and other relief workers, before the dining room could be made ready. Mrs. Paxton would recall years later trying to feed them with six eggs, a little bacon, a bushel of peaches, some prunes, and some frozen meat brought from Kansas City.[10]

The Paxton family remained at the Val Verde for nearly a half-century, providing the hotel with a statewide reputation for cordiality. Their daughter Peggy Paxton Dailey says, "It was not the ordinary small hotel of the time," and has treasured the evidence of its reputation in the form of newspaper clippings and letters of appreciation to her parents from guests such as New Mexico governors Clyde Tingley and John Simms. Peggy Dailey remembers, too, another of the benefits of being the daughter of hotelkeepers. Humorist Will Rogers and his wife drove up one day, persuaded by the local Business Men's Club to stop at the Val Verde during a trip across New Mexico. Rogers gave, she says, "quite a lengthy talk in the dining room. He also autographed a book for me."[11]

Margaret Paxton's long life with the Val Verde ended with her death in 1975. It was sold to a physician while still in operating condition, but by 1977, when the hotel was purchased by Charles Mandeville, the building needed extensive repair. Ceilings had caved in from water damage, and, said Mandeville, "There were over a hundred broken windows in it and this was where all the pigeons in Socorro lived at the time."[12] Mandeville, who bought the hotel because of memories of it from his days as a student at New Mexico Institute of Mining and Technology, undertook major rehabilitation. He was aided by his discovery of the original Trost drawings in the El Paso Public Library. Though the work on the building remains unfinished at present, the former hotel now houses offices, shops, apartments, and, in the dining room where Will Rogers once held forth, the Val Verde Steak House.

The Val Verde once styled itself the "Oasis in the Desert" and earned that name because its courtyard offered a rare patch of garden green amid the earthen colors of Socorro. Although much more of the town is watered and verdant today, the epithet still seems appropriate.

One day while the noon meal was being served in the restaurant, the pungent aroma of enchiladas with green chile and Socorro's constant sunlight filled the room. Beyond the courtyard oasis outside the restaurant windows rose the russet and dun Socorro Mountains. From them and others nearby, shaped by explosive eruptions, came the silver ore that brought a brief boom to Socorro in the 1880s.

Above diners' heads in the restaurant, a mural painted in a narrow band around the walls echoed the austere beauty of the desert surroundings. Dark woodwork, wainscot, and a wooden, walk-in cooler recalled the room's World War I era. A waiter, a student at New Mexico Tech, explained to me that he lived in an apartment in the building and that he was told the mural was painted by a tuberculosis patient in the early twenties who bartered his artistry for a place in the "Oasis." He was Peter Savage, a Taos artist. Today the art works of Socorro's Holly Hughes, who transforms cast-off materials into richly textured sculptures, also grace the hotel. Though still a work in progress, the Val Verde is itself an example of inspired recycling.

The Swastika Hotel in Raton

The town of Raton invented itself with the coming of the Santa Fe Railroad into New Mexico over Raton Pass in 1878, though a nearby settlement named Willow Springs preceded it as a stopover on the Santa Fe Trail.

The pass, allowing passage over lava-capped mountains at about 7,800 feet, had long provided a thoroughfare for change. The Army of the West under the command of Colonel Stephen Watts Kearny had marched over Raton Pass in 1846, intent on claiming New Mexico for the United States. The Utes, who trekked over the pass unrecorded for a time stretching far back in their communal memory, must have been puzzled by the establishment of a pay-as-you-go toll road in the 1860s. The keeper of the toll gate, Richens Lacy "Uncle Dick" Wootton, blasted twenty-seven miles of the old pass route to ease the way for wagons and stagecoaches on the Santa Fe Trail. (Writer Harvey Fergusson once said of Wootton that "He . . .made . . . Indians pay all the traffic would bear. He was the original go-getter." However, Miguel Otero, who knew him personally, claimed that Uncle Dick wisely declined to press the Indians to pay for passage.)[13] After railroad tracks advancing into New Mexico Territory were laid across the mountains, the Atchison, Topeka, and Santa Fe established a division headquarters where Willow Springs had been at the foot of the pass, and so Raton was born. Later, roadways for automobile traffic cut a swath over the mountains near the tracks.

Given that Raton is situated on such a strategic route, it is not surprising that the town possesses more historic hotels than most other New Mexico communities. If you stroll through Raton's Downtown Historic District with a guide brochure in hand, you can find, among others, the sprawling Seaberg European Hotel, still offering guest rooms under the name El Portal, as well as the Haven and Palace Hotels adjacent to one another. The 1896 Palace has suffered from misfortune in recent years: its furnishings, including a splendid back bar and stained glass, were stripped out and sold off. But the Swastika Hotel on Second Street has prospered.

When the Swastika opened in June 1929, Raton advertised its position as a crossroads center, located on U.S. Highway 64, "The Pawnee Bill Route"; U.S. Highway 485, "The Old Santa Fe Trail Route"; U.S. Highway 385, "The Gulf to Colorado Route"; as well as the main line of the Santa Fe Railway.[14] The good news of the opening shared the front page of the *Raton Daily Range* with that of the first public appearance of newlyweds Charles and Anne Lindbergh. The bad news of the Depression still lay ahead. The newspaper was optimistic, headlining the new hotel as a "Landmark in Building Progress of Raton."[15] Completely fireproof, six stories high with eighty guest rooms, and equipped with a cafe, restaurant, lobby lounge, and a "ladies' mezzanine floor," the Swastika was pretty snazzy.

Victor Allen, a former resident of Raton, recalled the hotel with nostalgia, "We thought it was the nicest thing that ever happened to Raton. When I went back for my twenty-fifth school anniversary, I had to take my family to show them that wonderful hotel."[16] Allen participated in an important moment in the building's history when he became one of several winners of a contest to rename the hotel in 1939 from the Swastika to the Yucca. The swastika, a Native American symbol still ornamenting the brick building, was a characteristic of its style, sometimes called Pueblo Deco, which incorporates design motifs from Native American craft patterns. But when a similar symbol became the mark of the Nazis in Germany, the hotel management wanted to remove the taint of association.

The hotel's decor was enhanced in the 1930s by well-known Raton muralist Manville Chapman, who also painted murals for the Shuler Theater under the auspices of the Public Works of Art Project, a program funded by the federal government early in the Depression recovery effort. Some paintings in the hotel were done by one of Chapman's students, William Warder, who also worked one summer in the hotel as a bellhop. Warder, who paints now in a studio in Albuquerque, laughed when he told how he began his career as a muralist in 1939 by repainting the south end of a horse in the Yucca Hotel's tavern because the original Chapman version had been deemed . . . well, too realistic. Warder was invited to return to Raton to paint additional murals for the hotel when it was remodeled for use as the International State Bank.[17]

The Yucca served as a hotel until 1969, but by that time competition from motels along the highway had cut its clientele. The International State Bank located across the street needed an occupant for this defunct hotel building it owned and also more space for itself, so it made sense for the bank to move into the Yucca. After all, as Thomas J. Boyle, long-time employee of the International State Bank and former head teller, put it, "It was the best-built building in Raton."[18]

The International State Bank opened in the newly rehabilitated hotel in 1971. Boyle could remember when the present banking lobby was a grocery store selling canned milk for nine cents and tomatoes at five cents a pound. Now the bank's quiet, electronic business of data processing goes on where cooks once prepared food in the steam and clamor of the hotel kitchen. But the original elegance of the Swastika remains intact, including the tile fountain and curved stairways at its entrance that were fashioned after the Blackstone Hotel in Chicago.[19]

When the Swastika opened in 1929, its announcement brochure had extolled Raton as, "The Gateway City to New Mexico, where the summers are always cool and the winters mild."[20] Boyle mused, "I remember limousines driving up to this entrance, lining up, full of Texans coming here to escape the heat."[21]

What are memories worth? The effort and expense required to save old buildings? To find, when necessary, new uses for those whose hospitality seems woven into the fabric of a community? In Las Cruces, Socorro, Raton, and other towns across New Mexico, the answer seems to be a strong yes.

Notes

Introduction

1. Max L. Moorhead, "Spanish Transportation in the Southwest, 1540–1846," *New Mexico Historical Review* 32, no. 2 (April 1957): 121.

2. Susan Shelby Magoffin, *Down the Santa Fe Trail and into Mexico*, ed. Stella M. Drumm (Lincoln: University of Nebraska, 1982), 208.

3. Manville Chapman, "Blazed Trails: A series of Colfax County Historical Narratives based on the mural paintings in the Shuler Auditorium of Raton, N.M., done under PWA project and written by the artist," (n.p., 1935), no page numbers, courtesy of William Warder, Albuquerque, N.Mex.; Richard A. Van Orman, *A Room for the Night: Hotels of the Old West* (New York: Bonanza Books, 1966), 15.

4. Roscoe Conkling and Margaret Conkling, *The Butterfield Overland Mail, 1857–1869* (Glendale, Calif.: The Arthur H. Clark Company, 1947), vol. 2: 57–154.

5. "No structures or sites established *solely as stage stops* [emphasis added], with the possible exception of a Butterfield stage stop site in southern New Mexico, have been architecturally or archaeologically identified in the state, although historic sources indicate that there were such sites." Cf. Boyd Pratt, Charles Biebel, and Dan Scurlock, *Trails, Rails, and Roads: The Central New Mexico East-West Transportation Corridor Regional Overview* (Santa Fe: New Mexico Historic Preservation Division, 1988), 1: 105.

6. A few other hotels preceded the Tremont, but it is usually cited as the ancestor of today's urban hotel.

7. Marian Meyer, *Mary Donoho: New First Lady of the Santa Fe Trail* (Santa Fe: Ancient City Press, 1991), 45–52. On the subject of lice, see Marc Simmons' "Hygiene, Sanitation, and Public Health in Hispanic New Mexico," *New Mexico Historical Review* 67, no. 3 (July 1992): 205–225.

8. The phrase "palaces of the people" is from Arthur White, *Palaces of the People: A Social History of Commercial Hospitality* (New York: Taplinger, 1970). The phrase "public as the parks" comes from Paul Goldberger's preface to Catherine Donzel, Alexis Gregory, and Marc Walter's *Grand American Hotels* (New York: Vendome Press, 1989), 9. For a discussion of the significance of the Tremont House and the differences between American and European hostelries, see White, especially pp. 127–146, and Jefferson Williamson, *The American Hotel* (New York: Knopf, 1930; facsimile reprint, New York: Arno Press, 1975), 8–37.

9. Catherine Massey, "Stories of a Few Special People Who Came to New Mexico in the Early 1900s" (unpublished manuscript, 1992), no page numbers.

10. Pratt, Biebel, and Scurlock, *Trails, Rails and Roads*, 2: 152.

11. Lawrence R. Borne, *Dude Ranching: A Complete History* (Albuquerque: University of New Mexico Press, 1983), 11.

12. *Las Cruces Historic Buildings Survey* (Las Cruces: Doña Ana County Historical Society, no date). According to Leslie Dorsey and Janice Devine in *Fare Thee Well: A Backward Look at Two Centuries of Historic American Hostelries, Fashionable Spas and Seaside Resorts* (New York: Crown, 1964), 174–5,

whole troupes of actors began to travel after the Civil War. They were not always welcomed by innkeepers because they brought along pets, slept late in the day, burned lights late at night, cooked in their rooms, and then didn't always pay the long-suffering host at the end. Information about the National Hotel is from an interview with Audrey Alpers and Henny Davies, 17 June 1991, in Cimarron, New Mexico.

13. These examples are from August Mencken, *The Railroad Passenger Car* (Baltimore: Johns Hopkins University Press, 1957), 159, 170, and 178. He quotes from J. W. Boddam-Whetham, *Western Wanderings*, 1874; W. G. Marshall, *Through America*, 1882; and Lady Duffus Hardy, *Through Cities and Prairie Lands*, 1881.

14. George H. Foster and Peter C. Weiglin, *The Harvey House Cookbook: Memories of Dining Along the Santa Fe Railroad* (Atlanta: Longstreet Press, 1992), 72–80.

15. See Marta Weigle, "From Desert to Disney World: The Santa Fe Railway and the Fred Harvey Company Display the Indian Southwest," *Journal of Anthropological Research*, 45 (1989): 115–137.

16. Brochures quoted in Marta Weigle and Peter White, *The Lore of New Mexico* (Albuquerque: University of New Mexico Press, 1988), 49, 59.

17. Conrad N. Hilton, *Be My Guest* (Englewood Cliffs: Prentice Hall, 1957), 15.

18. Ibid., 109.

19. Whitney Bolton, *The Silver Spade: The Conrad Hilton Story* (New York: Farrar, Straus, and Young, 1954), 152.

20. Ibid., 83.

21. Helen Kentnor, interview with author, 29 September 1990, in Taos, New Mexico.

Chapter One

1. Albuquerque Morning Journal, 27 September 1908.

2. "Fair Women and Brave Men at Alvarado," *Albuquerque Morning Journal*, 10 October 1908, 4.

3. "Climax of Social Gaieties of Fair is Reached in Brilliant Montezuma Ball," *Albuquerque Morning Journal*, 1 October 1916, 2.

4. Richard Worthen, interview with author, 31 December 1994 in Albuquerque, N.Mex. All subsequent quotes, unless otherwise indicated, are from this interview.

5. Marc Simmons, *Albuquerque: A Narrative History* (Albuquerque: University of New Mexico Press, 1982), 329.

6. James David Henderson, *Meals by Fred Harvey: A Phenomenon of the American West* (Fort Worth: Texas Christian University Press, 1969), 24.

7. *Albuquerque Journal-Democrat*, 11 May 1902, article on opening.

8. Christopher Wilson, "The Spanish Pueblo Revival Defined: 1904–1921," *New Mexico Studies in the Fine Arts* 7 (1982): 25.

9. The Alvarado was not the first California Mission-style building in New Mexico; the Castañeda Hotel in Las Vegas, built in 1898, was the first.

10. David Gebhard, "Architecture and the Fred Harvey Houses," *New Mexico Architecture*, July-August 1962, 13.

11. Directory of New Mexico Architects and folder 106, Boyd Pratt Archive, John Gaw Meem Collection, Center for Southwest Research, University of New Mexico.

12. Virginia L. Grattan, *Mary Colter: Builder Upon the Red Earth* (Flagstaff, Ariz.: Northland Press, 1980), 8. Grattan apparently quotes this from the original wire.

13. Quoted in Simmons, *Albuquerque*, 30, from George P. Hammond and Agapito Rey's translation of *Narratives of the Coronado Expedition, 1540–1542* (Albuquerque: University of New Mexico Press, 1940), 183.

14. *Albuquerque Journal-Democrat*, 11 May 1902.

15. Erna Fergusson, *Albuquerque* (Albuquerque:

Merle Armitage Editions, 1947), 20–21; Harvey Fergusson, *Rio Grande* (New York: Knopf, 1933), 282–283.

16. C. M. Graham, "Alvarado (Harvey House) Reveries," *New Mexico Railroader* 12 (July-August 1970): 7–8.

17. Byron Harvey III, "The Fred Harvey Collection, 1899–1963," *Plateau: Quarterly of the Museum of Northern Arizona* 36, no. 2 (Fall 1963):38; "Rare Minerals to Be Brought to Albuquerque," *Albuquerque Morning Journal*, 4 July 1907, 5.

18. Quoted from an advertisement in Grattan, *Mary Colter*, 11.

19. Harvey, "The Fred Harvey Collection," 39.

20. See David Gebhard, "Architectural Imagery, the Mission and California," *Harvard Architectural Review* 1 (Spring 1980): 139.

21. The term "commodify" is used in Marta Weigle's "From Desert to Disney World: The Santa Fe Railway and the Fred Harvey Company Display the Indian Southwest," *Journal of Anthropological Research* 45 (1989): 115–137.

22. For another discussion of the Santa Fe Railway and its relationship to the American Indian, see T. C. McLuhan, *Dream Tracks: The Railroad and the American Indian, 1890–1930* (New York: Harry N. Abrams, Inc., 1985).

23. Nancy Peake, "'If it came from Wright's, you bought it Right': Charles A. Wright, Proprietor, Wright's Trading Post," *New Mexico Historical Review* 66, no. 3 (July 1991): 267; Chalmers Lowell Pancoast, "Presidential Visit . . . 1903," *New Mexico Magazine*, June 1950, 45.

24. Simmons, *Albuquerque*, 352.

25. William Keleher, *The Fabulous Frontier: Twelve New Mexico Items* (Santa Fe: Rydal Press, 1945), 191–195.

26. Grattan, *Mary Colter*, 39; Newspaper clipping dated 11 September 1922, no source noted on it, from the Alvarado files of the city of Albuquerque, Planning Division, Planning Department.

27. "Alvarado Will Have Elaborate Beauty Scheme," newspaper clipping dated 19 April 1923, no source noted on it, from the Alvarado files of the city of Albuquerque.

28. Graham, "Reveries," 3, 8.

29. Jack Mullen, "America's Best-Fed Travelers," *The Santa Fe Magazine* 37, no. 12 (December 1943): 9.

30. Mullen, "America's Best-Fed," 36; Lesley Poling-Kempes, *The Harvey Girls* (New York: Paragon House, 1989), 195.

31. Mullen, "America's Best-Fed," 18.

32. Typescript entitled "Notes from the Discussion with Mrs. Opal Hill on November 4, 1969 at 3:00 P.M." from Alvarado files of the city of Albuquerque.

33. Quoted in Alexandra Roberts' unpublished essay dated 1 April 1980, "The Alvarado Hotel, A Reflection of the Railroad Years in Albuquerque," 16, Center for Southwest Research, University of New Mexico.

34. Grattan, *Mary Colter*, 99–100.

35. Opal Hill, "Notes from the Discussion," 2.

36. "Alvarado Remodeling 24 Rooms, Redecorating of Wing Completed," *Albuquerque Tribune*, 11 August 1952, clipping from Alvarado files, city of Albuquerque; brochure for Alvarado Hotel, dated 1959, from Special Collections, University of Arizona Library.

37. John Conron, "The Alvarado Hotel," *New Mexico Architecture*, May-June 1970, 17.

38. Susanne Burks, "Mystery and Misunderstanding: Death of the Alvarado—A Post-mortem," *Albuquerque News*, 19 February 1970.

39. Letter in Alvarado files, city of Albuquerque.

40. Inspection report in Alvarado files, city of Albuquerque.

41. Quoted in Conron, "The Alvarado Hotel," 19.

42. Letter in Alvarado files, city of Albuquerque.

43. Letter from Pete Domenici to Ben Raskob, 9 December 1969, in Alvarado files, city of Albuquerque. Committee members were Ben G. Raskob, Frank A. Mapel, Oscar Love, Dr. Eldred Harrington, Richard Worthen, George Pearl, and

Ruth Armstrong. Domenici initially asked Ben Raskob to chair the committee, but Richard Worthen ended up chairing it because, as he put it:

> I was young and foolish and energetic and had a mission. . . . But I couldn't even get [some members] to come to a meeting. They simply were not interested. . . . I've had a lingering feeling that . . . they had some other agenda, but they were just going along with this because Pete had asked them to.

44. *Albuquerque Tribune*, 2 January 1970, sec. B, p. 10.
45. Letter in Alvarado files, city of Albuquerque.
46. "Alvarado Buildings Have Had Day," *Albuquerque Journal*, 13 January 1970, clipping in Alvarado files, city of Albuquerque.
47. Newspaper clipping dated 17 January 1970, no source noted on it, in Alvarado files, city of Albuquerque.
48. Burks, "Mystery and Misunderstanding."
49. "Alvarado Hotel Not Worth Saving, Rail Officials Say," *Albuquerque Tribune*, 20 January 1970, clipping in Alvarado files, city of Albuquerque.
50. Letter in Alvarado files, city of Albuquerque; "Anderson Reveals Alvarado Declared National Treasure," *Albuquerque Journal*, 1 February 1970, sec. A, p. 2.
51. "Transcript of Testimony Given at the Public Meeting Held by the Alvarado Advisory Committee at the Civic Auditorium," 4 February 1970, in Alvarado files, city of Albuquerque; Pearl interview; Joline Daffer, "$2800 is Pledged to Save Alvarado," *Albuquerque Journal*, 10 February 1970, sec. A, pp. 1, 14.
52. Memo to Albuquerque City Commission from Citizens for Saving the Alvarado, in Alvarado files, city of Albuquerque.
53. David Walter Klein, "The Downtown Planning Process: An Analysis of the Albuquerque Experience," (master's thesis, University of New Mexico, 1974), 33; Laura Jamharian, *Albuquerque Tribune*, "Setbacks for Alvarado Cause," 17 February 1970, in Alvarado files, city of Albuquerque.
54. Mike Clancy, "The Alvarado—From Landmark to Lot," *Albuquerque Tribune*, 6 September 1975, sec. A, p. 2.
55. Ruth J. Luhrs, "A Classic Hotel Still Lives," *Impact: Albuquerque Journal Magazine*, 4 March 1980, 5.
56. V. B. Price, *A City at the End of the World* (Albuquerque: University of New Mexico Press, 1992), 54–55.
57. *Albuquerque Tribune*, 20 October 1995.
58. Lawrence Clark Powell, *Southwestern Book Trails: A Reader's Guide to the Heartland of New Mexico and Arizona* (Santa Fe: William Gannon, 1982), 2.

Chapter Two

1. Oliver La Farge, *Santa Fe: The Autobiography of a Southwestern Town* (Norman: University of Oklahoma Press, 1959), 420.
2. Quoted from *L'Amerique au jour le jour* in Catherine Donzel, Alexis Gregory, and Marc Walter, *Grand American Hotels* (New York: Vendome Press, 1989), 158.
3. Regge N. Wiseman was kind enough to provide me with two reports that were very helpful: Regge Wiseman, "Early Spanish Colonial Occupation of Santa Fe: Excavations at the La Fonda Parking Lot Site (LA 54000)," *Current Research on the Late Prehistory and Early History of New Mexico, no. 18* (Albuquerque: New Mexico Archaeological Council, 1992) and Regge Wiseman, "Pottery Production for the Spanish: A Preliminary Analysis of the Indian-Made Ceramics Recovered by the La Fonda Project, Santa Fe, New Mexico," *Laboratory of Anthropology*, note no. 499 (Santa Fe: Museum of New Mexico, 1988).

4. Reproduced in Andrew K. Gregg, *New Mexico in the Nineteenth Century: A Pictorial History* (Albuquerque: University of New Mexico Press, 1968), 84.

5. The descendent, Mrs. Evelyn Lara Martinez of Denver, Colorado, prepared information about her research and the model for La Fonda.

6. Marian Meyer, *Mary Donoho: New First Lady of the Santa Fe Trail* (Santa Fe: Ancient City Press, 1991), 7–8. Meyer discovered the existence of Mary Donoho when she found a newspaper article in *The Santa Fe New Mexican* from August of 1885 reporting an interview with James Donoho, Mary and William's son, who had returned to Santa Fe to visit his birthplace. He told the interviewer that his parents had "engaged in the hotel business on the plaza . . . and occupied the celebrated 'old Fonda' or Exchange hotel as it is now called."

7. Janet Lecompte, "When Santa Fe Was a Mexican Town," *Santa Fe: History of an Ancient City*, ed. David Grant Noble (Santa Fe: School of American Research Press, 1989), 83–84.

8. Meyer, *Donoho*, 46–47.

9. Susan Shelby Magoffin, *Down the Santa Fe Trail and into Mexico: The Diary of Susan Shelby Magoffin, 1846–47*, ed. Stella M. Drumm (New Haven: Yale University Press, 1962; reprint, Lincoln: University of Nebraska Press, 1982), 103.

10. Magoffin, *Down the Santa Fe Trail*, 103.

11. Ibid., 104.

12. Nancy E. Wood, "A History of Land Use: The La Fonda Hotel Parking Lot Project, 1984," (unpublished paper dated April 22, 1984), n.p., photocopy.

13. Quoted in John P. Bloom, "New Mexico Viewed by Anglo-Americans 1846–1849," *New Mexico Historical Review* 34, no.3 (July 1959): 172.

14. Frank McNitt, "Navajo Campaigns and the Occupation of New Mexico, 1847–1848," *New Mexico Historical Review* 43, no.3 (July 1968): 176.

15. From an advertisement reprinted in Peter Hertzog, *La Fonda: The Inn of Santa Fe*, Western Americana vol. 2 (Santa Fe: The Press of the Territorian, 1964), 4. Peter Hertzog was the pseudonym for Phillip St. George Cook III.

16. Quoted in Paul Horgan's foreword to La Farge, *Autobiography*, v and vi.

17. I had already written the above description of the postcard in my collection when I saw the same card reproduced in John Sherman's *Santa Fe: A Pictorial History* (Norfolk/Virginia Beach, Va.: Donning Company, 1983), 38. In his caption for it, Sherman mentions that it was alleged to be based on an old photograph but calls that a "dubious claim." I think it may have been based on the 1855 photograph, with the addition of a stagecoach arrival to add excitement to a static scene.

18. Paul Horgan, *Lamy of Santa Fe: His Life and Times*, (New York: Farrar, Straus, and Giroux, 1975), 122.

19. Ralph Emerson Twitchell, *Old Santa Fe* (Santa Fe: Santa Fe New Mexican Publishing Corp., 1925), 237 and 239.

20. Meyer, *Donoho*, 51.

21. James A. Bennett, *Forts and Forays: A Dragoon in New Mexico, 1850–1856*, ed. Clinton E. Brooks and Frank D. Reeve (Albuquerque: University of New Mexico Press, 1948), 27.

22. Twitchell, *Old Santa Fe*, 384 and 388; "The Death of Chief Justice Slough," *Santa Fe Weekly Gazette*, 21 December 1867, reprinted in Hertzog, *La Fonda*, 10–13.

23. Attributed to Sister Blandina in Mary J. Straw's *Loretto: The Sisters and their Santa Fe Chapel* (Santa Fe: Loretto Chapel Fund, 1983), 49.

24. For a discussion of these influences, see Carl Sheppard, *The Archbishop's Cathedral* (Santa Fe: Cimarron Press, 1995).

25. *The New Mexican*, 6 September 1879.

26. Ibid., 13 September 1879.

27. Quoted in Horgan, *Lamy*, 399. I found only references to the murder but no background or details until an endnote in Straw's *Loretto* led me to the original newspaper accounts. My retelling comes directly from the newspaper articles, but I am also indebted to Nancy Wood's "A History of Land Use: The La Fonda Hotel Parking Lot Project, 1984."

28. It should be noted that the name Zadoc

has variant spellings. It also appears as Zoldac and Zadok in different sources. Information about the Santa Fe Hotel Building Company came from Floyd S. Fierman, "The Staabs of Santa Fe: Pioneer Merchants in New Mexico Territory," *Rio Grande History* 13 (1983): 9, and William J. Parish, "The German Jew and the Commercial Revolution in Territorial New Mexico, Part 2," *New Mexico Historical Review*, 35, no. 2 (April 1960): 138. Other information came from Tigges, "Land Ownership," 172.

29. From a letter written by the correspondent of the Chicago "Hotel World" and quoted in Hertzog, *La Fonda*, 20.

30. Hertzog, *La Fonda*, 22–23.

31. The above is a highly simplified and compressed version of a complex story. The reader interested in much more detail about the origins of "Santa Fe style" may wish to start with Chris Wilson's *The Myth of Santa Fe* (Albuquerque: University of New Mexico Press, 1997); David Gebhard's "Architecture and the Fred Harvey Houses, the Alvarado and La Fonda," *New Mexico Architecture*, January-February 1964, 18–25; Carl Sheppard's *Creator of the Santa Fe Style: Isaac Hamilton Rapp, Architect* (Albuquerque: University of New Mexico Press, 1988); and Bainbridge Bunting's *John Gaw Meem: Southwestern Architect* (Albuquerque: University of New Mexico Press, 1983).

32. Hertzog, *La Fonda*, 28.

33. Quoted from the *Santa Fe New Mexican*, 14 December 1919, in La Farge, *Autobiography*, 247.

34. Sheppard, *I. H. Rapp*, 94–95.

35. Quoted in La Farge, *Autobiography*, 286.

36. T. C. McLuhan, *Dream Tracks: The Railroad and the American Indian, 1890–1930* (New York: Harry N. Abrams, 1985), 41.

37. From "The Golden Key to Wonderland" in *They Know New Mexico: Intimate Sketches by Western Writers* and quoted in Marta Weigle's "Exposition and Mediation: Mary Colter, Erna Fergusson, and the Santa Fe/Harvey Popularization of the Native Southwest, 1902–1940," *Frontiers: A Journal of Women Studies*, 12, no. 3 (1992): 130.

38. This question was an example provided by a former courier to Ann and Albert Manchester in "The Indian Detours: Couriers, Dudes, and Touring Cars," *Persimmon Hill*, Summer 1993, 31–35.

39. Edith Reid Dixon (Mrs. Joseph K. Dixon) to the Santa Fe Railway, 31 May 1927, Box 15, Fred Harvey Collection, Fred Harvey Company Papers, 1896–1945, University of Arizona Library Special Collections, Tucson.

40. Bunting, *Meem*, 73.

41. Ibid., *Meem*, 3–4.

42. Ibid., *Meem*, 14–15.

43. Ibid., *Meem*, 74; Wilson, *Myth*, 242–3.

44. Ibid., *Meem*, 74–75.

45. Virginia L. Grattan, *Mary Colter: Builder Upon the Red Earth* (Flagstaff, Ariz.: Northland Press, 1980), 54.

46. Bunting, *Meem*, 74; Grattan, *Mary Colter*, 52; Carl Sheppard (*I. H. Rapp*, 96–97) complains that in 1948 when Colter reorganized the San Francisco Street facade and added shops where the entrance patio had been, she was guilty of darkening the lobby.

47. *Santa Fe New Mexican*, 12 May 1928.

48. Grattan, *Mary Colter*, 54.

49. Bunting, *Meem*, 78.

50. Ernie Pyle, *Home Country* (New York: William Sloane Associates, 1947), 75–76.

51. Pyle, *Home Country*, 76.

52. Ibid., 79.

53. Ibid., 79.

54. Frederick Turner discusses Cather's interest in Lamy and where the manuscript may have been completed in *Spirit of Place: The Making of an American Literary Landscape* (Washington, D.C.: Island Press, 1989), 140, 143.

55. *Work of Art* deals with protagonist Myron Weagle's artistry as a hotelkeeper and has been denounced as one of Lewis's worst novels. If you don't let the critics stop you from reading it, the book offers an entertaining look at hotel life from the 1890s into the automobile era.

56. Keith L. Bryant Jr., *History of the Atchison, Topeka, and Santa Fe Railway* (Lincoln: University of Nebraska Press, 1974; reprint, 1982), 355; Sam Ballen, personal interview with author, 21 November 1995.

57. Grattan, *Mary Colter*, 106.

58. Ballen interview (see note 56).

59. October 22, 1986.

60. Paul Horgan, *The Centuries of Santa Fe* (New York: E. P. Dutton, 1956), 322.

61. John A. Jakle, *The Tourist: Travel in Twentieth-Century North America* (Lincoln: University of Nebraska Press, 1985), 299, 284.

62. Lewis Gannett, *Sweet Land* (Garden City, N.Y.: Doubleday, Doran, & Company, 1934), 53.

63. *USA Today*, 3 February 1994.

64. *The Diary of Anais Nin, 1947–55* (New York: Harcourt Brace Jovanovich, 1974), 201.

Chapter Three

1. The story up to this point appears with variations in details and graphic depiction in several sources, including these, listed in order of importance: *Santa Fe Weekly New Mexican*, 18 October 1870; Jim B. Pearson, *The Maxwell Land Grant* (Norman: University of Oklahoma Press, 1961), 34–5; Ralph Looney, *Haunted Highways* (Albuquerque: University of New Mexico Press, 1968), 95–96; Tom Hilton, *Nevermore, Cimarron, Nevermore* (Ft. Worth: Western Heritage Press, 1970), 37–43.

2. Willa Cather, *Death Comes for the Archbishop* (New York: Vintage Books Edition, 1971), 67.

3. I report here only what appeared on the marker. I can't explain why the date doesn't seem to jibe with the dates in October of 1870 for the events reported in other accounts, including the *Santa Fe Weekly New Mexican*.

4. This figure for the acreage of the grant comes from William A. Keleher, *Maxwell Land Grant* (New York: Argosy-Antiquarian, 1964; Albuquerque: University of New Mexico Press, 1984), 29.

5. Marc Simmons, *Following the Santa Fe Trail: A Guide for Modern Travelers* (Santa Fe: Ancient City Press, 1984), 140.

6. Zane Grey, *Fighting Caravans* (New York: Grosset & Dunlap, 1929), 145.

7. Agnes Morley Cleaveland, *Satan's Paradise* (Boston: Houghton Mifflin Company, 1952), 57.

8. Pearson, *Maxwell*, 28.

9. I draw this conclusion from stories associated with the St. James that date from 1870 and 1871 as well as from Customer Ledgers of the St. James Hotel, 3 vols., from 1871 to 1900, ed. Laurel E. Drew and comp. Howard W. Henry, 1994.

10. Robert Julyan, *The Place Names of New Mexico* (Albuquerque: University of New Mexico Press, 1996), 84.

11. Keleher, *Maxwell*, 19–20; Pearson, *Maxwell*, 8.

12. Marc Simmons, "Coal Oil Jimmy: One Slick Outlaw," *New Mexico Magazine*, February 1993, 42–47; Coal Oil Jimmy's story is also told in Pearson, *Maxwell*, 35–37.

13. The *Santa Fe New Mexican* told of this episode and is quoted in Simmons, "Coal Oil," 47. The reward is variously reported as $1,200 and $3,000.

14. The account of the killing of Pancho Griego and discussions of Clay Allison can be found in the following sources: Ruth Armstrong, *The Chases of Cimarron: Birth of the Cattle Industry in Cimarron County, 1867–1900* (Albuquerque: New Mexico Stockman, 1981), 26; Keleher, *Maxwell*, 76–81; Miguel A. Otero, *My Life on the Frontier, 1864–1882* (New York: Press of the Pioneers, 1935; Albuquerque: University of New Mexico Press, 1987), 121–127; Pearson, *Maxwell*, 68–69; Philip Rasch, "The People of the Territory of New Mexico versus the Santa Fe Ring," *New Mexico Historical Review* 47, no. 2 (April 1972): 192.

15. Monroe Lee Billington, *New Mexico's Buffalo Soldiers, 1866–1900* (Niwot, Colo.: University Press of Colorado, 1991), xvi; and inter-

pretive information for visitors provided at Fort Union, N.Mex.

16. Pearson, *Maxwell*, 38.

17. For accounts of the shootout, see Armstrong, *Chases*, 50; Billington, *Buffalo Soldiers*, 66–67; Pearson, *Maxwell*, 38 and 70; Rasch, "People vs. the Santa Fe Ring," 196; and Keleher, *Maxwell*, 69. Note that Keleher is actually telling a different story: some of the incidents he relates match other accounts, but these are not the same soldiers, and, according to Keleher, the incidents occur in May rather than March of 1876. For a look at the type of holster the cavalrymen wore, you can visit the museum in the Visitors' Center at Fort Union.

18. Hilton, *Nevermore*, 25, but not always a reliable source.

19. Cleaveland, *Paradise*, 25.

20. *Cimarron News and Press*, 20 November 1879.

21. Cleaveland, *Paradise*, 59. Lew Wallace would later stay in room 9, now known as the Governor's Room.

22. Cleaveland, *Paradise*, 99–100.

23. Ibid., 103.

24. Betty A. Griffin, *The Folsom Hotel Story* (1988), 35; and interview with author, 18 June 1991.

25. The stories about Thomas Ketchum and his gang are often garbled and contradictory. I found a consistent and reasonably clear account of the events around Cimarron in Ed Bartholomew, *Black Jack Ketchum: Last of the Hold-up Kings* (Houston: The Frontier Press of Texas, 1955), 67–78. Bartholomew mentions variant versions of events and tries to untangle them.

26. Judy Romero-Oak, "Wild West Hotel: St. James transports guests back in time," *New Mexico Magazine*, January 1990, 55.

27. Tom Hilton (*Nevermore*, 105–6) does mention the Abernathys, though not by name, in this way:

> The next to attack the St. James, or now Diego, was a new owner, Texan by birthright. The place was bought for daughter and carousing son-in-law. Oh, they worked on it, spent thousands on modern furniture and while they were at it, they stripped the place of its original furnishings. . . . Beds that had held the heads of Mace Bowman, Dick Wooten [Wootton], Tom Boggs, and Annie Oakley were sent to a mountain empire [Vermejo Park Ranch], doomed in less than a year to be burned in an accidental fire [the burning of the largest guest house in 1955].

28. Sitzberger, interview with author, 27 December 1989. Unless otherwise indicated, all quotes from Ed Sitzberger are from this interview.

29. Cleaveland, *Paradise*, 270.

30. Otero, *Life on the Frontier*, 89. Audrey Alpers and Henny Davies, interview with author, 17 June 1991. For information about the former owners of the Santa Fe Trail Inn, see Sandra D. Lynn, "Cowboy is Real McCoy Down to his Rawhide," *New Mexico Magazine*, October 1993, 17–18, and "Donn Davies: A Man Who Loves the West," *Persimmon Hill: Magazine of the National Cowboy Hall of Fame and Western Heritage Center*, Autumn 1992, 55–56.

31. This phrase came from Angie Papadakis, quoted by Bob Beck in the San Pedro, California, *News-Pilot* and reprinted in *Reader's Digest*, October 1990, 25.

32. Fritz Thompson, "Enchanted Tales Ring Across State," *Albuquerque Journal*, 30 October 1988.

33. Rick Nathanson, "Ghosts as Guests," *Albuquerque Journal*, 29 October 1989.

Chapter Four

1. Rita Hill, *Then and Now Here and Around Shakespeare* (Lordsburg, New Mexico: First edition in cooperation with the Lordsburg, Hidalgo

County, Chamber of Commerce, 1963; second edition, Shakespeare Ghost Town, 1986), 6.

2. Roscoe Conkling and Margaret Conkling, *The Butterfield Overland Mail, 1857–1869* (Glendale, Calif.: Arthur H. Clark Company, 1947), vol. 3, map of the southern route; Rita Hill and Janaloo Hill, "Alias Shakespeare: The Town Nobody Knew," *New Mexico Historical Review* 42, no. 3 (July 1967): 213; Janaloo Hill, personal correspondence with author, 26 August 1993; Oscar O. Winther, "The Southern Overland Mail and Stagecoach Line, 1857–1861," *New Mexico Historic Review* 32, no. 2 (April 1957). John Evensen told his experiences to Emma Marble Muir, who recounted them to Rita Hill. See Rita and Janaloo Hill's discussion of the reliability of these accounts in endnote 1 to their article cited above from the *New Mexico Historical Review*.

3. Janaloo Hill, "Stratford Hotel—Shakespeare, N.M.," a single typescript page, n.d.

4. Janaloo Hill, personal correspondence, 29 November 1996.

5. Janaloo Hill, interview with author, 17 July 1991. Unless otherwise indicated, quotes from Janaloo Hill are from this interview.

6. R. Hill, *Then and Now*, 15; Marc Simmons, "The McComas Massacre," *New Mexico Magazine*, January 1996, 60–65.

7. Emma Marble, whose married name was Emma Muir, published some of her stories in *New Mexico Magazine* in 1948: "The Stage to Shakespeare," July 1948, 25–27, 52, 59; "The Great Diamond Swindle," August 1948, 26–27, 46–49; "Bonanza Days at Shakespeare," September 1948, 26–27, 41–46; "Shakespeare Becomes a Ghost Town," October 1948, 25–27, 47–51. These articles, Janaloo Hill wrote to the author on 29 November 1996, were altered enough during the publication process that they told a somewhat different story from Mrs. Muir's accounts to the Hill family.

8. Janaloo Hill, interview.

9. Hill and Hill, "Alias Shakespeare," 224.

10. Janaloo Hill, interview; Michael Rozek, "Souls," *Rozek's* 2, no. 3 (1994–95): 3.

11. Janaloo Hill, interview, and in *Shakespeare Quarterly* 11, no. 2 (July 1996).

12. Janaloo Hill, personal correspondence, undated (late 1991).

Chapter Five

1. George G. Street, *Che! Wah! Wah! The Modern Montezumas in Mexico* (Rochester, N.Y.: E. R. Andrews, Printer and Bookbinder, 1883), 93–94.

2. Street, *Montezumas*, 94–95.

3. *Las Vegas Optic*, 28 and 29 October 1982.

4. A quote from the *Chicago Inter-Ocean* of 27 April 1882 that appeared in an 1883 promotional booklet entitled "Las Vegas Hot Springs." Excerpts were reprinted by the Citizens' Committee for Historic Preservation in the Preservation Bulletin, Las Vegas, N.Mex., September 1987. My thanks to Diana Stein for providing me with a copy.

5. Keith Bryant Jr., *History of the Atchison, Topeka, and Santa Fe Railway* (Lincoln: University of Nebraska Press, 1974; 1982), 111.

6. Louise H. Ivers, "The Architecture of Las Vegas, New Mexico" (Ph.D. diss., University of New Mexico, 1975), 128; Jefferson Williamson, *The American Hotel* (New York: Knopf, 1930; New York: Arno Press, 1975), 69.

7. Ivers, "Architecture of Las Vegas," 131.

8. For further comment on this, see "Other-directed Houses," in *Landscapes: Selected Writings of J. B. Jackson*, ed. Ervin H. Zube (University of Massachusetts Press, 1970).

9. William Herbert Carruth, *Las Vegas Hot Springs, New Mexico* (Chicago: Rand McNally, 1887), 42.

10. Earl Pomeroy, *In Search of the Golden West: The Tourist in Western America* (New York: Knopf, 1957), 16–17.

11. For a fascinating discussion of the differences between resorts and city hotels and between men's and women's spaces in hotels, see Warren Belasco's *Americans on the Road From Autocamp to Motel, 1910–1945* (Cambridge: MIT Press, 1979).

12. Carruth, *Las Vegas Hot Springs*, 14.

13. Lynn I. Perrigo, *Gateway to Glorieta* (Boulder, Colo.: Pruett Publishing Company, 1982), 22. Louise Ivers in "Architecture of Las Vegas," 118, said the first building was a hospital and cited an article written by Clarence Pullen for *Harper's Weekly*, 28 June 1890. In that article Pullen wrote:

> In 1846, the first year of the Mexican war, after New Mexico had been conquered by forces led by Doniphan and Kearny, the United States military authorities established a hospital here—a long one-story adobe house, fronted by a veranda with posts of natural logs. It served for military hospital purposes as late as 1862, and afterward was made a hotel.

14. Perrigo, *Gateway*, 22; Arthur Olivas, chronology of Las Vegas Hot Springs in Montezuma files, Photography Archives, Museum of New Mexico, Santa Fe; Milton Callon, "Montezuma," *New Mexico Magazine*, September 1960, 30. Callon quoted from a book called *Bear City and Other Frontier Sketches* by George T. Buffum.

15. Perrigo, *Gateway*, 22; Howard Bryan, *Wildest of the Wild West* (Santa Fe: Clear Light Publishers, 1988), 101–102; Miguel Antonio Otero, My *Life on the Frontier* (Press of the Pioneers, 1935; Albuquerque: University of New Mexico Press, 1987), 177. Also, Robert Utley mentioned the meeting in *Billy the Kid: A Short and Violent Life* (Lincoln: University of Nebraska Press, 1989), 123, and cited Henry Hoyt's *A Frontier Doctor* (Chicago: R. R. Donnelley & Sons, 1979), 183–87.

16. The Adobe Hotel burned in 1881, according to Sally Kabat, "Home Away from Home: The Architectural Geography of Hotels in the American Southwest, 1880–1920" (Ph.D. diss., University of New Mexico, 1994), 134.

17. Perrigo, *Gateway*, 22; Bruce Ashcroft, "The Montezuma Hotel: Playground of Kings and Cowboys," *El Palacio* 91, no. 3 (Winter/Spring 1986): 9; Ivers, "Architecture of Las Vegas," 119.

18. Charlie Dambmann's story may be found in detail in Otero, *Life on the Frontier*, 260–265; Ashcroft, "Playground," 10.

19. Otero, *Life on the Frontier*, 276.

20. Marta Weigle pointed out in "From Desert to Disney World," 117, that:

> The Southwestern encounter with guardian Indians and stately Montezuma of a 'civilized' but vanquished Aztec nation was rendered symbolically equivalent to encountering Europe, the classical world, and biblical lands during . . . the Grand Tour.

21. James David Henderson, *Meals by Fred Harvey: A Phenomenon of the American West* (Fort Worth: Texas Christian University Press, 1969), 13.

22. Bryant, *History*, 112.

23. *Las Vegas Daily Optic*, 17 January 1884.

24. Kabat, "Home Away From Home," 134.

25. Harriet Monroe, *John Wellborn Root* (New York: Houghton Mifflin and Company, 1896; Park Forest, Ill.: Prairie School Press, 1966), 121–124.

26. Monroe, *Root*, 151–2.

27. Thomas S. Hines Jr., "Daniel Hudson Burnham A Study in Cultural Leadership" (Ph.D. diss., University of Wisconsin, 1971), 62.

28. *Las Vegas Daily Optic*, 20 April 1885.

29. The only change from the second to the third Montezuma Hotel was in the roofing material. The second hotel had a slate roof; the rebuilt version of 1886 had a terneplate roof, according to an undated typescript history by Ellen Threinen in George Pearl's files.

30. *Las Vegas Daily Optic*, 20 April 1885.

31. Reports of numbers varied. The *Las Vegas*

Daily Optic, 20 April 1885, said, "The bathhouse has a capacity of 500 baths per day." Five years later, Clarence Pullen said, "The capacity of the establishment for baths is 1000 per day, embracing every variety usually found in a complete water-cure establishment, and the attendants, male and female, are carefully selected and well trained." "The Las Vegas Hot Springs," *Harper's Weekly*, June 28, 1890.

32. Pullen, "The Las Vegas Hot Springs," and Carruth, *Las Vegas Hot Springs*, 41. Pullen's description of the mud bath was very similar in wording to Carruth's.

33. Carruth, *Las Vegas Hot Springs*, 17; Pullen, "The Las Vegas Hot Springs."

34. A german was a dancing party featuring the german cotillion, which involved complicated figures.

35. *Las Vegas Daily Optic*, 19, 22, and 23 August, 1893.

36. Ibid., 28 August 1893.

37. Kabat, "Home Away from Home," 152; Ashcroft, "Playground," 14.

38. Monte Montgomery, telephone interview with author, 16 January 1996; Perrigo, *Gateway*, 62 and 147.

39. This figure is the most commonly found, though others appear.

40. Armand Hammer with Neil Lyndon, *Hammer* (New York: G. P. Putnam's Sons, 1987), 513. Although I have taken a couple of innocuous quotes from this autobiography of Hammer, I must caution the reader that Hammer's autobiographies are not necessarily to be trusted. See Edward Jay Epstein's "The Last Days of Armand Hammer" in *The New Yorker*, 23 September 1996, 37. Epstein claims that in his autobiographies Hammer "would sculpt events to his liking."

41. Eric Pace, "Armand Hammer Dies at 92; Executive Forged Ties," *New York Times*, 11 December 1990, and *New York Times*, 12 December 1990, editorial.

42. Hammer, *Hammer*, 510.

43. The reference to Lord Mountbatten's death and his dream of an American campus comes from a quote from Theodore Lockwood in *The Dallas Morning News*, 12 September 1982.

44. Steve Weinberg, *Armand Hammer: The Untold Story* (Boston: Little, Brown and Company, 1989), 394–396.

45. George Pearl to Joseph D. Cohen, personal correspondence, 18 October 1982.

46. *Las Vegas Optic*, 29 May 1990; see also *Historic Preservation News*, July 1990, for news brief.

47. When Armand Hammer died, many of his projects could not be funded according to the hopes of those who had claims on his fortune. Hammer's estate turned out to be worth about $40 million encumbered with numerous liabilities and legal battles. See Epstein, "Last Days," 44.

48. Phillip Geier, telephone interview with author, 25 January 1996.

49. *New Mexico Business Weekly*, 1 April 1996.

50. Dave Condon, "Las Vegas Landmark," *New Mexico Magazine*, January 1945, 11, 39.

51. Stanley Marcus and Lonnie Lucero, *The Plaza Hotel in Las Vegas*, interview by Harold Rhodes (Albuquerque: KNME-TV, 1983), videorecording. Additional note: Byron T. Mills ended up selling the hotel to Mrs. John G. Ortiz.

52. Perrigo, *Gateway*, 8, 16, 68, 70.

53. Bryan, *Wildest of the Wild West*, 2.

54. Ivers, "Architectural History of Las Vegas," 166; H. Ward Jandl, "Rehabilitating Historic Storefronts," Preservation Briefs no. 11, Technical Preservation Services, National Park Service, U.S. Department of the Interior.

55. For a more detailed account of Ford and Liddil's stay in Las Vegas, see "The Dirty Little Coward" in Bryan, *Wildest of the Wild West*, 200–207.

56. Katherine Slick, interview with author, 18 March 1989.

57. David Wesner, "Mama Lucy," *Albuquerque Journal*, 12 December 1982.

58. Katherine and Wid Slick, interview, 18 March 1989.

59. From Elmo Baca, in Chris Wilson et al., *Architecture and Preservation in Las Vegas 2*, His-

toric Resources Nomination prepared for the Citizens' Committee for Historic Preservation, 1984, 7–8.

60. Katherine and Wid Slick, interview, 18 March 1989.

61. Lance Chilton et al., *New Mexico: A New Guide to the Colorful State* (Albuquerque: University of New Mexico Press, 1984), 199.

62. The ruins of a stone main house and some other buildings remain, along with remnant fruit trees. There is some evidence that Mills' house served as a hotel for stagecoach passengers. Files of the Kiowa National Grasslands, Clayton, New Mexico, including Nomination Form for inclusion of the Mills Canyon Orchard site on the National Register of Historic Places, 1990; Robin McKinney, "Land of Memories: Harding County's Kiowa National Grasslands," *New Mexico Magazine*, November 1978, 29–45; Marc Simmons, "Call of the Canadian" *New Mexico Magazine*, June 1990, 35–43; Fritz Thompson, "Melvin Mills: A Faded Legacy," *Impact: Albuquerque Journal Magazine*, 2 December 1980, 4–9.

63. Henderson, *Meals by Fred Harvey*, 24; H. F. Thatcher, Director Curator of the Las Vegas Rough Rider and City Museum, "Castañeda The Hotel and The Man," photocopy of manuscript dated 8 November 1978.

64. Ivers, "Architecture of Las Vegas," 219; Kabat, "Home Away from Home," 178–180; Lynn I. Perrigo, "The Castañeda Hotel, Las Vegas, New Mexico," photocopy of manuscript dated 1974.

65. Jocelyn Lieu, "The Castañeda: New Owner Halts Decline of Opulent Hotel," *New Mexico Magazine*, February 1991, 72–73; Don Eldh, interviews with author, 30 and 31 March 1996.

Chapter Six

1. The whole story is told in "Christmas in Kingston" in *Black Range Tales*, first published in 1936, reprinted by Rio Grande Press (Chicago) in 1965. In the foreword to the 1965 edition, Lucien File explains how to view this work: "[McKenna's] book is hardly the gospel truth from cover to cover, but most of his tales are based on truth." The reference to Sierra Diablo, apparently an old name for the mountains, comes from McKenna, *Tales*, 9.

2. Ibid., 93.

3. Fayette Jones, president of New Mexico Institute of Mining and Technology, quoted in Bill Rakocy, *Ghosts of Kingston and Hillsboro* (El Paso: Bravo Press, 1983), 84.

4. McKenna, *Tales*, 108–9.

5. Elliott West, *The Saloon on the Rocky Mountain Mining Frontier* (Lincoln: University of Nebraska Press, 1979), 74–75.

6. John S. Sinclair, *New Mexico: The Shining Land* (Albuquerque: University of New Mexico Press, 1980), 140.

7. Martin Ansell, "Such is Luck: The Mining Career of Edward L. Doheny in New Mexico, 1880–1891," *New Mexico Historical Review* 71, no. 1 (January 1995): 50–52.

8. McKenna, *Tales*, 292.

9. See Warren Belasco, *Americans on the Road: From Autocamp to Motel, 1910–1945* (Cambridge, Massachusetts: MIT Press, 1979), 58. Belasco says that "the register was not considered suitable reading for the gentler sex," but I speculate that ladies' names were also omitted from the register in an effort to ensure their privacy and protection.

10. The register for 1886–87 is in the Geronimo Springs Museum in Truth or Consequences, New Mexico. When I read it on December 30, 1993, the museum staff was unaware of President Cleveland's signature in it and could thus offer no explanation for his apparent presence in Kingston.

11. Except, that is, for a single reference in Rakocy, *Ghosts*, 96. Rakocy's book, however, is not a reliable source, though it is useful for its lengthy excerpts from various other sources, particularly several interesting newspaper articles from El Paso.

12. *Sierra County Advocate*, 29 January 1887, 4.

13. Erna Fergusson, *New Mexico: A Pageant of Three Peoples* (New York: Knopf, 1966), 294.

14. Jacqueline Meketa, *From Martyrs to Murderers: The Old Southwest's Saints, Sinners, and Scalawags* (Las Cruces: Yucca Tree Press, 1993), 150.

15. Betty Reich, "Stagecoach Days," unpublished manuscript dated 27 March 1937, file 127, New Mexico Federal Writers Project, State Records and Archives, Santa Fe, N.Mex.

16. William Swilling Wallace, "Short-line Staging in New Mexico," *New Mexico Historical Review* 26, no. 2 (April 1951): 89–100. John Sinclair in his portrait of Sadie in *Shining Land*, 141, quoted correspondence from Adlai Feather, a writer and historian: "The story of Sadie's stage-driving rests entirely upon her own authority, and is perhaps of her own manufacture."

17. Fergusson, *Pageant*, 294.

18. William Keleher, *The Fabulous Frontier: Twelve New Mexico Items* (Santa Fe: Rydal Press, 1945), 238.

19. Mrs. Orem Lewis, formerly Margarethe Tittman, telephone interview with author, 8 February 1994.

20. *The Black Range Museum on the Scenic Route Through Hillsboro, New Mexico: The Land of Enchantment*, museum pamphlet, no date.

21. B. Franklin, telephone interview with author, 6 July 1994. Mr. Franklin helped haul the stones used to construct the lodge and recalls a small building there that had been an assay office. But according to the Sierra County Historical Society's *History of Sierra County, New Mexico* (Truth or Consequences, 1979), 54, "The basic structure [of the Black Range Lodge] is said to have been an old miners' dormitory dating back to the 1880s."

22. McKenna, *Tales*, 291, 299.

23. "Black Range Road Opened," *El Paso Times*, 19 August 1935, 10.

24. *Silver City Daily Press*, 17 June 1938, 11.

25. The post office opened in 1882 and closed in 1957.

26. This information comes from an interview the author had with Margaret Vetter on 31 December 1993 and from William P. Diven, "Boomtown Revival," *New Mexico Magazine*, July 1993, 56–63.

27. Sierra County Historical Society, *History*, 142–3.

28. Mike Sherlock and Catherine Wanek, interview with author, 25 May 1990.

29. Catherine Wanek, telephone interview with author, 9 December 1991; Diven, "Boomtown Revival," 58; David Steinberg, "Hillsboro Casts Its Spell Over Visiting Movie Crew," *Albuquerque Journal*, 23 August 1992, G2.

Chapter Seven

1. Much of this story comes from Dr. Lee's daughter Margaret "Peggy" Kuula, interview with the author, 14 April 1995, and from a clipping from the *El Paso Times*, November 1916, in Peggy Kuula's files. The clipping begins, "Doesn't it give you a nice thrilly feeling to find out a real romance of the story book variety?" It provides details of the courtship and wedding of Luisa Griggs-Fegan and Ernest C. Lee, as well as the role of "that chubby little rogue, Danny Cupid." All subsequent quotes from Peggy Kuula, unless otherwise noted, come from the interview of 14 April 1995.

2. Dorothy Jensen Neal, *The Lodge, 1899–1969* (Alamogordo, N.Mex.: Alamogordo Printing Company, 1969), 1; Marie Wuersching and Sacramento Mountains Historical Society, *Railroad to Cloudcroft* (Cloudcroft: 1988), 1.

3. Neal, *The Lodge*, 2.

4. Jeanie P. Fleming, "Six Historic Hotels," *New Mexico Magazine*, January 1985, 70.

5. Sally Kabat, "Home Away From Home: The Architectural Geography of Hotels in the American Southwest, 1880–1920" (Ph.D. diss., University of New Mexico, 1994), 196; Cyril Harris, ed., *Illustrated Dictionary of Historic Architecture* (New York: Dover Publications, 1977), 308.

6. *Albuquerque Journal-Democrat*, April 1901, quoted in Neal, *The Lodge*, 3. She did not supply an exact date, but identified the quote as from an issue in "mid-April." The hotel opened in June.

7. "Cloudcroft—A Pen Picture," *El Paso Journal*, September 1901, 7.

8. Ibid., 1.

9. Marjorie White, "The Cloud-Climbing Route," *Railroads and Railroad Towns in New Mexico* (Santa Fe: New Mexico Magazine, 1989), 31.

10. Ibid., 31; Neal, *The Lodge*, 15.

11. Wuersching and Historical Society, *Railroad*, 4–5. The Mexican Canyon Trestle was placed on the State Register of Cultural Properties in 1970 and on the National Register of Historic Places in 1979.

12. White, "Cloud-Climbing Route," 32.

13. "Cloudcroft Lodge Gone up in Smoke," *The Silver Lining*, 19 June 1909. I am indebted to Marie Wuersching for providing me with a photocopy of this article and others.

14. Neal, *The Lodge*, 13.

15. Ibid., 15.

16. William Douglas Lansford, *Pancho Villa* (Los Angeles: Sherbourne Press, 1965), 91.

17. Neal, *The Lodge*, 15.

18. Martin Luis Guzman, *Memoirs of Pancho Villa*, trans. Virginia H. Taylor (Austin: University of Texas Press, 1965), 53.

19. Gene Z. Hanrahan, ed., *The Murder of Madero and Role Played by U.S. Ambassador Henry Lane Wilson*, vol. 4 of *Documents on the Mexican Revolution* (Salisbury, N.C.: Documentary Publications, 1981), 113–114.

20. Neal, *The Lodge*, 18.

21. Paul Hernandez, letter to author, 19 April 1994. All subsequent quotes from Paul Hernandez are from this correspondence unless otherwise noted. Though Hernandez was not sure of the year, it would not likely have been in 1916; after the raid on Columbus, Villa was a hunted man. It may have been possible in 1915, when Villa came to Juarez-El Paso several times to meet with General Hugh L. Scott from Fort Bliss. The dates for events between 1915 and 1920 given by Paul Hernandez and by Dorothy Jensen Neal do not agree.

22. The advertisement is quoted in Neal, *The Lodge*, 3.

23. It is perhaps worth noting that the first time a woman wore shorts on the Lodge golf course was in the early 1940s. Soletta Schwartz persuaded Rufus Wallingford, the manager, to grant her permission—"permission," his wife said, "*I* never did get" (Neal, *The Lodge*, 28).

24. Sally Kabat, "Land of Cool Pines," *New Mexico Architecture*, July-August 1988, 13.

25. Wilfred McCormick, "High Country Holiday," *New Mexico Magazine*, August 1939, 59.

26. Neal, *The Lodge*, 44.

27. The information in this section on golf comes from Neal's detailed account of the history of golf at the Lodge in a chapter entitled "Golf Above the Clouds"; Kabat, "Land of Cool Pines," 13; Dale Chaney, "Golfing in the Clouds," *New Mexico Magazine*, June 1990, 26–31; Paul Hernandez and Peggy Kuula.

28. State of New Mexico, Governor's Organized Crime Prevention Commission, Charitable Bingo Investigative Summary (October 1993), 2; Marc Simmons, *Albuquerque: A Narrative History* (Albuquerque: University of New Mexico Press, 1982), 287; New Mexico Statutes, art. 19 of the Criminal Code and art. 2B of Business Licenses (1978).

29. Neal, *The Lodge*, 18–21.

30. Conrad Hilton, *Be My Guest* (New York: Prentice Hall Press, 1957), 171.

31. William A. Keleher, *Memoirs, 1892–1969* (Santa Fe: Rydal Press, 1969), 149–152.

32. Neal, *The Lodge*, 32.

33. Ibid., 37.

34. Ibid., 2.

35. Ibid., 9; *The Otero County Advertiser*, 3 August 1912; *The Weekly Cloudcrofter*, 11 June 1915.

36. McCormick, "High Country Holiday," 59.

37. Martha Wallingford West, interview with Marie Wuersching, 28 October 1988.

38. Neal, *The Lodge*, 38–39.

39. Dianne deLeon-Stallings, "Snow Play in Cloudcroft," *New Mexico Magazine*, March 1993, 19; Gary Wood, "Sanders Sells the Lodge and Snow Canyon," *Mountain Monthly*, January 1993, 1.

40. Neal, *The Lodge*, 27–29.

41. Ibid., 35.

42. Paul Hernandez.

43. *Alamogordo Daily News*, 4 September 1988, 5.

44. "Lodging's 400 Top Performers," *Lodging Hospitality*, August 1986, 82.

45. This story is based on an interview with Judy Montoya by Fritz Thompson, quoted in "Enchanted Tales Ring Across State," *Albuquerque Journal*, 30 October 1988, C1, 10.

46. Application for registration, New Mexico State Register of Cultural Properties, files of the Historic Preservation Division, State of New Mexico, Santa Fe. The Lodge was placed on the State Register of Cultural Properties in 1987.

47. Jefferson Williamson, *The American Hotel* (New York: Knopf, 1930; facsimile reprint New York: Arno Press, 1975), 229.

48. Neal, *The Lodge*, 14, and Peggy Kuula.

49. *The Weekly Cloudcrofter*, 6 November 1914.

50. Postcard from the author's collection.

Chapter Eight

1. William H. Bartlett to H. A. Smith, 6 September 1912, William H. Bartlett papers, Vermejo Park Ranch, N.Mex. (hereafter cited as Bartlett/Vermejo).

2. Veronica E. Velarde Tiller, *The Jicarilla Apache Tribe: A History* (Lincoln: University of Nebraska Press, 1992), 4–5.

3. Jim Berry Pearson, *The Maxwell Land Grant* (Norman: University of Oklahoma Press, 1961), 16.

4. Karen Pillmore Laurie, "History of Vermejo Park," *New Mexico Geological Society Guidebook*, 27th Field Conference (Vermejo Park, 1976), 88; Pearson, *Maxwell*, 21.

5. Pearson, *Maxwell*, 80.

6. William A. Keleher, *Maxwell Land Grant* (New York: Argosy-Antiquarian, 1964; Albuquerque: University of New Mexico Press, 1984), 110–111.

7. Pearson, *Maxwell*, 112.

8. Laurie, "History of Vermejo Park," 89; John Neary, "The Oil Baron Buys a Park," *Audubon*, September 1974, 43; Joe Torres, "Life with the Rancheros," *Denver Post Empire Magazine*, 11 August 1974, 14–17.

9. Pearson, *Maxwell*, 231.

10. Charles D. Michaels, "William H. Bartlett," obituary in *The Price Current Grain Reporter*, 18 December 1918.

11. Bartlett to George Patten, Esq., 19 August 1898, Bartlett/Vermejo.

12. William Barnes to Bartlett, 29 July 1899, William H. Bartlett papers, Special Collections, University of New Mexico, Albuquerque, N.Mex. (hereafter cited as Bartlett/UNM).

13. Adams to Bartlett, 7 August 1899, Bartlett/UNM.

14. Pearson, *Maxwell*, 231. In 1903 Bartlett was still withholding $10,000 of the purchase amount from the Maxwell Land Grant Company because of 600 acres still held by Hispanic settlers. Bartlett to Adams, 8 May 1903, Bartlett/Vermejo.

15. Frank Andrews to Bartlett with clipping attached dated 20 January 1902, Bartlett/UNM.

16. William H. Bartlett Jr. to Bartlett Sr., 9 February 1904, Bartlett/UNM.

17. Laurie, "History of Vermejo Park," 89.

18. Bartlett to H. L. Leupp, 15 December 1914, Bartlett/Vermejo.

19. Ann Haslanger, Oral History Project, photocopy of transcript of "Casa Grande Tour" (tour led by Haslanger), 26 May 1976. All subsequent references to the Oral History Project will refer to transcript photocopies by name or title and date.

20. Adams to Bartlett, 2 September 1906, Bartlett/UNM.

21. Ann C. Haslanger, *A History of Vermejo Park* (n.p., n.d.), 6.

22. Adams to Edwin Crampton, 21 October 1913, Bartlett/UNM.

23. Bartlett to Bureau of Fisheries, Department of the Interior, 19 March 1909, Bartlett/Vermejo; Laurie, "History of Vermejo Park," 89.

24. Pennzoil Company, *Vermejo Park Ranch* (Houston: 1982), 41; United States Department of the Interior, United States Department of Agriculture, State of New Mexico, *Study of Management Options: Vermejo Ranch New Mexico/Colorado,* July 1979, 52; Brownlow Wilson, *Reminiscences of a Nautical Rancher* (New York: Exposition Press, 1971), 138.

25. Bartlett to Frank C. Hatch, 17 September 1917, Bartlett/Vermejo.

26. Haslanger, transcript, "Mrs. Marie Riley on Vermejo History," 10 December 1975, 17.

27. Bartlett to James A. Patten, 17 July 1911, Bartlett/Vermejo.

28. As told here the story comes from Haslanger, transcript of interview with Ted Haddon, undated, and transcript, "Casa Grande Tour," 26 May 1976.

29. Lawrence R. Borne, *Dude Ranching: A Complete History* (Albuquerque: University of New Mexico Press, 1983), 51.

30. Wilson, *Reminiscences,* 153.

31. Ibid., 152.

32. Haslanger, *A History,* 7; Wilson, *Reminiscences,* 166.

33. Vermejo Club Guest Accounts, 25 September 1927 to 15 October 1927.

34. Wilson, *Reminiscences,* 172.

35. "Prescribed Recreation," booklet by All-Year Guest Ranches, Inc., ca. 1934.

36. Elliott Barker, *When the Dogs Bark 'Treed'* (Albuquerque: University of New Mexico Press, 1946), preface.

37. Barker, *Dogs,* 135.

38. Ibid., 144.

39. Ibid., 206.

40. From Elliott Barker, quoted in *The Vermejo Park Gazette,* a tabloid designed, researched, and written by Charlotte A. Hollis and published for Vermejo Park Ranch by *The Sangre de Cristo Chronicle,* 1991, 8.

41. Laurie, "History of Vermejo Park," 92.

42. *Vermejo Park Gazette,* 8.

43. Haslanger, transcript of interview with O. D. "Judd" Knight, 23 September 1979.

44. Haslanger, transcript of interview with Brownlow Wilson, 7 June 1978.

45. James H. Cook, "Six Gun Days," *New Mexico Magazine,* March 1936, 12–13, 43–45; Brownlow Wilson, "Open Range," *New Mexico Magazine,* June 1938, 26–27, 42–43; Wilson, *Reminiscences,* 24–25.

46. Pearson, *Maxwell,* 276.

47. Lee Gourley Wootten, niece-in-law of W. J. Gourley, telephone interview with author, 1 July 1996.

48. Haslanger, transcript, "Casa Grande Tour," 26 May 1976.

49. Ibid.

50. Neary, "Oil Baron," 37.

51. Laurie, "History of Vermejo Park," 92.

52. John Peterson, "For Sale—750 Miles of Majestic Ranchland; Terms—Strictly Cash," *The National Observer,* 25 December 1971, 7.

53. Neary, "Oil Baron," 45.

54. Peterson, *National Observer,* 7.

55. *Chicago Tribune,* 3 December 1972.

56. *Raton Daily Range,* 25 May 1971.

57. The subtitle comes from titles of articles in *New Mexico Magazine* in 1972 and 1975.

58. Neary, "Oil Baron," 46.

59. *Albuquerque Journal,* 26 June 1988.

60. United States Department of the Interior et al., *Study of Management Options,* 2; Pennzoil, *Vermejo Park Ranch,* 20.

61. United States Department of the Interior et al., *Study of Management Options,* 6.

62. Ibid., 123.

63. Pearson, *Maxwell,* 166, 240–42; James E. Sherman and Barbara Sherman, *Ghost Towns and Mining Camps of New Mexico* (Norman: University of Oklahoma Press, 1975), 34–35.

64. Sherman, *Ghost Towns,* 131.

65. Ibid., 21, 202.

66. From a clipping in the vertical files of the Arthur Johnson Memorial Library in Raton, New Mexico. The clipping is dated January 24, 1982, but bears no indication of the newspaper source. Ann Haslanger used the same phrase in *A History*, 8.

67. These are the Ring and McCrystal Ranches and Ponil Park.

68. Howard Fineman, "A Ground War Begins," *Newsweek*, 6 July 1992, 37. Hugh Liedtke, Pennzoil's chairman, had been Bush's oil partner in Texas in the 1950s.

69. *Albuquerque Tribune*, 19 June 1996.

Chapter Nine

1. Clem Shaffer, handwritten and typed manuscripts of memoir dated 1942, from the private collections of G. Harding Kayser and Jackie Shaffer Hudgeons in Mountainair, New Mexico.

2. This and all subsequent quotes from Ernie Pyle are from his columns published in *The Albuquerque Tribune*, 13 April 1942, 7, and 14 April 1942, 8.

3. Dewey Tidwell, "John Barleycorn, Beans, and Bad Guys," *Impact: Albuquerque Journal Magazine*, 24 January 1984, 12.

4. Pauline "Polly" Shaffer, interview with author, 23 March 1990.

5. Marcus Whiffen and Carla Breeze, *Pueblo Deco* (Albuquerque: University of New Mexico Press, 1984), 55.

6. Jackie Shaffer Hudgeons, interview with author, 12 March 1991. All subsequent quotes from Jackie Hudgeons are from this interview unless otherwise indicated.

7. Quoted from the National Register of Historic Places Nomination Form prepared by Ellen Threinen, 5 September 1978, in the files of the State of New Mexico Historic Preservation Division in Santa Fe.

8. William S. Greever, "Railway Development in the Southwest," *New Mexico Historical Review* 32, no. 2 (April, 1957): 178–179; Torrance County Historical Society, *History of Torrance County* (1979), 36–40.

9. All quotes from Clem "Pop" Shaffer, unless otherwise indicated, are from his 1942 handwritten memoir. I have retained his original spelling and punctuation.

10. G. Harding Kayser Jr., interview with author, 12 March 1991. All subsequent quotes from G. Harding Kayser Jr. come from this interview unless otherwise indicated.

11. Sue Schofield, "The Life and Times of the Shaffer Hotel, Mountainair, New Mexico" (paper presented at the annual meeting of the Historical Society of New Mexico, Montezuma Hotel, Las Vegas, New Mexico, June 1986), 2.

12. Quoted in Boyd Pratt, Charles Biebel, and Dan Scurlock, *Trails, Rails, and Roads: The Central New Mexico East-West Transportation Corridor Regional Overview* (Santa Fe: New Mexico Historic Preservation Division, 1988) 1: 253.

13. State Highway Department Map of New Mexico, 1923, and *Official Automobile Blue Book: 1925 Standard Touring Guide of America*, vol. 4 (Chicago: Automobile Blue Books, 1925), 439.

14. Schofield, "Life and Times," 2.

15. However, I was told by a woman who lived in the hotel as a young school teacher that Pop worked hard butchering the meat served in the dining room.

16. Dewey Tidwell, "John Barleycorn," 14; Maxine Block, ed., *Current Biography* (New York: H. W. Wilson Co., 1941), 207; Marjorie Dent Candee, ed., *Current Biography* (New York: H. W. Wilson Co., 1953), 146.

17. Dewey Tidwell, "John Barleycorn," 14.

18. John Proctor, "Zany Zoo," *The Family Circle*, 15 January 1943, 16–17.

19. *New Mexico Statistical Abstract* (Albuquerque: Bureau of Business and Economic Research, University of New Mexico, 1989), 105.

20. Dixie Reid, "Pop's Art," *Impact: Albuquerque Journal Magazine*, 5 June 1984, 9.

Chapter Ten

1. Conrad Hilton, *Be My Guest* (New York: Prentice Hall Press, 1957), 102.

2. "Albuquerque Takes Another Step Forward With Opening of Hilton Hotel," *Albuquerque Journal*, 9 June 1939, sec. 2, p. 1.

3. "Hilton Occupies Stable Location," sec. 2, p. 13. Marc Simmons, *Albuquerque: A Narrative History* (Albuquerque: University of New Mexico Press, 1982), 10–11 and 334–335.

4. See also National Register of Historic Places Nomination Form prepared by Mary Davis, 29 November 1983, 3, New Mexico Historic Preservation Division, Santa Fe, N.Mex.

5. "'Northern' Windows to Prevent Drafts;" "Elevators in New Hilton Hotel Here Are Latest in Vertical Transportation;" "Authentic Native Furniture is Bought for Use in New 10-Story Hilton Hotel;" *Albuquerque Journal*, 9 June 1939, sec. 2, pp. 9, 10, 14.

6. Whitney Bolton, *The Silver Spade: The Conrad Hilton Story* (New York: Farrar, Straus, and Young, 1954), 83.

7. Hilton, *Be My Guest*, 103.

8. Ibid., 113.

9. Ibid., 181–2.

10. Thomas Ewing Dabney, *The Man Who Bought The Waldorf* (New York: Duell, Sloan, and Pearce, 1950), 125; "Herndon Happy as Hilton Hotel Opens to Public," *Albuquerque Journal*, 9 June 1939, sec. 2, p. 14.

11. Tommy McMullan, interview with author, 22 February 1993. All subsequent quotes from Mr. McMullan are from this interview.

12. When Tommy McMullan told me this story on February 22, 1993, he said the events took place on the day *before* opening day and reiterated that when questioned. Others have said he told it to them as occurring *on* opening day, which seems more likely, as the hotel invited the public to visit on opening day between 10:30 A.M. and 3:30 P.M. The doors may have been locked before the announced opening time. I have thus chosen to tell the story as if it happened on June 9.

13. Descriptions of these uniforms came from Tommy McMullan and from "Bellboys Have Novel Uniforms," *Albuquerque Journal*, 9 June 1939, sec. 2, p. 12.

14. Hilton, *Be My Guest*, 186, 190–91.

15. "Conrad Hilton, Georgia Gabor to Wed Friday Noon in Rites at Santa Fe," *Albuquerque Journal*, 10 April 1942, 14; "Hilton Hotel President Weds Sari Gabor, Former Wife of Turkish Propaganda Minister," *Santa Fe New Mexican*, 10 April 1942, 3.

16. Sherry Robinson, "Coming Back in Style," *Albuquerque Journal*, 6 June 1984, sec. D, p. 1.

17. Simmons, *Albuquerque*, 366.

18. According to the *New Mexico Statistical Abstract* (Albuquerque: Bureau of Business and Economic Research, University of New Mexico, 1984), 60, the city of Albuquerque grew from 35,449 in 1940 to 96,815 in 1950.

19. Lansing Lamont, *Day of Trinity* (New York: Atheneum, 1965), 34–89.

20. Walter Schneir and Miriam Schneir, *Invitation to an Inquest* (New York: Pantheon Books, 1983), 377.

21. Schneir and Schneir, *Inquest*, 380–388.

22. Ibid., 385.

23. Lamont, *Trinity*, 188.

24. Ibid., 9, 240.

25. Ibid., 242.

26. Neil Clark, "Albuquerque," *Saturday Evening Post*, 8 April 1950, 139.

27. Harrison W. Mason, "Albuquerque Atom City," *San Diego Uptown Examiner*, 25 May 1950, 5.

28. Tony Montoya, interview and tour of the building with author, 5 February 1993.

29. "Senator Kennedy Remembered from Days of PT Boat Fighting in South Pacific," *Albuquerque Journal*, 29 March 1957, 23.

30. Wayne C. Scott, "Kennedy Blasts Administration Spending Policy," *Albuquerque Journal*, 30 March 1957, 1; "Kennedy to Arrive Here Today," *Albuquerque Journal*, 29 March 1957, 1.

31. John F. Kennedy, *Profiles in Courage*,

Memorial Edition (New York: Harper & Row, 1964), 146.

32. I received valuable assistance in pinning down the date of Senator Kennedy's first visit to Albuquerque from the staff of the John F. Kennedy Library in Boston, Massachusetts.

33. Howard Bryan, "Ok, La Posada Hotel is historic" *Albuquerque Tribune*, 9 June 1984, sec. A, p. 6.

34. "Todd Brushes Off 'Big Shot' Sirens," *Albuquerque Tribune*, 19 March 1958. The plane crash in which Todd was killed occurred near Grants, New Mexico, while he was bound for New York from Los Angeles.

35. Susan Dewitt, "New & Old—A City Mix," *New Mexico Architecture*, November/December 1977, 11, 15.

36. Daniel Gibson, "Plush Plaza Hotel Rich with History," *Downtowner*, 22 August 1979, 7.

37. Bart Ripp, "Giant Sale On at Hotel," *Albuquerque Journal*, 6 May 1982, sec. B, p. 1.

38. The information about the objects sold came from several sources: "Lighting Fixtures are Outstanding," *Albuquerque Journal*, 9 June 1939, sec. 2, p. 4; Ripp, "Giant Sale," sec. B, p. 1; National Register of Historic Places Nomination Form, 3; Robinson, "Back in Style," sec. D, p. 1.

39. Robinson, "Back in Style," sec. D, p. 1.

40. Theresa McFerrin, interview with author, 18 May 1993.

41. Hilton, *Be My Guest*, 182–183.

Chapter Eleven

1. Martin Amador filed a petition with the U.S. Court of Claims in 1892 for compensation for the Apache attack almost three decades earlier. The basis for his claim was that the Apaches had been at the time "in amity and under treaty" with the United States Government. See petition, 30 September 1892, MS 427, Legal Documents of Martin Amador, Amador Papers, Rio Grande Historical Collections, New Mexico State University Library, Las Cruces, N.Mex.

2. The attack in Grant County was only one of forty-one such incidents reported in a speech delivered by Colonel W. Rynerson, a member of the Territorial Senate in 1870. Colonel Rynerson prepared a list of "Indian depredations" occurring in 1869 in Doña Ana and Grant Counties. The list was printed in the *Rio Grande Republican*, 30 June 1889, to remind readers that "two decades ago it was as much as man's life was worth to travel throughout the section of country surrounding Las Cruces." Quoted in George Griggs, *History of Mesilla Valley or The Gadsden Purchase* (Las Cruces: Bronson Print Co., 1930), 99.

3. Dates given for the establishment of the building that became Amador Hall and was later incorporated into the Amador Hotel vary widely, from 1850 (*Las Cruces Historic Buildings Survey*, n.d.) to 1859 (Sytha Motto's *Old Houses of New Mexico and the People Who Built Them* [Albuquerque: Calvin Horn, 1972]) to as late as 1870 (Hispanic Heroes Project, *Hispanic Heroes of New Mexico: Portraits of New Mexicans Who Have Made a Difference* [Albuquerque: Starlight Publishing, 1993]). Since Martin Amador was born in 1839 and lived away from Las Cruces much of the time before 1863, it is unlikely that he built Amador Hall as early as the 1850s. Though most accounts attribute the construction to Amador himself, it seems possible to me that his mother, Doña Gregoria Rodela, a businesswoman, could have had the building constructed as early as the 1850s.

4. *Rio Grande Republican*, 13 June 1885, 3.

5. Ibid., 7 March 1886, 3, and 20 March 1886, 3.

6. Fred Shaw, "New Mexico's Slaphappy Hostelry," *Holiday*, November 1946, 63; Rio Grande Historical Collections, New Mexico State University Library.

7. *Rio Grande Republican*, 8 January 1887, 3.

8. For a detailed description of the road conditions around Socorro in those days, see John DeWitt and Spencer Wilson, "Leave the Back of Garage and Turn Left," *New Mexico Architecture*, November/December 1975, 11–19.

9. Conrad N. Hilton, *Be My Guest* (Englewood Cliffs: Prentice Hall, 1957), 102.

10. Leona Klipsch, "Mrs. Paxton on Birthday Recalls Val Verde Past," Socorro's *El Defensor Chieftain*, 3 May 1966, 9.

11. Peggy Paxton Dailey, telephone interviews with author, 27 January 1994 and 15 May 1994, and personal correspondence, 9 March 1994.

12. Charles Mandeville, interview with author, 7 April 1990.

13. Harvey Fergusson, *Rio Grande* (New York: Alfred A. Knopf, 1933), 149; Miguel Otero, *My Life on the Frontier, 1864–1882* (n.p.: Press of the Pioneers, 1935; Albuquerque: University of New Mexico Press, 1987), 147.

14. Brochure announcing the hotel's opening, Arthur Johnson Memorial Library, Raton.

15. "New Structure Represents Land Mark in Building Progress of Raton," *Raton Daily Range*, 7 June 1929, 1.

16. Victor G. Allen, telephone interview with author, 28 May 1991.

17. William Warder, interview with author, 21 February 1992.

18. Thomas J. Boyle, telephone interview with author, 22 February 1994.

19. "New Structure," *Raton Daily Range*, 7 June 1929, 1.

20. Brochure announcing the hotel's opening, Arthur Johnson Memorial Library, Raton.

21. Thomas J. Boyle, interview with author while touring the International State Bank, 19 June 1991.

Selected Bibliography

Archives

Albuquerque Public Library vertical files. Albuquerque, N.Mex.

Alvarado Hotel files. Planning Department, Planning Division, City of Albuquerque, N.Mex.

Amador, Martin. Papers. Rio Grande Historical Collections, New Mexico State University Library, Las Cruces, N.Mex.

Arthur Johnson Memorial Library vertical files. Raton, N.Mex.

Bartlett, William H. Papers. Special Collections, Center for Southwest Research, General Library, University of New Mexico, Albuquerque.

Bartlett, William H. Papers. Vermejo Park Ranch, N.Mex.

Fergusson, Erna. Papers. Manuscript Collection, Center for Southwest Research, General Library, University of New Mexico, Albuquerque.

Fred Harvey Company. Papers, 1896–1945. Special Collections, University of Arizona Library, Tucson.

Haslanger, Ann C. Oral History Interview Transcripts. Oral History Project, Vermejo Park Ranch, N.Mex.

Kiowa National Grasslands files. Clayton, N.Mex.

La Fonda Hotel files. Santa Fe, N.Mex.

Montezuma Hotel file. Including a chronology of Las Vegas Hot Springs and its hotels prepared by photographic archivist Arthur L. Olivas. Museum of New Mexico Photography Archives, Santa Fe.

Montezuma Hotel file. Personal documents of architect George C. Pearl. Albuquerque, N.Mex.

New Mexico Department of Tourism files. Santa Fe, N.Mex.

New Mexico Historic Preservation Division files. Santa Fe, N.Mex.

Pratt, Boyd. Archive. John Gaw Meem Collection, Center for Southwest Research, General Library, University of New Mexico, Albuquerque.

Sacramento Mountains Historical Museum. Cloudcroft, N.Mex.

Sierra County property records. County Courthouse, Truth or Consequences, N.Mex.

Vermejo Club Guest Accounts, 1927 and 1929. Vermejo Park Ranch, N.Mex.

Books, Pamphlets and Periodicals

All-Year Guest Ranches, Inc. *Prescribed Recreation*. N.d. (circa 1934). Photocopied pamphlet.

Ansell, Martin. "Such is Luck: The Mining Career of Edward L. Doheny in New Mexico, 1880–1891." *New Mexico Historical Review* 71, no. 1 (January 1995): 47–65.

Ascensio, Luis M., S.J. *Montezuma Intimo Su Escenario, Su Gente, Su Vida*. Editorial Jus S.A. Mexico, 1962.

Ashcroft, Bruce. "The Montezuma Hotel: Playground of Kings and Cowboys." *El Palacio* 91, no. 3 (Winter/Spring 1986): 8–15.
Baca, Elmo. "Return to Mission Style." *New Mexico Magazine*, April 1994, 22–33.
Barker, Elliott. *When the Dogs Bark 'Treed'*. Albuquerque: University of New Mexico Press, 1946.
Barnhart, Jan. *An Albuquerque Bibliography*. Albuquerque: University of New Mexico General Library and Museum of Albuquerque, 1980.
Bartholomew, Ed. *Black Jack Ketchum: Last of the Hold-up Kings*. Houston: Frontier Press of Texas, 1955.
Belasco, Warren J. *Americans on the Road: From Autocamp to Motel, 1910–1945*. Cambridge, Mass.: MIT Press, 1979.
Bennett, James A. *Forts and Forays: A Dragoon in New Mexico, 1850–1856*. Edited by Clinton E. Brooks and Frank D. Reeve. Albuquerque: University of New Mexico Press, 1948.
Beverley, Mary F. "Sadie Orchard was a Good Ol' Girl." *New Mexico Magazine*, July 1983, 40–42.
Billington, Monroe L. *New Mexico's Buffalo Soldiers, 1866–1900*. Niwot, Colo.: University Press of Colorado, 1991.
The Black Range Museum on the Scenic Route Through Hillsboro, New Mexico: The Land of Enchantment. N.d. Pamphlet.
Bloom, John P. "New Mexico Viewed by Anglo-Americans 1846–1849." *New Mexico Historical Review* 34, no. 3 (July 1959): 165- 198.
Bolton, Whitney. *The Silver Spade: The Conrad Hilton Story*. New York: Farrar, Straus, and Young, 1954.
Borne, Lawrence R. *Dude Ranching: A Complete History*. Albuquerque: University of New Mexico Press, 1983.
Bryan, Howard. *Wildest of the Wild West*. Santa Fe: Clear Light Publishers, 1988.
Bryant, Keith L., Jr. *History of the Atchison, Topeka, and Santa Fe Railway*. Lincoln: University of Nebraska Press, 1974. Reprint, 1982.
Bunting, Bainbridge. *John Gaw Meem: Southwestern Architect*. Albuquerque: University of New Mexico Press, 1983.
Callon, Milton. "Montezuma." *New Mexico Magazine*, September 1960, 30–33, 40.
Carruth, William H. *Las Vegas Hot Springs, New Mexico*. Chicago: Rand McNally, 1887.
Cather, Willa. *Death Comes for the Archbishop*. New York: Knopf, 1927. Reprint, New York: Vintage Books Edition, 1971.
Chaney, Dale. "Golfing in the Clouds." *New Mexico Magazine*, June 1990, 26–31.
Clark, Neil. "Albuquerque." *Saturday Evening Post*, 8 April 1950, 27, 139, 141–142, 144–45.
Cleaveland, Agnes M. *Satan's Paradise*. Boston: Houghton Mifflin Company, 1952.
Condon, Dave. "Las Vegas Landmark." *New Mexico Magazine*, January 1945, 11, 39.
———. "Montezuma." *New Mexico Magazine*, November 1942, 12, 32.
Conkling, Roscoe and Margaret Conkling. *The Butterfield Overland Mail, 1857–1869*, 3 vols. Glendale, Calif.: Arthur H. Clark Company, 1947.
Conron, John. "The Alvarado Hotel." *New Mexico Architecture* (May–June 1970): 16–19.
Conron, John P. *Socorro: A Historic Survey*. Albuquerque: University of New Mexico Press, 1980.
Dabney, Thomas E. *The Man Who Bought the Waldorf: The Life of Conrad N. Hilton*. New York: Duell, Sloan, and Pearce, 1950.
Dewitt, Susan. "New & Old—A City Mix." *New Mexico Architecture*, (November-December 1977): 11–15.
Doña Ana County Historical Society. *Las Cruces Historic Buildings Survey*. N.d.
Donzel, Catherine, Alexis Gregory, and Marc Walter. *Grand American Hotels*. New York: Vendome Press, 1989.
Dorsey, Leslie, and Janice Devine. *Fare Thee Well: A Backward Look at Two Centuries of Historic American Hostelries, Fashionable Spas and Seaside Resorts*. New York: Crown, 1964.

Epstein, Edward J. "The Last Days of Armand Hammer." *The New Yorker*, 23 September 1996, 36–49.

Fergusson, Erna. *Albuquerque*. Albuquerque: Merle Armitage Editions, 1947.

———. New Mexico: *A Pageant of Three Peoples*. New York: Knopf, 1966.

Fierman, Floyd S. "The Staabs of Santa Fe: Pioneer Merchants in New Mexico Territory." *Rio Grande History* 13 (1983).

Folsom, Franklin. *Black Cowboy: The Life and Legend of George McJunkin*. Niwot, Colo.: Roberts Rinehart Publishers, 1992.

Foster, George H., and Peter C. Weiglin. *The Harvey House Cookbook: Memories of Dining Along the Santa Fe Railroad*. Atlanta: Longstreet Press, 1992.

Gannett, Lewis. *Sweet Land*. Garden City, N.Y.: Doubleday, Doran, & Company, 1934.

Gebhard, David. "Architectural Imagery, the Mission and California." *Harvard Architectural Review* 1 (Spring 1980):137–145.

———. "Architecture and the Fred Harvey Houses." *New Mexico Architecture* (July-August 1962): 13–17.

———. "Architecture and the Fred Harvey Houses: The Alvarado and La Fonda." *New Mexico Architecture* (January–February 1964): 18–25.

Graham, C. M. "Alvarado (Harvey House) Reveries." *New Mexico Railroader* 12, no. 4 (July–August 1970): 3–9.

Grattan, Virginia L. *Mary Colter: Builder Upon the Red Earth*. Flagstaff, Ariz.: Northland Press, 1980.

Greever, William S. "Railway Development in the Southwest." *New Mexico Historical Review* 32, no. 2 (April 1957): 151- 203.

Gregg, Andrew K. *New Mexico in the Nineteenth Century: A Pictorial History*. Albuquerque: University of New Mexico Press, 1968.

Gregory, Kathleen. "Salud! to the Old Amador." *New Mexico Magazine*, February 1981, 42–51.

Grey, Zane. *Fighting Caravans*. New York: Grosset & Dunlap, 1929.

Griffin, Betty. *The Folsom Hotel Story*. N.p., 1988. Pamphlet.

Hammer, Armand, with Neil Lyndon. *Hammer*. New York: G.P. Putnam's Sons, 1987.

Harvey, Byron III. "The Fred Harvey Collection, 1899–1965." *Plateau* 36, no. 2 (Fall 1963): 33–53.

Haslanger, Ann C. *A History of Vermejo Park*. N.p., n.d. Pamphlet.

Henderson, James D. *Meals by Fred Harvey: A Phenomenon of the American West*. Fort Worth: Texas Christian University Press, 1969.

Hertzog, Peter. *La Fonda: The Inn of Santa Fe*. No. 2., Western Americana Series. Santa Fe: Press of the Territorian, 1964.

Hill, Rita. *Then and Now Here and Around Shakespeare*. 2d ed. Shakespeare Ghost Town, N.Mex., n.p., 1986. Pamphlet.

Hill, Rita, and Janaloo Hill. "Alias Shakespeare: The Town Nobody Knew." *New Mexico Historical Review* 42, no. 3 (July 1967): 211- 227.

Hilton, Conrad. *Be My Guest*. New York: Prentice Hall Press, 1957.

Hilton, Tom. *Nevermore, Cimarron, Nevermore*. Fort Worth, Tex.: Western Heritage Press, 1970.

Hiss, Tony. *The Experience of Place*. New York: Knopf, 1990.

Horgan, Paul. *The Centuries of Santa Fe*. New York: E.P Dutton, 1956.

———. *Lamy of Santa Fe: His Life and Times*. New York: Farrar, Straus, and Giroux, 1975.

Ivers, Louise H. "The Hotel Castañeda, Las Vegas, N. M.—A Fred Harvey Inn on the Santa Fe Railway." *New Mexico Architecture* (May–June 1974): 19–24.

———. "The Montezuma Hotel." *New Mexico Architecture* (May-June 1977): 13–25.

Jackson, J. B. *The Necessity for Ruins and Other Topics*. Amherst: University of Massachusetts Press, 1980.

Jakle, John A. *The Tourist: Travel in Twentieth-Century North America*. Lincoln: University of Nebraska Press, 1985.

Julyan, Robert. *The Place Names of New Mexico*.

Albuquerque: University of New Mexico Press, 1996.
Kabat, Sally. "Land of Cool Pines." *New Mexico Architecture* (July–August 1988): 11–17.
Keleher, William. *Maxwell Land Grant*. 2d ed. New York: Argosy- Antiquarian, 1964. Reprint, Albuquerque: University of New Mexico Press, 1984.
King, Scottie. "The Challenge of Paradise—A Follow-up." *New Mexico Magazine*, March 1975, 33–34.
Kline, Doyle. "A Challenge in Paradise." *New Mexico Magazine*, Winter 1972, 38–39.
La Farge, Oliver. *Santa Fe: The Autobiography of a Southwestern Town*. Norman: University of Oklahoma Press, 1959.
Laine, Don. "Valle Vidal." *New Mexico Magazine*, July 1991, 58–67.
Lamont, Lansing. *Day of Trinity*. New York: Atheneum, 1965.
Lewis, Sinclair. *Work of Art*. New York: Doubleday, Doran & Company, 1935.
Lieu, Jocelyn. "The Castañeda: new owner halts decline of opulent hotel." *New Mexico Magazine*, February 1991, 70–73.
Limerick, Jeffrey W., Nancy Ferguson, and Richard Oliver. *America's Grand Resort Hotels*. New York: Pantheon Books, 1979.
Looney, Ralph. *Haunted Highways*. Albuquerque: University of New Mexico Press, 1968.
Luhrs, Ruth J. "A Classic Hotel Still Lives." *Impact: Albuquerque Journal Magazine*, 4 March 1980, 4–8.
McKee, John D., and Spencer Wilson. "Leave the Back of the Garage and Turn Left," *New Mexico Architecture* (November–December 1975): 11–19.
McKenna, James. *Black Range Tales*. 1936. Reprint, Chicago: Rio Grande Press, 1965.
McLuhan, T. C. *Dream Tracks: The Railroad and the American Indian, 1890–1930*. New York: Harry N. Abrams, 1985.
Magoffin, Susan Shelby. *Down the Santa Fe Trail and into Mexico: The Diary of Susan Shelby Magoffin, 1846–47*. Edited by Stella M. Drumm. New Haven: Yale University Press, 1962. Reprint, Lincoln: University of Nebraska Press, 1982.
Manchester, Ann and Albert Manchester. "The Indian Detours, Couriers, Dudes, and Touring Cars." *Persimmon Hill*, Summer 1993, 31–35.
Mead, P. L. "The Hotel with a Personality." *New Mexico Sun Trails*, June 1954, 4–7.
Meketa, Jacqueline. *From Martyrs to Murderers: The Old Southwest's Saints, Sinners, and Scalawags*. Las Cruces, N.Mex.: Yucca Tree Press, 1993.
Mencken, August. *The Railroad Passenger Car*. Baltimore: Johns Hopkins University Press, 1957.
Meyer, Marian. *Mary Donoho: New First Lady of the Santa Fe Trail*. Santa Fe: Ancient City Press, 1991.
Miller, Michael, ed. and comp. *A New Mexico Scrapbook*. Huntsville, Ala.: Honeysuckle Imprint, 1991.
Monroe, Harriet. *John Wellborn Root*. New York: Houghton Mifflin Company, 1896. Reprint, Park Forest, Ill.: Prairie School Press, 1966.
Moorhead, Max. L. "Spanish Transportation in the Southwest, 1540–1846." *New Mexico Historical Review* 32, no. 2 (April 1957): 107–122.
Moul, Harry, and Linda Tigges. "The Santa Fe 1912 City Plan: A 'City Beautiful' and City Planning Document." *New Mexico Historical Review* 71, no. 2 (April 1996): 135–155.
Muir, Emma M. "The Stage to Shakespeare." *New Mexico Magazine*, July 1948, 25–27, 52, 59.
———. "The Great Diamond Swindle." *New Mexico Magazine*, August 1948, 26–27, 46–49.
———. "Bonanza Days at Shakespeare." *New Mexico Magazine*, September 1948, 26–27, 41–46.
———. "Shakespeare Becomes a Ghost Town." *New Mexico Magazine*, October 1948, 25–27, 47–51.
Mullen, Jack. "America's Best-Fed Travelers." *The Santa Fe Magazine* 37, no. 12 (December 1943): 9–36.

Neal, Dorothy Jensen. *The Lodge, 1899–1969*. Alamogordo, N.Mex.: Alamogordo Printing Company, 1969.

Neary, John. "The Oil Baron Buys a Park." *Audubon*, September 1974, 35–46.

Nickens, Eddie. "Mining the Past." *Historic Preservation*, July–August 1992, 16–19.

Noble, David Grant, ed. *Santa Fe: History of an Ancient City*. Santa Fe: School of American Research Press, 1989.

Official Automobile Blue Book: 1925 Standard Touring Guide of America. Vol. 4. Chicago: Automobile Blue Books, 1925.

Otero, Miguel A. *My Life on the Frontier, 1864–1882*. Press of the Pioneers, 1935. Reprint, Albuquerque: University of New Mexico Press, 1987.

———. *My Nine Years as Governor of the Territory of New Mexico, 1897–1906*. Albuquerque: University of New Mexico Press, 1940.

Pancoast, Chalmers Lowell. "Presidential Visit . . . 1903." *New Mexico Magazine*, June 1950, 25,45.

Pearson, Jim B. *The Maxwell Land Grant*. Norman: University of Oklahoma Press, 1961.

Perrigo, Lynn I. *Gateway to Glorieta*. Boulder, Colo.: Pruett Publishing Company, 1982.

Poling-Kempes, Lesley. *The Harvey Girls*. New York: Paragon House, 1989.

Pomeroy, Earl. *In Search of the Golden West: The Tourist in Western America*. New York: Knopf, 1957.

Post, Emily. *By Motor to the Golden Gate*. New York: Appleton, 1916.

Powell, Lawrence Clark. *Southwestern Book Trails: A Reader's Guide to the Heartland of New Mexico and Arizona*. Santa Fe: William Gannon, 1982.

Pratt, Boyd, Charles Biebel, and Dan Scurlock. *Trails, Rails, and Roads: The Central New Mexico East-West Transportation Corridor Regional Overview*. 2 vols. Santa Fe: New Mexico Historic Preservation Division, 1988.

Price, V. B. *A City at the End of the World*. Albuquerque: University of New Mexico Press, 1992.

Proctor, John. "Zany Zoo." *The Family Circle*, 15 January 1943, 16–17.

Pullen, Clarence. "The Las Vegas Hot Springs." *Harper's Weekly*, 28 June 1890.

Pyle, Ernie. *Home Country*. New York: William Sloane Associates, 1947.

Railroads and Railroad Towns in New Mexico. Santa Fe: *New Mexico Magazine*, 1989.

Rakocy, Bill. *Ghosts of Kingston and Hillsboro*. El Paso: Bravo Press, 1983.

Reid, Dixie. "Pop's Art." *Impact: Albuquerque Journal Magazine*, 5 June 1984, 5–9.

Romero-Oak, Judy. "Wild West Hotel: St. James transports guests back in time." *New Mexico Magazine*, January 1990, 53–56.

Rozek, Michael. *"Souls." Rozek's* 2, nos. 3, 4, 5, and 6 (1994–1995).

Schauer, Sandy. "Edmund Ross' Second Coming." *New Mexico Magazine*, January 1994, 20–25.

Schneir, Walter, and Miriam Schneir. *Invitation to an Inquest*. New York: Pantheon Books, 1983.

Shakespeare Quarterly newsletters from 1987 to 1996, Vols. 2–11: Shakespeare Ghost Town, NM.

Shaw, Fred. "New Mexico's Slaphappy Hostelry." *Holiday*, November 1946, 62–65.

Sheppard, Carl D. *Creator of the Santa Fe Style: Isaac Hamilton Rapp, Architect*. Albuquerque: University of New Mexico Press, 1988.

Sherman, James E., and Barbara H. Sherman. *Ghost Towns and Mining Camps of New Mexico*. Norman: University of Oklahoma Press, 1975.

Sherman, John. *Santa Fe: A Pictorial History*. Norfolk/Virginia Beach, Va.: Donning Company, 1983.

Sierra County Historical Society. *History of Sierra County, New Mexico*. Truth or Consequences, 1979.

Simmons, Marc. *Albuquerque: A Narrative History*. Albuquerque: University of New Mexico Press, 1982.

———. "Call of the Canadian." *New Mexico Magazine*, June 1990, 35–43.

———. "Coal Oil Jimmy: One Slick Outlaw." *New Mexico Magazine*, February 1993, 42–47.

———. *Following the Santa Fe Trail: A Guide for Modern Travelers*. Santa Fe: Ancient City Press, 1984. Vols. 2 to 11. Shakespeare: Ghost Town, New Mexico.

Sinclair, John L. *New Mexico: The Shining Land*. Albuquerque: University of New Mexico Press, 1980.

Street, George G. *Che! Wah! Wah! The Modern Montezumas in Mexico*. Rochester, N.Y.: E. R. Andrews, Printer and Bookbinder, 1883.

Thompson, Fritz. "Melvin Mills: A Faded Legacy." *Impact: Albuquerque Journal Magazine*, 2 December 1980, 4–9.

Tidwell, Dewey. "John Barleycorn, Beans, and Bad Guys." *Impact: Albuquerque Journal Magazine*, 24 January 1984, 12–13.

Tiller, Veronica E. Velarde. *The Jicarilla Apache Tribe: A History*. Lincoln: University of Nebraska Press, 1992.

Torrance County Historical Society. *History of Torrance County*. New Mexico: 1979.

Trumbo, Theron M. "The House of Amador." *New Mexico Magazine*, April 1946, 18, 45, 47, 49.

Twitchell, Ralph Emerson. *The Leading Facts of New Mexican History*. Vol. 3. Cedar Rapids, Iowa: Torch Press, 1917.

———. *Old Santa Fe*. Santa Fe: Santa Fe New Mexican Publishing Corp., 1925.

Tydeman, William E., ed. *The Pueblo Revival Architecture of John Gaw Meem*. Exhibition catalog. Albuquerque: The Albuquerque Museum, City of Albuquerque and the Regents of the University of New Mexico, 1989.

Van Orman, Richard. *A Room for the Night: Hotels of the Old West*. New York: Bonanza Books, 1966.

Varney, Philip. *New Mexico's Best Ghost Towns*. Flagstaff, Ariz.: Northland Press, 1981.

Wallace, William S. "Short-line Staging in New Mexico." *New Mexico Historical Review* 26, no. 2 (April 1951): 89–100.

Wallis, Michael. "La Fonda: Gathering place at the end of the trail." *New Mexico Magazine*, November 1992, 34–45.

Weigle, Marta. "Exposition and Mediation: Mary Colter, Erna Fergusson, and the Santa Fe/Harvey Popularization of the Native Southwest, 1902–1940." *Frontiers: A Journal of Women Studies* 12, no. 3 (1992): 117–150.

——— "From Desert to Disney World: The Santa Fe Railway and the Fred Harvey Company Display the Indian Southwest." *Journal of Anthropological Research* 45 (1989): 115–137.

Weigle, Marta, and Peter White. *The Lore of New Mexico*. Albuquerque: University of New Mexico Press, 1988.

——— and Kyle Fiore. *Santa Fe and Taos: The Writer's Era, 1916–1941*. Santa Fe: Ancient City Press, 1982.

Weinberg, Steve. *Armand Hammer: The Untold Story*. Boston: Little, Brown and Company, 1989.

West, Eliott. *The Saloon on the Rocky Mountain Mining Frontier*. Lincoln: University of Nebraska Press, 1979.

Whiffen, Marcus, and Carla Breeze. *Pueblo Deco*. Albuquerque: University of New Mexico Press, 1984.

White, Arthur. *Palaces of the People: A Social History of Commercial Hospitality*. New York: Taplinger, 1970.

Williams, Jerry L., ed. *New Mexico in Maps*. 2d ed. Albuquerque: University of New Mexico Press, 1986.

Williamson, Jefferson. *The American Hotel*. New York: Knopf, 1930. Facsimile reprint, New York: Arno Press, 1975.

Wilson, Brownlow. *The Devil's Staircase*. New York: Exposition Press, 1962.

———. *Reminiscences of a Nautical Rancher*. New York: Exposition Press, 1971.

Wilson, Chris. *The Myth of Santa Fe*. Albuquerque: University of New Mexico Press, 1997.

Wilson, Chris, Anita Vernon, and Hilario Romero. *Architecture and Preservation in*

Las Vegas. Vol. 2. Prepared for the Citizens' Committee for Historic Preservation. Las Vegas, N.Mex., 1982.

Wilson, Chris, Elmo Baca, Tamara Coombs, Anita Vernon, Sven Govaars, and Dick Highes. *Architecture and Preservation in Las Vegas*. Vol. 3. Prepared for the Citizens' Committee for Historic Preservation. Las Vegas, N.Mex., 1984.

Wilson, Christopher. "The Spanish Pueblo Revival Defined, 1904- 1921." *New Mexico Studies in the Fine Arts* 7 (1982): 24–30.

Winther, Oscar O. "The Southern Overland Mail and Stagecoach Line, 1857–1861." *New Mexico Historical Review*, 32, no. 2 (April 1957): 81–106.

Wiseman, Regge. "Early Spanish Colonial Occupation of Santa Fe: Excavations at the La Fonda Parking Lot Site (LA 54000)." *Current Research on the Late Prehistory and Early History of New Mexico*. No. 18. Albuquerque: New Mexico Archaeological Council, 1992.

———. "Pottery Production for the Spanish: A Preliminary Analysis of the Indian-Made Ceramics Recovered by the La Fonda Project, Santa Fe, New Mexico." *Laboratory of Anthropology*. Note no. 499. Santa Fe: Museum of New Mexico, 1988.

Wuersching, Marie, and Sacramento Mountains Historical Society. *Railroad to Cloudcroft*. Cloudcroft, N.Mex.: 1988. Pamphlet.

Zube, Ervin H. *Landscapes: Selected Writings of J. B. Jackson*. Amherst: University of Massachusetts Press, 1970.

Documents

Drew, Laurel E., ed., and Howard W. Henry, comp. Customer Ledgers of the St. James Hotel, 1871 to 1900. 3 vols. Special Collections of the Rio Grande Valley Library System, Albuquerque, N.Mex., 1994. Photocopy.

———. Guest Register of the St. James Hotel. Special Collections of the Rio Grande Valley Library System, Albuquerque, N.Mex., 1994. Photocopy.

Guest Register of the Victorio Hotel, 1886–87. Geronimo Springs Museum, Truth or Consequences, N.Mex.

Laurie, Karen Pillmore. "History of Vermejo Park." *New Mexico Geological Society Guidebook*. 27th Field Conference. Vermejo Park, 1976.

United States Department of the Interior, United States Department of Agriculture, and State of New Mexico. *Study of Management Options: Vermejo Ranch New Mexico/Colorado*. July 1979. Photocopy from Technical Information Center, National Park Service, Denver Service Center, Denver, Colorado.

Vermejo Park Gazette. A special tabloid publication for Vermejo Park Ranch by *The Sangre de Cristo Chronicle*, 1991.

Interviews

Allen, Victor G., former resident of Raton, N.Mex. Telephone interview with author, 28 May 1991.

Alpers, Audrey, historian, and Henny Davies, owner of the Santa Fe Trail Inn. Interview with author. Cimarron, N.Mex., 17 June 1991.

Anders, Gloria June, curator of Black Range Museum. Interview with author. Hillsboro, N.Mex., 31 December 1993.

Apodaca, Rudy S., chief judge, State of New Mexico Court of Appeals. Interview with author. Las Cruces, N.Mex., 14 January 1994.

Baker, Jim, game manager of Vermejo Park Ranch. Interview with author. Vermejo Park Ranch, N.Mex., 20 June 1991.

Ballen, Sam, chairman of the board and CEO of Corporación de La Fonda, Inc. Interview with author. Santa Fe, N.Mex., 21 November 1995.

Boyle, Thomas J., former head teller and security officer of International State Bank. Interviews with author. Guided tour of International State Bank, Raton, N.Mex., 19 June 1991, and

by telephone, 22 February 1994.
Charlesworth, Jim, president, Vermejo Park Ranch Corporation. Interview with author. Vermejo Park Ranch, N.Mex., 20 June 1991.
Conner, John, guest services manager, Vermejo Park Ranch. Interview with author. Vermejo Park Ranch, N.Mex., 20 June 1991.
Dailey, Peggy Paxton, daughter of Mr. and Mrs. Walter Paxton, who owned and operated the Val Verde Hotel. Telephone interviews with author, 27 January 1994 and 15 May 1994.
Drinkard, Tilden, general manager of La Posada de Albuquerque. Interview with author. Albuquerque, N.Mex., 5 February 1993.
Duggan, Dan, vice president and director of marketing, Citizens Bank. Interview with author. Las Cruces, N.Mex., 14 January 1994.
Eldh, Don, owner of Castañeda Hotel. Interviews with author. By telephone, 30 March 1996, and guided tours of Castañeda Hotel, Las Vegas, N.Mex., 31 March, and 13 and 23 April 1996.
Franklin, B., Hillsboro resident. Telephone interview with author, 6 July 1994.
Geier, Phillip, president, Armand Hammer United World College of the American West. Telephone interview with author, 25 January 1996.
Griffin, Betty, owner of Folsom Hotel. Interview with author. Folsom, N.Mex., 18 June 1991.
Hill, Janaloo, owner of Shakespeare Ghost Town. Interview with author. Shakespeare, N.Mex., 17 July 1991.
Hudgeons, Jackie Shaffer, Pauline and Don Shaffer's daughter. Interview with author. Mountainair, N.Mex., 12 March 1991.
Kayser, G. Harding Jr., owner of the Shaffer Hotel. Interview with author. Mountainair, N.Mex., 12 March 1991.
Kelley, George, retired employee of the Santa Fe Railway. Interview with author. Albuquerque, N.Mex., 13 January 1995.
Kentnor, Helen, founder of Sagebrush Inn. Interview with author. Taos, N.Mex., 29 September 1990.
Knight, O. D. "Judd," cowboy with WS and Vermejo Park Ranch. Telephone interview with author, 15 June 1991.
Kuula, Margaret L., "Peggy," daughter of Ernest C. Lee. Interview with author. Albuquerque, N.Mex., 14 April 1995.
Lewis, Mrs. Orem, formerly Margarethe Tittman, daughter of Edward Tittman. Telephone interview with author, 8 February 1994.
Mandeville, Charles, owner of the Val Verde Hotel. Interview with author. Socorro, N.Mex., 7 April 1990.
McFerrin, Theresa, former general manager of La Posada de Albuquerque. Interview with author. Albuquerque, N.Mex., 18 May 1993.
McMullan, Tommy, retired employee of the Albuquerque Hilton/La Posada de Albuquerque. Interview with author. Albuquerque, N.Mex., 22 February 1993.
Montgomery, Monte, former Baptist College student. Telephone interview with author, 16 January 1996.
Montoya, Tony, long-time employee of the Albuquerque Hilton/La Posada de Albuquerque. Interview with author. Albuquerque, N.Mex., 5 February 1993.
Olsen, Anne Hilton, cousin of Conrad Hilton. Interview with author. Socorro, N.Mex., 23 November 1990.
Pearl, George, architect appointed to the Alvarado-Santa Fe Station Complex Advisory Committee and consulting architect to Armand Hammer. Series of interviews with author. Albuquerque, N.Mex., 1991 and 1996.
Shaffer, Pauline or "Polly," Clem Shaffer's daughter-in-law, wife of Donald Shaffer. Interview with author. Albuquerque, N.Mex., 23 March 1990.
Sherlock, Mike and Catherine Wanek, owners of the Black Range Lodge. Interview with author. Kingston, N.Mex., 25 May 1990.
Sitzberger, Ed, owner of St. James Hotel. Interviews with author. Cimarron, N.Mex., 27 December 1989, and by telephone, 4 June 1996.
Slick, Katherine and Wid, partners in Plaza

Partnership Limited. Interview with author. Las Vegas, N.Mex., 18 March 1989.
Slick, Wid, of Slick and Associates, a preservation development firm. Guided tour of the Montezuma Hotel for author, 19 June 1989.
Trujillo, Dan, public information officer, Doña Ana County. Interview with author. Las Cruces, N.Mex., 14 January 1994.
Vetter, Margaret, resident of Kingston. Interview with author. Kingston, N.Mex., 31 December 1993.
Wanek, Catherine. Telephone interview with author, 9 December 1991.
Warder, William, artist. Interview with author. Albuquerque, N.Mex., 26 February 1992.
West, Martha Wallingford, daughter of Rufus Wallingford, manager of the Lodge at Cloudcroft. Interviewed by Marie Wuersching. Cloudcroft, N.Mex., 28 October 1988.
Whiteman, Ben, caretaker for former Victorio Hotel. Interview with author. Kingston, N.Mex., 1 January 1994.
Wootten, Lee Gourley, niece-in-law of W. J. Gourley. Telephone interview with author, 1 July 1996.
Worthen, Richard, interior designer and chair of Alvarado-Santa Fe Station Complex Advisory Committee. Interview with author. Albuquerque, N.Mex., 31 December 1994.

Manuscripts

Ballen, Sam. "History." Typescript document prepared for the Historic Santa Fe Foundation in 1994. Photocopy.
Fergusson, Erna. "The Tingleys of New Mexico." Unpublished manuscript, Box 13, Folder 7 of Erna Fergusson Papers, Center for Southwest Research, General Library, University of New Mexico, Albuquerque. Carbon copy.
Hines, Thomas S., Jr. " Daniel Hudson Burnham: A Study in Cultural Leadership." Ph.D. diss., University of Wisconsin, 1971.
Hunt, G. R. "Montezuma Hotel, Las Vegas Hot Springs." Manuscript dated 19 February 1954. Photocopy.
Ivers, Louise H. "The Architecture of Las Vegas, New Mexico." Ph.D. diss., University of New Mexico, 1975.
Kabat, Sally. "Home Away From Home: The Architectural Geography of Hotels in the American Southwest, 1880–1920." Ph.D. diss., University of New Mexico, 1994.
Klein, David W. "The Downtown Planning Process: An Analysis of the Albuquerque Experience." Master's thesis, University of New Mexico, 1974.
Martinez, Evelyn L. "The Alarid Home." Typescript document prepared for La Fonda. Photocopy.
Martinez, Mary Ann F. "Land Ownership of the La Fonda Parking Lot." Unpublished paper dated December 17, 1985 (a continuation of Nancy Wood's paper).
Massey, Catherine. "Stories of a Few Special People Who Came to New Mexico in the Early 1900s." Unpublished paper, University of New Mexico, 1992. Typescript in author's files.
Perrigo, Lynn I. "The Plaza Hotel: Las Vegas, New Mexico." Manuscript dated 1974. Photocopy.
———. "The Castañeda Hotel: Las Vegas, New Mexico." Manuscript dated 1974. Photocopy.
Reich, Betty. "Stagecoach Days." Unpublished manuscript dated 27 March 1937. New Mexico Federal Writers Project, file 127, State Records and Archives, Santa Fe, N.Mex.
Roberts, Alexandra. "The Alvarado Hotel: A Reflection of the Railroad Years in Albuquerque." Unpublished essay dated 1 April 1980. Center for Southwest Research, University of New Mexico, Albuquerque.
Schofield, Sue. "The Life and Times of the Shaffer Hotel, Mountainair, New Mexico." Paper presented at the annual meeting of the Historical Society of New Mexico, June 1986. Montezuma Hotel: Las Vegas, New Mexico.
Shaffer, Clem. Typescript and handwritten versions of an unpublished memoir dated 1942. Private collections of G. Harding Kayser,

Mountainair, N.Mex., and Jackie Shaffer Hudgeons, Queen Valley, Ariz.
Thatcher, H. F. "Castañeda: The Hotel and the Man." Manuscript dated 8 November 1978. Photocopy.
Vaden, Clay W. "Sadie Orchard: One of Few New Mexico Women Stage Drivers." Unpublished manuscript dated 10 August 1936. New Mexico Federal Writers Project files, 5–4–1 #23, Museum of New Mexico History Library, Santa Fe.
Wood, Nancy E. "A History of Land Use: The La Fonda Hotel Parking Lot Project, 1984." Unpublished paper dated 22 April 1984, prepared for Marcia Jackson, registrar, Site Survey, Laboratory of Anthropology, as part of Public History 366, University of New Mexico, 1984.

Videotapes

Early Albuquerque: The Railroad Boom Years, 1880–1912. Albuquerque Museum, City of Albuquerque, 1991.
Marcus, Stanley, and Lonnie Lucero. *The Plaza Hotel in Las Vegas*. Interview by Harold Rhodes. Albuquerque: KNME-TV, 1983.

Index